Misadventures *in* Nature's Paradise

Supporting Organisations

Misadventures *in* Nature's Paradise
Australia's Cocos (Keeling) Islands and
Christmas Island during the Dutch era

Graeme Henderson, Robert de Hoop
and Andrew Viduka

First published in 2022 by
UWA Publishing
Crawley, Western Australia 6009
www.uwap.uwa.edu.au

UWAP is an imprint of UWA Publishing
a division of The University of Western Australia

This book is copyright. Apart from any fair dealing for the purpose of private study, research, criticism or review, as permitted under the *Copyright Act 1968*, no part may be reproduced by any process without written permission. Enquiries should be made to the publisher.

The authors have made every effort to contact copyright holders for material used in this book. Any person or organisation that may have been overlooked should contact the authors.

Copyright © Graeme Henderson, Robert de Hoop, Andrew Viduka 2022

The moral right of the author has been asserted.

ISBN: 978-1-76080-233-2

 A catalogue record for this book is available from the National Library of Australia

Cover image: Magellan's *Victoria*. Detail from a 1590 Ortelius map. Background images from Istockphoto.
Cover design by Nada Backovic
Typeset in 12 point Bembo Book
Printed by Lightning Source

 uwapublishing

Contents

Series introduction by Peter Veth	vii
1. Islands of Misadventure	1
2. Marco Polo's islands and the Cantino planisphere	7
3. Discovery of the Cocos (Keeling) Islands	33
4. Exploration of the Cocos (Keeling) Islands	81
5. Discovery of Christmas Island	117
6. Exploration of Christmas Island	127
7. Casualties along the spice-trade route	153
8. Conclusions	179
Acknowledgements	187
Illustration sources and credits	191
References and notes	199
Select bibliography	225
Author biographies	231
Index	235

The Oceans Institute Monograph Series

Peter Veth

This is the inaugural edition of the UWA Oceans Institute Monograph Series. The concept of the series was initiated during my tenure as the director of the Oceans Institute in 2020 following workshops with colleagues and members of the board, chaired by Mr Jock Clough, and with support of the then Deputy Vice-Chancellor (Research) Professor Robyn Owens. The Oceans Institute straddles all schools of the University of Western Australia and embraces researchers from a wide range of disciplines, including oceanography, marine biology, ocean engineering, marine geoscience, coastal planning, environmental law, history and archaeology. Many of the researchers are global leaders in their fields, having active links with international hubs of marine research expertise, such as Woods Hole Oceanographic Institute and the Scripps Institution of Oceanography, and with many other researchers from universities with marine programs from around the world.

UWA is also part of the Indian Ocean Marine Research Centre (IOMRC), which brings together the CSIRO, the Australian Institute of Marine Science and the Department of Primary Industries and Regional Development. Together, staff from across the IOMRC partnership present a formidable set of research, management and community-outreach skills that ensure a new century of work unfolds in the Indian Ocean. UWA is optimally positioned to lead many of these actions, having centrality through geography and research engagement in Indian Ocean themes. It was therefore pleasing to be approached by Graeme Henderson with the offer of a major manuscript on the history of discovery of the remote Indian Ocean Territories. Graeme has had a long and fruitful relationship with UWA and its publishing arms. This volume is entitled *Misadventures in Nature's Paradise: Australia's Cocos (Keeling) Islands and Christmas Island*

INTRODUCTION

during the Dutch Era, and is authored by Graeme Henderson, Robert de Hoop and Andrew Viduka.

Graeme Henderson is a leading maritime historian and author, having discovered the seventeenth-century shipwreck *Vergulde Draeck*, or *Gilt Dragon*, in 1963 – one of the most significant shipwreck finds in Australian maritime history and also the catalyst for Western Australia's ground-breaking legislation to protect historic wreck sites. He has led many excavation and history programs, including on the ex-slaver *James Matthews*, and served as director of the Western Australian Maritime Museum. He was also the first site director I volunteered under on the excavations of the American China Trader *Rapid*, lost in 1811 off Point Cloates and located on the Ningaloo coast of WA.

Robert de Hoop is a maritime and underwater archaeologist who works at the International Programme for Maritime Heritage at the Cultural Heritage Agency of the Netherlands (RCE). He has worked at this agency, which is part of the Ministry of Education, Culture and Science, since 2017. As a maritime heritage expert Robert has travelled all over the world to cooperate with countries managing underwater cultural heritage. Robert participated in several national and international projects, including the excavation of the Dutch East Indiaman (VOC) ship the *Rooswijk* and writing the process and best practice guidelines for the EU-project SASMAP.

Finally, Andrew (Andy) Viduka is a maritime archaeologist and objects conservator who has been assistant director of Maritime and Commonwealth Heritage in Canberra for 14 years. Andy co-drafted the Australian Government's *Underwater Cultural Heritage Act, 2018*, which he also administers. He leads the Australian Underwater Cultural Heritage Program, and Australia's consideration of ratification of the UNESCO 2001 Convention on the Protection of the Underwater Cultural Heritage. Andy and I were co-investigators on the Australian Historic Shipwrecks Preservation Project, supported by the Australian Research Council and heritage departments and delegates from around Australia.

It would be hard to think of a stronger team coming together to recast the history of the Cocos (Keeling) Islands and Christmas Island and particularly their incorporation into global histories and imaginations.

INTRODUCTION

These remote islands now constitute Australia's Indian Ocean territories, the most isolated and westward islands of the nation. They have larger-than-life profiles for reasons ranging from their high marine biodiversity, their contested history of Malay communities, the plantation and guano history and the 'founding' Clunies-Ross dynasty, the battle between HMAS *Sydney* and SMS *Emden*, and, last but not least, the visit of Charles Darwin in HMS *Beagle*. What tends to be forgotten, however, is that these two islands were some of the last oceanic islands in the world to have been visited, let alone settled. This puts them in a fairly unique class globally of being able to register the impacts of the Anthropocene without any previous local modifications of their lands or waters until the 1820s. There is no previous evidence of Polynesian settlement of the islands from markers such as pottery sherds or remains of the Polynesian rat. Nor is there clear evidence of visitation by seafarers from South-East Asia, China or Arabia, despite their centuries-long history of maritime movements across the Indian Ocean.

Misadventures is, according to the authors, 'a story about the earliest history of these islands ... [including] the events leading to the discovery of these islands, and, later, to their settlement in the nineteenth century'. This monograph, through meticulous archival, cartographic and archaeological research, resets the earliest history of these islands. Although the northern waters of the Indian Ocean were heavily plied by the fifteenth century, local folkloric accounts of terrible currents, pervasive shadows and avian monsters kept trade and exploration at bay. Before the Brouwer Route of 1611, which directed vessels down to the roaring forties of the Southern Ocean to halve the passage time from Europe to the Indies, cartographers were producing maps for 'safer' passage just south of the equator. Intersections with the very isolated and exposed submarine summits and atolls of Cocos (Keeling) Islands and Christmas Island were just a matter of time in this age of European mercantile expansion.

The current project was initiated by an invitation to the authors to locate the wrecks of the Dutch East Indiamen *Fortuyn* (lost in 1724) and *Aagtekerke* (lost in 1726). During the archival and fieldwork searches, many other stories of discovery, exploration, shipwreck and endurance emerged. The authors build on a lofty pedigree of previous travellers and writers, including Marco Polo, Antonio Pigafetta, Cornelis de Houtman, Hendrik Brouwer, Jonathan Swift and William Dampier. These explorers had, through various publications, increased Europe's interest in the southern Indian Ocean without them ever having stepped ashore on either the Cocos (Keeling) Islands or Christmas Island.

The research outlined in this monograph concludes that, because the early European trade routes to the Indonesian archipelago were from the west, both the Cocos (Keeling) Islands and Christmas Island had not been sighted by Europeans until the beginning of the seventeenth century. The push by the Dutch in the early 1600s to decrease travel time with shipping routes from the south of the Indonesian archipelago led to the discovery and exploration of these islands by the Dutch and the English.

A 1612 chart by Dutch cartographer Hessel Gerritsz is the earliest evidence that the Cocos (Keeling) Islands were first found and recorded by Dutch mariners. The modest Dutch appetite for birds, coconuts and water from these southern hemisphere islands did not compare with their rapidly expanding interests in the spice trade of Maluku. Possibly for similar reasons, the British Government did not actively seek control of the Cocos (Keeling) Islands, despite lobbying from several quarters. In 1646 British cartographer Robert Dudley named North Keeling Island as 'Killing Island', and in 1787 hydrographer Alexander Dalrymple saw this island name as referring back to a supposed 1609 British discovery (with the implication of British rights to possession) by William Keeling. Following an 1829 petition by John Clunies-Ross, and subsequent confusion in Britain between the names of the Cocos (Keeling) Islands and Coco Island in the Bay of Bengal, the islands were mistakenly annexed as British territory by Captain Stephen Fremantle in 1857.

The earliest recorded sighting of Christmas Island was made by English merchant John Milward, who sailed past in 1615. The first extensive exploration was conducted, albeit unwillingly, by the survivors of the wreck of the Dutch ship *Vice Admiraal Rijk*, who spent 57 days on the island in 1852, foraging and actively seeking rescue. Despite the island's proximity to the Sunda Strait, settlement did not occur until the 1880s, when phosphate deposits were sampled, the island was formally annexed for Britain, and George Clunies-Ross and family initiated a settlement. In 1891 John Murray and Clunies-Ross obtained a lease for phosphate mining.

As seems to be inevitably concluded from most studies of human forays into pristine island microcosms, the results of these colonising ventures were anything but a celebration of nature's paradise. *Misadventures* allows us to reflect on the origins and genesis, as well as the outcomes, of mercantile expansion into the Indian Ocean; the myths that surround sovereignty; and the extraordinary window that these oceanic pinpoints can provide into the Anthropocene of the Indian Ocean.

Chapter 1

Islands of Misadventure

Inkblots, representing the tracks of sailing ships, scurried like ghost crabs across successive European maps of the southern Indian Ocean during the Age of Exploration. Then a couple of those inkblots settled in the central-eastern part of the Indian Ocean, becoming the Australian territories of the Cocos (Keeling) Islands and Christmas Island. This is a story about the earliest history of these islands – a period that might be termed the Dutch Era given the preponderance of Dutch East Indiamen traversing the area. Our story includes the events leading to the discovery of these islands and, later, to their settlement in the nineteenth century.

Seafarers from Africa, the Middle East and Asia developed trade routes across the northern waters of the Indian Ocean. The Europeans who ventured eastward across this ocean, the first venue of global trade, relied on local pilots, some of whom had travelled southward, collecting tradeable natural products from the inhabitants of occupied islands. The local pilots told the Europeans of terrible dangers in the unknown waters to the south, including strong currents, dark shadows and giant birds of prey. These stories both frightened and attracted the young, unsophisticated European sailors attempting to cope with unfamiliar environments and cultures:

> Lands distant from the teller are natural settings for exotic and mythical wonders, not only because distance makes the stories difficult to refute, but also because distance creates possibilities: who knows what might be possible at the ends of the world, what unheard of things the earth might produce, or what bizarre customs might prevail?[1]

The development by the Dutch of shorter trade routes between South Africa and the Spice Islands of what is now Indonesia took European vessels southward, into the vicinity of the Cocos (Keeling) Islands and Christmas Island. Cartographers produced charts intended to make voyaging safer in the southern Indian Ocean (meaning, here, the ocean south of the equator rather than just the 'roaring forties' Southern Ocean route), but this did not prevent the odd shipwreck misadventure in the waters of these beautiful islands.

The two Australian territories had developed on top of old volcanic mountains rising steeply from a water depth of 5,000 metres. This environment has influenced their accessibility, the condition and location of the shipwrecks, and the experiences of the survivors of those shipwrecks. The two coral atolls of the Cocos (Keeling) Islands lie between 11.8° and 12.2° south, approximately 1,600 nautical miles northwest of Fremantle and 500 nautical miles west-southwest of Christmas Island. North Keeling Island is uninhabited, but West Island and Home Island on the South Keeling atoll are permanently inhabited. Christmas Island, also permanently inhabited, is the exposed summit of a submarine

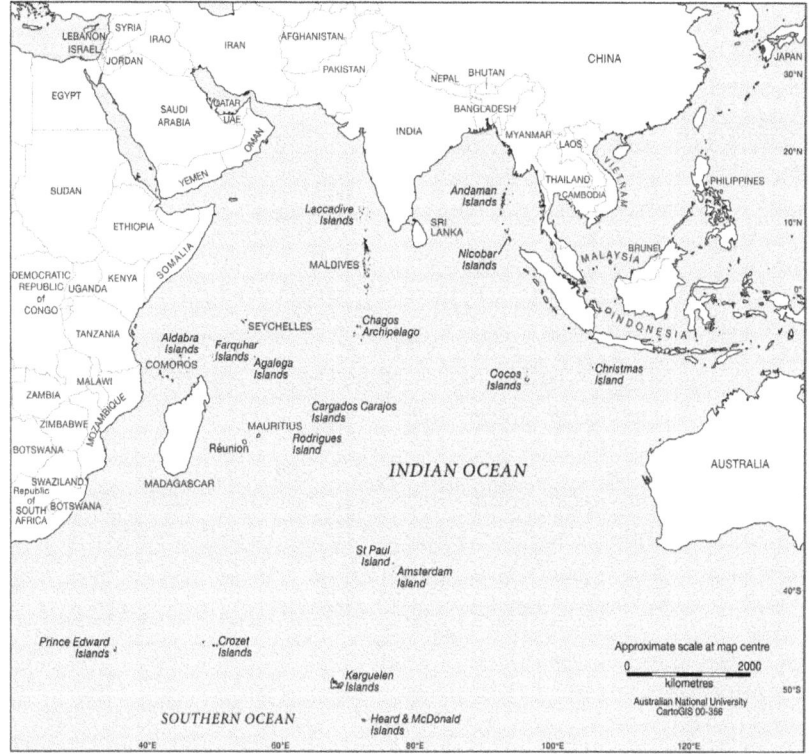

Figure 1. The Cocos (Keeling) Islands and Christmas Island lie in the tropical eastern waters of the Indian Ocean.

mountain, lying at 10.4° south, 265 nautical miles south of Sunda Strait and 1,400 nautical miles northwest of Fremantle.

The stories told here are an amalgam of archival and desktop historical research, discussions with island community members, collaboration with various scientists about artefact analysis, and two short archaeological survey expeditions conducted by Wreck Check, an Australian not-for-profit group formed to research maritime cultural heritage.[2]

The project started as a search for two Dutch shipwrecks. Willem Andreae, the Dutch ambassador to Australia, had called for expressions of interest by researchers to develop projects for the 2016 Dirk Hartog 400th anniversary celebrations – Hartog having been captain of the first European vessel to visit Western Australia. Wreck Check members formed a partnership with the Cultural Heritage Agency of the Netherlands (RCE) to review the archival sources and conduct searches in the waters surrounding the Cocos (Keeling) Islands and Christmas Island during 2015 and 2016, using a magnetometer to identify seabed anomalies. One of the objectives was to locate the wrecks of the Dutch East Indiamen *Fortuyn* (lost in 1724) and *Aagtekerke* (lost in 1726), or to show that those wrecks do not lie in water less than 30 metres deep. During the archival and fieldwork searches, many other stories of discovery, exploration, shipwreck and endurance emerged.

The terms Age of Discovery and Age of Exploration have been used to describe the time between the beginning of the fifteenth century and the middle of the seventeenth century, when overseas exploration became an important part of European culture, signalling the beginning of globalisation. Lands previously unknown to Europeans were 'discovered' and colonised. In 1493 Pope Alexander VI issued a Papal Bull stating that any lands not inhabited by Christians were available to be 'discovered', claimed and exploited by Christian rulers.[3] European monarchies promulgated this Doctrine of Discovery to legitimise their colonisation of lands outside of Europe, seizing lands already inhabited by Indigenous peoples, but ignoring uninhabited lands, because in such places there was no prospect of trade and no supply of labour.

The 1494 Treaty of Tordesillas divided newly 'discovered' lands outside of Europe between the empires of Portugal and Spain, along a meridian 1,184 nautical miles west of the Cape Verde Islands. It allocated lands to the east (Africa, India and Indonesia, but also the tip of Brazil) to Portugal and lands to the west (the rest of the Americas and the Pacific region) to Spain. The other side of the world was further divided between the two empires by the Treaty of Zaragoza in 1529. In the interim period, a conflict began when both kingdoms claimed the Molucca Spice Islands – the source of nutmeg, mace and cloves.

Christmas Island and the Cocos (Keeling) Islands were somewhat ignored by the Europeans until the latter phases of the Ages of Discovery and Exploration. It was their interest in establishing a shorter and quicker southern sea route past the Cape of Good Hope to the East Indies that led to the detailed charting of these islands and, ultimately, to their settlement. Thousands of ships headed across the southern Indian Ocean, passing Christmas Island and the Cocos (Keeling) Islands on the routes to and from the Spice Islands. These small islands along the way had no populations to cultivate spices, so, before the nineteenth century, although situated on the major sea highway to the spice markets of Java and Sumatra, they remained uninhabited. However, as a visiting naturalist observed, 'the drama of history loses nothing by reason of the smallness of its stage'.[4]

Chapter 2

Marco Polo's islands and the Cantino planisphere

Timeline

50–500 CE Austronesian-language people developed coastal trade routes between Asia and Africa.

8th century Trade developed between Java and southern India.

Circa 1000 The Chinese traded with a Javanese Empire.

1467 Cartographer Nicolaus Germanus depicted a triangle of islands southwest of the Malay peninsula.

Late-13th century Marco Polo's *The Travels of Marco Polo* was published.

1498 Vasco da Gama, who had read Marco Polo's book, reached India via the Cape of Good Hope.

1502 Alberto Cantino acquired a map depicting islands c. 25° south, south of the Maldive-Chagos archipelago.

1503 Thome Lopes, returning from India on da Gama's fourth Portuguese India Armada, recorded sighting Seychelles.

1520 Cartographer Petrus Apianus' world map of 1520 showed 'CALLENSVAZ' beside the Malay peninsula.

1522 Juan Elcano of Magellan's fleet sailed south of Java to return to Spain.

1522 Cartographer Nuño García de Toreno's map showed 'Calensuan' to the south of Sumatra.

1555 A Gerard de Jode map showed 'S. Apolonia' (after Saint Apollonia) east of Madagascar in c. 20° south.

1569 A Gerardus Mercator map specified separately Diego Garcia, 'Pousada', and 'Jona' (Iona).

1570 Ortelius showed 'Poueada', suggesting edible birds (*poulard* meaning a fat pullet) in 12° south, below India.

1593 Cartographer Gerard de Jode depicted a triangle of islands south of Sunda Strait.

1596 Cornelis Ceullen, *Duyfken*'s helmsman in Houtman's fleet, reported passing the vicinity of Polvera/Poluara.

1597 Dutch merchant seaman Cornelis de Houtman returned home to Europe via the south coast of Java.

1598 Jan Huygen van Linschoten showed 'Poluara' island as an inverted triangle similar to the Cantino map's depiction.

In this chapter we examine the stages whereby mariners familiarised themselves with the waters and coastlines of the northern rim of the Indian Ocean and then ventured southward into the oceanic region occupied by Christmas Island and the Cocos (Keeling) Islands.

The earliest seafarers

The earliest known deliberate seafaring on planet Earth started off the South-East Asian mainland, not far from Australia and Christmas Island, over 65,000 years ago. Eighteen thousand years ago only 62 nautical miles separated the Wallacea Archipelago (now Indonesia) from Sahul, which incorporated Australia and New Guinea.[1] Smoke from fires on either side of such a narrow strait would have been easily visible, confirming landfall, so the humans from Wallacea who settled in Sahul would have known, initially, that they could return with the seasonally reversing winds.

How did they navigate? Knowledgeable Indigenous Australians have used what have been described as 'songlines' or 'dreaming tracks' to navigate vast distances across the land by repeating stories, songs, dances and paintings, and to describe locations of waterholes and other important features.[2] It has been suggested that a similar strategy was used for crossings from islands.[3]

The Borobudur ship, a bas relief carved on a Buddhist monument in central Java, shows a large eighth-century vessel fitted with double outrigger, a typical feature of Austronesian (meaning Austronesian-language speakers) vessels. It is thought to have been of a type used in trade between Java, Ceylon and southern India. Before the European entry into the Indian Ocean leg of the spice trade, Indian textiles were in demand in the Spice Islands of eastern Indonesia, and in Java and Sumatra. South-East Asian goods were re-exported from the west coast of India overland to the Middle East and on to Europe.

Figure 2. Relief panel of the Borobudur ship.

Researchers also argue that there was well-maintained contact between Sunda Strait and the Maldives in the late-fifteenth century. Pierre Yves Manguin wrote:

> The easiest and most common way of navigating was to run along a parallel, keeping a star at the same height above the horizon. This technique was well known to Pacific navigators and to other Asian navigators of the Indian Ocean. The 6° south parallel route described by early 16th century Portuguese sources leads precisely from the Sunda Strait to the Chagos archipelago, a convenient watering-place from which it was easy to sail north to the main atolls of the Maldives.[4]

Being separated from the star could mean disaster for mariners. The sixteenth-century Italian word *disastro* (from 'dis-', expressing negation, and 'astro', meaning star) means an ill-starred event. Nevertheless, some researchers see the Austronesian contact as having extended further west, and south (more distant from the star), of the Maldives. In 2003 a replica of the Borobudur ship, built under the supervision of Nick Burningham, an Australian expert on Indonesian watercraft, was sailed directly from Indonesia, past the Seychelles, to Madagascar on a trans–Indian Ocean voyage rather than coasting via India and Arabia, to suggest that long-distance trade could have occurred.[5]

Other researchers developed computer simulations based on wind and current data for vessels with the capacity to sail windward. They used the results of these simulations, coupled with linguistic and genetic data, to develop theories about migration routes to Madagascar by Austronesians wanting to colonise new islands. Another study involved the paleoclimate reconstruction of storm tracks in the South Pacific during the 1400s and 1500s CE that opened climate windows for voyaging between Easter Island and South America and broadened colonisation possibilities. The authors of that study argue that the method represents a globally applicable approach to understanding patterning in prehistoric maritime migration.[6]

These researchers argue that, before the arrival of the first Europeans, Austronesians had been making a direct sea crossing of about 3,200 nautical miles between Sunda Strait and Madagascar. Their course, best commenced in March, would have taken them to the Maldives archipelago, and the Chagos archipelago (now the British Indian Ocean Territories) may have been a stopping point. If the direct-route voyage simulations and the paleoclimate reconstruction study accurately reflect the Austronesian voyaging, they can be read as leaving open the possibility that some vessels on their westward passage to Madagascar would have been swept further south than intended, coming close to, or visiting, Christmas Island and the Cocos (Keeling) Islands.

Such visitors from South-East Asia would have been prompted to land, if sea conditions allowed, to dig wells for water, to collect any coconuts and to catch edible birds, such as the boobies or the Cocos Rail (the Malay name being *ayam hutan*, meaning 'chicken of the forest'). However, they had few reasons to leave traceable cultural materials behind.

Local pilots

Before the development of modern nautical charts, Arab pilots of the eleventh century recorded their navigational knowledge in the form of pilot guides, as poems and prose. Portuguese explorer Vasco da Gama relied on them for his crossing of the Indian Ocean to India. This form of navigation had reached a high level by the fifteenth century, but the European entry into the Indian Ocean brought realisation by the peoples of the Indian Ocean rim of the need for standardised charts.

Religious beliefs and navigational knowledge were spread by traders, and trade centres became learning centres:

> Knowledge was transferred from the foreigners to the local communities, from one group of foreign traders to another (from Indians to Chinese, Arabs to Indians, Europeans to Arabs, etc) as well as from the local communities to the foreign traders. The transferred knowledge included religious, commercial and nautical knowledge and the transfer took place in institutionalized modes of knowledge transfer (schools of religious learning, art) as well as in un-institutionalized ways (spontaneous exchange of knowledge through interaction with a trader from a different ethnic group).[7]

Several factors slowed the development of an accurate understanding of the existence and location of the Cocos (Keeling) Islands and Christmas Island. These factors were inaccurate or non-existent longitude attribution, 'phantom' islands (accepted as real by mapmakers but not existing in the purported location), and the sometimes confusing tendency to name numerous islands after their accessible resources, rather than using a unique descriptor. Those resources included villages, water and edible birds, as well as the refreshing fruit and other products of the coconut palm. Early charts of Sumatra, for example, show four separate islands with names denoting coconuts along the south coast alone.[8]

Marco Polo
The late-thirteenth-century publication titled *The Travels of Marco Polo* was composed by Venetian merchant Marco Polo and Italian romance writer Rustichello da Pisa. The book described for Europeans the then mysterious culture of the Eastern World, giving the first comprehensive look at many Asian countries. It is important also in appreciating the confused state of knowledge of the southern Indian Ocean islands at that time, islands which Polo's book described without him ever visiting them. The Polo book stated that when navigators left Java and sailed for 700 miles on a course between south and southwest, they would arrive at two islands, a greater and a lesser:

> The one is called SONDUR and the other CONDUR. As there is nothing about them worth mentioning, let us go on five hundred miles beyond Sondur, and then we find another country which is called LOCAC. It is a good country and a rich; [it is on the mainland]; and it has a king of its own.[9]

Marco Polo has been called the greatest traveller and the most magnificent observer of the Middle Ages, but full awareness of his book was delayed until the mid-fifteenth century, when Venetian cartographer Fra Mauro included Polo's toponyms – place names – on his 1450 map of the world.[10]

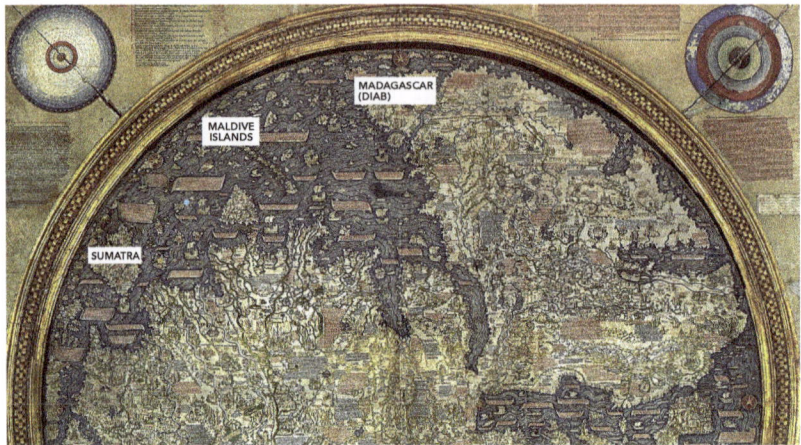

Figure 3. Section of the 1450 Fra Mauro map showing Sumatra, the Laccadive-Maldive-Chagos Ridge and Madagascar.

Nicholas Germanus

A Germanus map of 1467, following the coordinates of Ptolemy's world map from his *Geographica*, depicted a triangle of islands to the southwest of the Malay peninsula – the location of Sumatra, but also the general direction of the Cocos (Keeling) Islands. In 1482 another map in the Ptolemaic form, by Lienhart Holle, showed groups of islands (probably Ceylon and thereabouts) southwest of the Malay peninsula, with legends referring to products grown or traded, such as cinnamon and cotton.[11]

Vasco da Gama

When Portuguese explorer Vasco da Gama entered the Indian Ocean via the Cape of Good Hope in 1498, becoming the first European to reach India by sea, the monsoon routes already linked the Mediterranean, Africa, India and China in a global trade network. Monsoon voyagers followed familiar coastlines. Da Gama's early outward and homeward sea routes ran around the ports of the northern rim of the Indian Ocean, although some later Portuguese vessels travelled further south.

Alberto Cantino

An envoy of the duke of the northern Italian city-state of Ferrara, Cantino acted as a spy in the Portuguese court. In 1502 he smuggled out of Portugal an anonymous Portuguese world map (Figure 4), made up of six glued parchment sheets, thought to have been created in 1501 and now known as the Cantino planisphere.[12] The Cantino planisphere is the earliest extant example of the so-called 'latitude chart', developed following the introduction of astronomical navigation in the second half of the fifteenth century. A scale of latitudes is implicit in the positions of the equator, the tropics and the Arctic Circle. It is also the earliest map showing Portuguese discoveries in the Indian Ocean. However, those 'discoveries' were generally limited at that time to already occupied places on the east African coast, Madagascar, and along the ocean's western and northern hemisphere rim visited by Bartolomeu Dias, Vasco da Gama, Pedro Cabral and Joao da Nova.

Latitudes are only indicated for several sections of the Cantino map, and the distortions are immense, the southern end of the Malay peninsula being shown as just north, and the Cape of Good Hope as just south, of the Tropic of Capricorn. No islands are shown in the area immediately south and southeast of the Malay peninsula, where we now know the islands of Indonesia lie. Midway across the southern Indian Ocean, represented as a little south of the tropic, directly south of the Laccadive-Maldive archipelago, and southwest of what might be the expected location of the Cocos (Keeling) Islands, the Cantino map depicts three features in a triangular format: two islands and a shoal or reef, with legends detailing their potentially profitable products.

Information about southern Indian Ocean islands shown in these particular legends was obtained from Arab or Javanese traders or sea captains, who then provided that information to Polo, da Gama or Cabral, or sent it overland to the Mediterranean, ultimately leading to the briefing of a Portuguese cartographer. Given the multiple transmissions of the information, there is room for gross errors to have been included in the positioning of islands and the

Figure 4. The Cantino planisphere of 1502.

information about the local products in the toponyms on these maps. Nevertheless, the natural resources and other information given in the legends makes it clear that the islands are from the tropical zone. On the back of the map is an Italian inscription, which translates as 'Navigational chart of the islands recently [discovered]…in part of the Indies: from Alberto Cantino to Duke Hercole'. Some of the toponyms appear to have been damaged and partly obscured by the joins in the Cantino planisphere.

Portuguese historians Jaime Cortesão and Avelino Teixeira da Mota have translated the Cantino planisphere's Portuguese captions into English.[13] They read the caption on the blue island as 'Ilha gauaa: mesta ilha ha muito benjoim e seda porcelana' and concluded

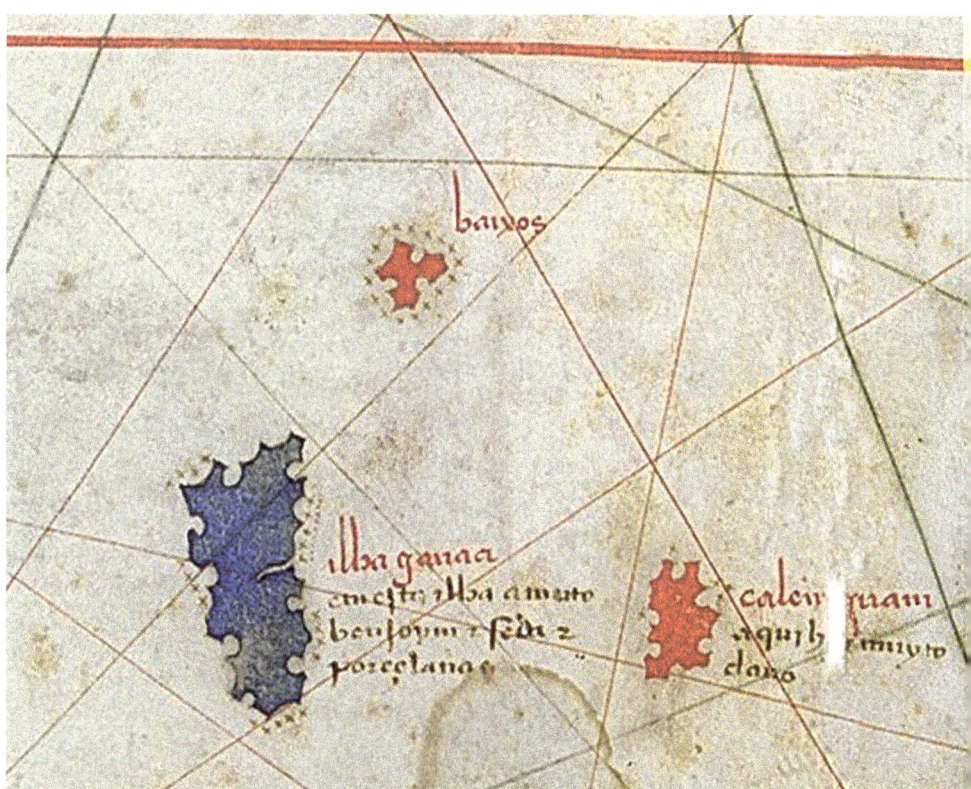

Figure 5. Detail from the 1502 Cantino planisphere showing a blue island and a red island.

that this island represents Java.¹⁴ So their translated caption reads, 'Island Java: on this island there is much benzoin, silk and porcelain'. The word *gauaa* is phonetically similar to 'Java'. Benzoin, from the Benjamin tree (*Styrax benzoin*), is a source of frankincense, an aromatic resin. Mesta, or 'Roselle', is a species of hibiscus cultivated for its fibre, which is used in making rope and baskets, and used in folk medicine as a diuretic. The silk industry has a long history in Java, being used in traditional handicrafts, particularly in batik clothing and textiles.

Marco Polo used the term *porcellana* to describe hard-paste ceramic pottery he saw in China, but the old Italian term was also used to refer to cowrie shells. This might have added to confusion about the Cantino map because the Maldives, rather than the Spice Islands, were the acknowledged centre of the cowrie-shell-money trade. The shells were used as money across Africa, South and East Asia (including China), and Oceania. From the tenth century, sailors from Arabia and East Africa, who dominated the trade routes around the Maldives, stopped in the Maldives to trade for cowrie shells, which were used as currency in Africa and the Arabian Peninsula. Cowries are attractive to look at, durable and difficult to hoard, as King Gezo of Dahomey told explorer Richard Burton.¹⁵ They were carried, initially by Arabs, from the Maldives to the Mediterranean, for further transport via Morocco across the Sahara to communities such as the Dagaare-speaking people in the northwestern corner of Ghana.¹⁶ To a lesser extent, they were distributed through Africa from the East African coast and islands. Competing Portuguese, Dutch, English and French slave traders took them to Europe for forwarding to the West African coast as an exchange for the enslaved people they exported to the New World.¹⁷ However, various cowrie types are plentiful among the islands of Indonesia, so the likelihood is that Spice Islands cowries were also a part, albeit a lesser-known one, of the trade.

Cortesão and Mota read the caption on the red island as 'Caleirciram aqui he muyto clauo' and concluded that this island (...ciram) is Ceram, which lies further to the east in the southern part of the Moluccas.[18] The caption then translates as 'Hot Ceram: here there is much clove'. Ceram (now Seram) is the largest island of the Moluccas, which were known as the Spice Islands because of the nutmeg, mace and cloves that were exclusively found there. It was the presence of these spices that sparked interest from Europe in the sixteenth century. It appears from this interpretation that the Cantino map's Portuguese cartographer moved the Spice Islands 3,500 miles westward from the contested Portuguese–Spanish longitude, further westward than on the Ptolemaic maps of Germanus and Holle, and well into Portuguese trading-rights territory under the Treaty of Tordesillas.

Figure 6. The modern 1-cedi coin of Ghana bears the cowrie image, recalling the shell money.

Figure 7. Cowries from Diego Garcia.

Given the reference to cloves, the Cortesão and Mota account is a compelling explanation for those islands that Cantino marked in the middle of the Indian Ocean. However, Cantino had placed them equidistant between the island-grouping locations of Java-Seram, and Diego Garcia-Gan. Gan is the southernmost island of the Addu Atoll, as well as the southernmost island of the Maldives. It is relatively large by Maldive standards. The origin of the word 'Gan' is in the Sanskrit word *Grama*, meaning 'village', so, not surprisingly, two other Maldive islands are also named Gan.[19]

Some of those who saw the Cantino map would have been misled into thinking that the real islands of Indonesia must be present where they were shown, far to the west of their actual location, while others would have been led to believe that extensions of the Maldives (Diego Garcia and Gan) extended far to the south, or that the Mascarene Islands lay in the middle of the Indian Ocean, far to the east of their actual position.

In 1909 French naturalist A. A. Fauvel saw the Cantino planisphere as the first document showing the position of the Seychelles islands. Vasco da Gama had travelled past the Seychelles on his voyages to and from India between 1498 and 1503, and Fauvel may have interpreted the island name Ganaa as relating to that great explorer.[20] However, the Seychelles lie to the north of Madagascar, far from where Cantino has depicted three islands. Fauvel made no attempt to explain the island name he read as Calensuam, or the island products listed in the Cantino planisphere.

The Cantino planisphere shows three small islands close to the southeast coast of Madagascar representing the Mascarene Islands of Réunion (in early times referred to as Apollonia), Mauritius and Rodriguez, likely seen by Europeans before 1502. It may be that the creators of the Cantino map, unsure of the location of the Mascarenes, have simply drawn a repeat version of them further to the east – Englishman Robert Dudley placed 'Apoluara' island (derived from Apollonia) to the south of the Maldives on his 1646 chart. However, the Mascarenes also lacked the products, such as silk, that were listed on the Cantino planisphere. The word interpreted by Cortesão and Mota as 'gauaa' could easily be read as 'ganaa', in which case it might be seen to relate to the island of Gan, the southernmost island of the Maldives, rather than to Java.

For all the above reasons, it is not surprising that cartographers during the rest of the sixteenth century came up with various interpretations of the island groups to the west of Indonesia and the meaning of the Cantino toponyms. An interesting example is the word read by Cortesão and Mota as 'caleirciram' and translated as 'hot Ceram'. The toponym runs across a joint in the map where several letters appear to have been obliterated, and it has perhaps been interpreted by others as the Latin *calceamentum*, meaning a covering for the foot. *Calcaneum* is the great bone of the heel, *calceus* means a shoe or half-length boot, *caligatus* or *caligo* refers to wearing heavy boots, and *caliga*, connected with *calceus*, refers to a soldier's boot. Such an interpretation of the Cantino map may have been in the mind of mapmaker Pierre Desceliers in 1550 when he showed, in the southern Indian Ocean section of his chart, a boot shape representing the Diego Garcia atoll. A recent NASA satellite image of Diego Garcia (Figure 23) shows the atoll as what can be described (almost uniquely within the Indian Ocean) as a boot or the great bone of the heel. So if the intended meaning of the Cantino map inscription was *Calcagno* (Italian), meaning heel, or *calceamentum* (Latin), implying a foot- or boot-shaped island, it would indicate that the map represents Diego Garcia and nearby islands such as Gan, rather than Java and Seram.[21] Additionally, it would indicate that the overall shape of Diego Garcia had been carefully examined by Indigenous Maldivian fishermen and/or Arab pilots with substantial knowledge of charting before any known European presence in that part of the Indian Ocean. The first European, Portuguese Captain Pedro Mascarenhas, is thought to have visited Diego Garcia in 1512.

Martin Waldseemuller

In 1507, five years after Alberto Cantino purchased the Cantino planisphere, cartographer Martin Waldseemuller had his chart of the Indian Ocean published. As on the Cantino map, Waldseemuller, influenced by Ptolemy and Polo, set a group of islands southwest of the Malay peninsula. He has depicted one island with an upright profile that could be likened to the ancient Roman women's hair net (the *caliendrum*), and he has titled that island 'Callen Zuam', a similar name to Cantino's 'Caleirciram'. Against the east side of the Malay peninsula, he has placed 'Seylam', representing Ceylon. To the west of Callen Zuam his legend identifies 'Iona' (meaning Java), the largest island, with 'porcellana', suggesting ceramics. On his later (1516) map, he has moved Iona (now an inverted triangle, shaped like Cantino's Ila Gauaa) westward, closer to the locations of Diego Garcia and Madagascar.[22] The toponym Iona is discontinued by later cartographers, yet its inverted-triangle shape was apparently continued on later maps with the toponym 'Pousada'. The game of Chinese whispers comes to mind, whereby in a sequence of repetitions of a story (in this case a toponym), each one differs slightly from the next, so that eventually the telling bears only a scant, and then no, resemblance to the original.

Ferdinand Magellan/Juan Sebastian Elcano voyage 1519–1522

The first circumnavigation of the Earth was achieved by Spain's Magellan-Elcano expedition, one of the greatest exploring voyages of all time. Magellan sailed westward from Seville in 1519, in command of five ships manned by 270 crew. In 1521, in the Philippines, he was killed in battle – shot with a poison arrow. Elcano, with a depleted group of 60 men under his command, took the fleet further westward to the Moluccan Spice Islands, in what is now Indonesia. Finally, in 1522, he arrived back in Spain with 18 surviving crew on their one remaining ship, the 90-ton *Victoria*, having crossed the Atlantic, Pacific and Indian oceans.

The travails of the men still on the *Victoria* after leaving the Moluccas were documented by crew member Antonio Pigafetta, an Italian from the Republic of Venice, who had served as Magellan's assistant earlier in the voyage. His account shows that, in addition to his fear of the Portuguese, he had fears of the unknown, of disease and of women. Pigafetta had good reason to long for the open ocean and to escape from Portuguese territory in the Indies.

During *Victoria*'s stopover at Timor, the disease of St Jop, a neurodegenerative disease that he called the Portuguese disease (or St Job, interpreted by journal translator James Robertson as syphilis), was more prevalent than at other places, and there was a mutiny, resulting in some of the men being beheaded for their crimes.[23] Pigafetta wrote that: '...we left the island of Timor and took to the great open sea called Laut Chidol. Laying our course to the west southwest, we left the island of Zamatra, formerly called Traprobana, to the north of our right hand, for fear of the king of Portoghala'.[24]

Pigafetta frequently lent a credulous ear to the Malay pilots on the *Victoria* and they obliged, telling him fearful stories about the open ocean ahead:

> Our oldest pilot told us that in an island called Acoloro, which lies below Java Major [Java], there are found no persons but women, and that they become pregnant from the wind. When they bring forth if the offspring is a male, they kill it, but if it is a female, they rear it. If men go to that island of theirs, they kill them if they are able to do so.[25]

Sailing initially southeast from Timor, the *Victoria*'s pilot, Francisco Albo, wrote that on 13 February:

> ... the latitude came to 10° 32′, and we were in the neighbourhood of islands of which we do not know the names, nor whether they are inhabited. They lie E.S.E. and W.N.W. with the west cape of Timor, and from here we took our course to the Cape of Good Hope, and went to W.S.W.[26]

Figure 8. Magellan's *Victoria*. Detail from a 1590 Ortelius map.

The islands were Bathurst and Melville, off the coast of the Northern Territory of Australia. Moving on to a west-southwest homeward course, *Victoria*'s crew must have passed reasonably close to the south of both Christmas Island and the Cocos (Keeling) Islands. Then they sailed southward to 42°, where they saw the lofty Amsterdam Island while en route to the Cape of Good Hope.[27]

Nuño García de Toreno

Soon after *Victoria*'s arrival back home in 1522, a Sevillian, García de Toreno, produced or more likely added to a portolan map depicting the Treaty of Tordesillas antemeridian demarcation line bisecting Sumatra at the 100° east meridian. He has placed the inscription 'Line Divisionis Castellanorum et Portugallensium' (dividing line between Castilians and Portuguese) beside the antemeridian. On the Portuguese side of the Tordesillas demarcation, the map shows three islands marked Calensuan, the name following the Cantino map's 'Caleirciram' and Waldseemuller's 'Callen Zuam'. Modified versions of the toponym Calensuan were later used to depict phantom islands as 'Calenfuan' on the first map to name the Pacific Ocean, and as 'Calenfua'/'Calensua', again on other maps in the Pacific.[28]

Portuguese cartographers marked charts of the 1590s with the words 'baixos' (shallow) and 'guaon', south and east of Java. The latter toponyms may indicate interest by the Portuguese in 'guanas', that is iguanas or goannas – the giant monitor lizards known as Komodo dragons and found on the islands of Komodo, Rinca, Flores and Gili Motang to the east of Sunda Strait. In 1699 William Dampier referred to lizards on Dirk Hartog Island, Western Australia, as 'guanos'.[29] An alternative word association is 'guano' – bird manure present on islands, including Bathurst and Melville in what are now Australian waters; although, for Western nations, the attraction of guano as fertiliser developed in the nineteenth century. It may also be that guaon refers to 'guan', loosely applied to mean game birds generally. On a later date, Dampier went fowling for parrots and cockatoos on Timor.

Figure 9. Parrot-hunting on Mauritius in 1598, by Johann Theodor de Bry. The long-legged birds are thought to be erroneous depictions of dodos.

During much of the sixteenth century, the south coast of Java was avoided by European traders because of the strong currents there. Ferdinand Magellan's *Victoria* (1522), Francis Drake's *Golden Hind* (1580), and Thomas Cavendish's *Desire* (1588) all traversed well offshore.[30]

The Dutch merchant, trader and historian Jan Huygen van Linschoten, based for a time in Goa, gathered information from local traders who had visited other parts of the region, such as Malacca, and he wrote of the south coast of Java in 1596 that:

> ... touching the breadth, it is not found, because as yet it is not discovered, nor by the Inhabitants themselves knowne. Some think it to be firme land, of the countrie called Terra Incognita.[31]

Cornelis de Houtman returned home to Europe via the south coast of Java in March 1597 after circumnavigating Java, and he commented:

> ... we found that Iava is not so broade, nor stretcheth it selfe so much Southwarde, as it is set downe in the Carde: for if it were, we should have passed clean through the middle of the land.[32]

Meanwhile, cartographers of the second half of the sixteenth century began to place more islands on the south side of Sunda Strait in the general vicinity of Christmas Island, not far from the coasts of Sumatra and Java. Gerardus Mercator was the first cartographer to draw meridians and parallels as straight lines. With Mercator's projection, the positions of places relative to one another remained correct, but only if the correct coordinates were given for those islands. His 1569 world map shows islands along the south coast of Sumatra to the west of Sunda Strait.[33] These islands can be interpreted, respectively, as the Mentawai Islands, Enggano and, perhaps, Christmas Island.

A 1593 map of the southern hemisphere by Belgian cartographer Gerard de Jode (Figure 10) also shows islands to the south of Sunda Strait. De Jode was based in Antwerp, an important trade centre for the Portuguese involved in the spice trade. Influenced by Polo's writings, he gave the name 'Sondur' to a group of three islands forming a triangle off the south coast of Sumatra, with a fourth island, Augama, pointing north.[34]

Linguist Jan Tent has examined the question of the discovery of Christmas Island, and the toponyms given by de Jode on his chart may have some additional bearing as to who was aware of the islands south of Sunda Strait in 1593.[35] In Sanskrit, an ancient Indo-European language of India in which the Hindu scriptures and classical Indian epic poems are written, the toponym Agama can be read as 'coming near', or 'approaching', which might be seen to apply to vessels approaching Sunda Strait from the south. The name Agamidae refers to small dragon lizards, but they may also have been associated in people's minds with stories of Komodo dragons.[36] Mercator had given the same name to an island in front of the Strait of Malacca in 1569.

The use of such toponyms suggests that they came to de Jode and Mercator from Portuguese traders and to Polo from reports by traders from China, India and the Malay peninsula, who travelled the region in large seagoing junks and proas (a type of sailing boat,

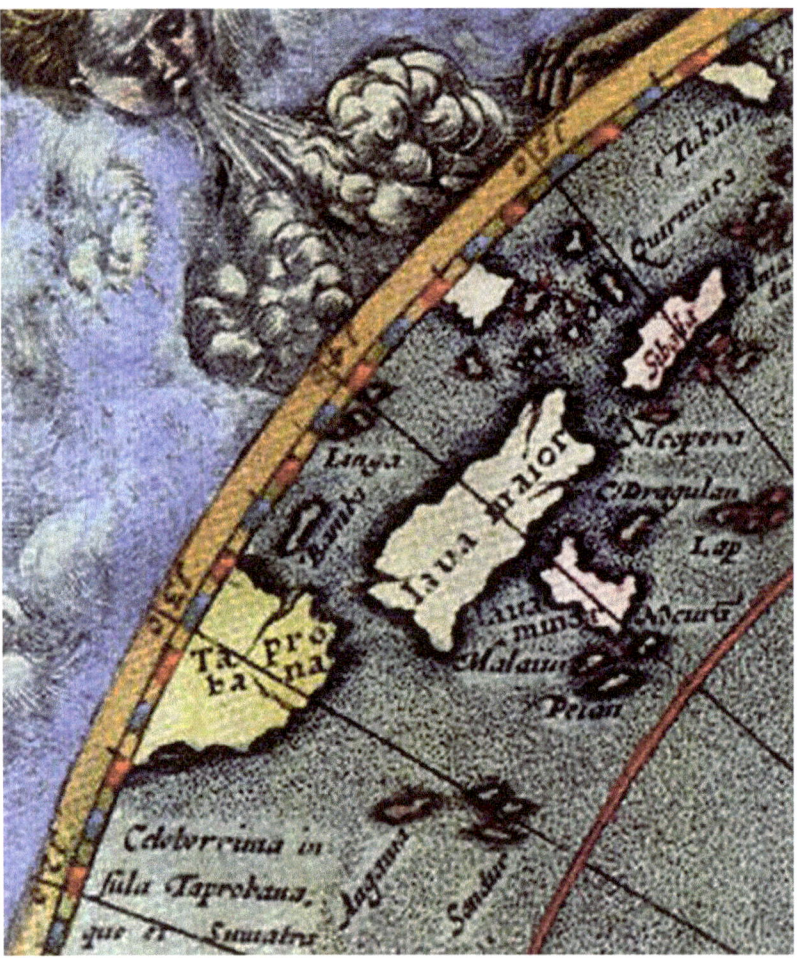

Figure 10. Section of Gerard de Jode's 1593 chart. Note the islands of Augama and Sondur below Java Major and Taprobana (Sumatra).

typically having a large triangular sail and an outrigger, originating in Malaysia and Indonesia). Some of these South-East Asian traders would, like later Europeans, have traded with the inhabitants of islands along the south coast of Sumatra, or been blown south from Sunda Strait by the monsoon winds. Austronesians are thought to have deliberately sailed south from Sunda Strait before turning west on their voyages to Madagascar. Over the years of this theorised route, some vessels likely strayed far enough to see Christmas Island, 265 nautical miles south of Sunda Strait, and the Cocos (Keeling) Islands, 100 miles further south.

Polo's islands of Sondur and Condur lasted well into the eighteenth century, appearing to the southwest of Java on a chart produced by English engraver Emanuel Bowen (Figure 11), and published by Pieter van der Aa in 1729. Text on the chart indicates that it was engraved 'according to the itinerary of Marco Polo, traveller to Asia in 1252'.[37]

However, those Polo islands to the south of Java were named through a misunderstanding. It appears that the Polo manuscript had incorrectly used the name Java instead of 'Champa' – what is today central and southern Vietnam. On the Champa interpretation, Polo's islands of Sondur and Condur represent the group now known as Pulo Condor (or Con Son) off the coast of Vietnam.[38]

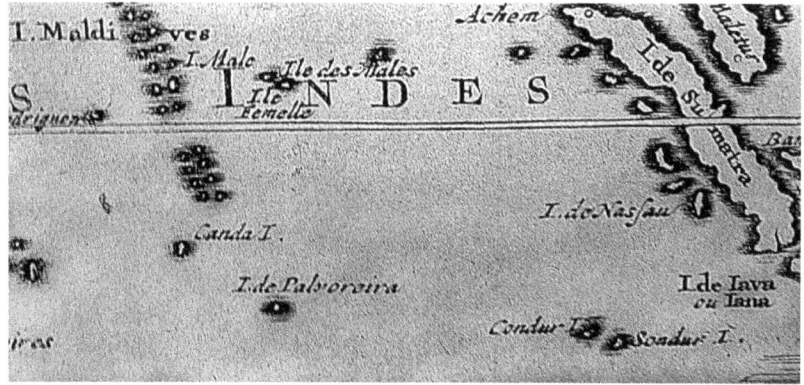

Figure 11. Bowen's 1729 chart shows Polo's Sondur and Condur in the location of the Cocos Islands, and 'Palvoreira' further west.

Polo's islands were not along the south coast of Sumatra, but real islands – the Mentawai Islands and Enggano – were. Then further afield, to the west-southwest, lay the Cocos (Keeling) Islands, rather than Sondur and Condur.

The Borobudur replica ship voyage and the subsequent computer simulations envisage a trading route between Sunda Strait and Madagascar relying on winds occurring around 6° south. Some

Figure 12. Marco Polo in Tartar costume.

vessels conceivably strayed further southward. No hard evidence has been found of Christmas or Cocos (Keeling) Islands sightings or landings before the seventeenth century. However, with increasing European activity to the south of Sunda Strait, initiated by the Dutch, it was inevitable that both the Cocos (Keeling) Islands and Christmas Island would be seen by European vessels.

Figure 13. Detail of 'The probable view of Marco Polo's own geography', drawn by Henry Yule in 1871, showing Sondur and Condur off Vietnam.

Chapter 3

Discovery of the Cocos (Keeling) Islands

Timeline

1450 A Fra Mauro chart detailed a giant Chrocho bird on the island of Madagascar.

1522 Antonio Pigafetta described thrush-sized dead birds at Bachian Island as 'birds of God'.

1522 Pigafetta was told of Garuda birds that could carry an elephant.

1522 The García de Toreno chart showed giant birds west-southwest of the Malay peninsula.

1538 Mercator showed Zanzibar Island east of Madagascar and 'Los roccos insula' south of Java.

1546 Pierre Desceliers showed an island named 'A: defponoada' in 10° south, the approximate latitude of the Cocos (Keeling) Islands.

1569 Mercator replaced A: defponoada with 'Pousada'.

1569 Marco Polo's Java and Locach were shown on a Mercator world map.

1595–97 A Theodor de Bry chart showed islands west-southwest of Sunda Strait.

1609 William Keeling sailed back from Java to the Cape of Good Hope but did not report seeing the Cocos.

1610 Cartographer Jodocus Hondius placed 'Polvero' in the proximity of the Cocos (Keeling) Islands.

1611 Hendrik Brouwer established a shorter southern Indian Ocean route.

1612 Petrus Plancius introduced a new constellation, Gallus (the cockerel), south of the Tropic.

1612 A Hessel Gerritsz chart showed the South Keeling Islands southwest of Sunda Strait.

1622 A Gerritsz chart showed Linschoten's 'Poluara' as 'Polverara' (giant chickens), added an atoll that can be construed as North Keeling, and named South Keeling as 'Cocos Eylanden'.

1646 Dudley labelled South Keeling 'discovered by the English', and North Keeling 'Riling Iland', then 'Killing Iland'.

1780 English cartographer Samuel Dunn referred to 'Killing or Coco Islands' in the location of the Cocos.

1787 Dalrymple was first to use the Keeling toponym, labelling southern atoll 'Keeling or Cocos Islands'.

Mythological islands and creatures in the southern Indian Ocean

The word 'myth' denotes a traditional story, especially one concerning the early history of a people or explaining some natural or social phenomenon, and typically involves supernatural beings or events. 'Mythology' denotes a set of stories or beliefs about a particular person, institution or situation, especially when exaggerated or fictitious. Either term can also be used to refer to a widely held but false belief or idea. The mythological stories of the Indian Ocean are interesting, but do they have any bearing on the course of history? Should they be regarded merely as fairytales – stories for children involving fantastic forces and beings?

In the following sections, we put the argument that some of them do have a bearing on the course of history. From early times, mariners, travellers and mapmakers were spreading fables – stories conveying a moral principle – that identified islands (frequently phantom islands) with giant birds. There were other threatening stories – an island of giants, or of strong ocean currents and shipwreck – encouraging mariners to turn back from unfamiliar territory before it was too late to do so. The folklore of Arabian sailors, notably in the collection titled *One Thousand and One Nights*, popularised stories of an enormous bird of prey called a 'Rukh', a 'Ruc', a 'Roc', and other names, living in the southern Indian Ocean. Gerardus Mercator, in one of the inscriptions on his 1538 map, showed 'Los roccos insula' (islands of the Roc) south of Java. On his 1569 map he referred to Marco Polo's Los Romeros Isles (Amsterdam Island), on which, at a certain time of year, 'the bird Ruc of vast body appears'.[1] Scottish orientalist and geographer Sir Henry Yule, in his annotated translation of Polo's work, observed that:

> The fable of the RUKH was old and widely spread. ... one accidental circumstance or another would give it a local habitation, now here, now there. The *Garuda* of the Hindus, the *Simurgh* of the old Persians, the *'Angka* of the Arabs, the *Bar Yuchre* of the Rabbinical legends, the *Gryps* (Griffins) of the Greeks, were probably all versions of the same original fable.[2]

Marco Polo located more monsters on Indian Ocean islands, at the southern edge of the world, than elsewhere. During his journey to the East in the late-thirteenth century, he mentioned hearing of very large birds, shaped like an eagle, with a wingspan of 30 paces (versus the 12 feet wingspan of the wandering albatross), living on southern Indian Ocean islands.[3] Fra Mauro's 1450 map (see Figure 3) shows, on the lower section of 'Diab' (perhaps Madagascar), reference to a giant bird called 'Chrocho', with eggs the size of

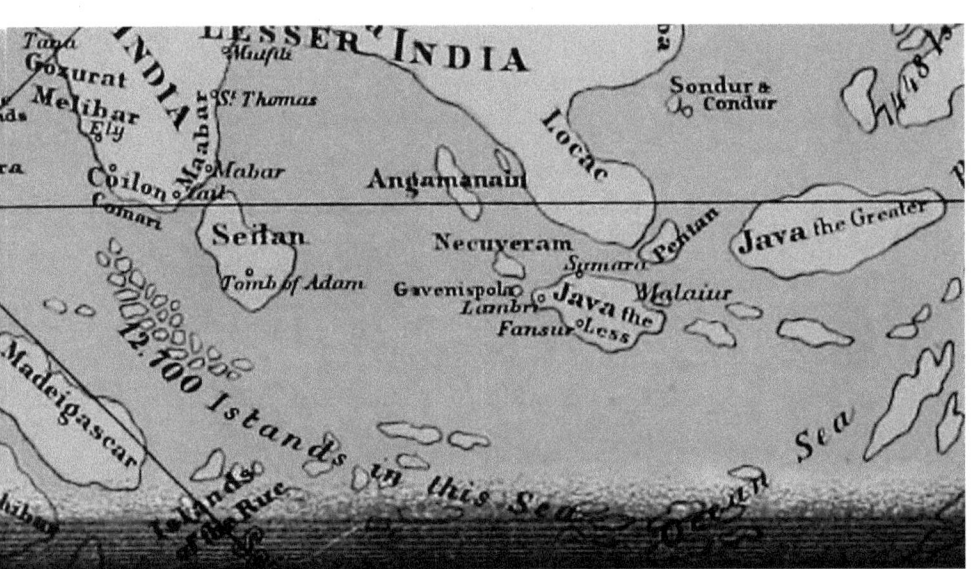

Figure 14. Henry Yule showed the Islands of the Ruc as lying eastward of Madagascar.

a cask. On the same chart appear the words 'Qui comenza el mar scuro' (Here begins the dark sea) – a warning that terrible dangers are to be expected in the southern Indian Ocean.[4] In his 1871 edition of the Marco Polo work, Yule included a map titled 'Probable view of Marco Polo's own geography' (Figure 14). He placed a group of four islands, 'Islands of the Ruc', to the east of Madagascar, where lie the Mascarene Islands of Mauritius, Réunion and Rodrigues, the Maldives, the Chagos archipelago including Diego Garcia and, further east again, the Cocos (Keeling) Islands.

Antonio Pigafetta, writing immediately after Elcano completed his circumnavigation of the world, told of having purchased, in the Spice Islands, some extremely beautiful preserved birds of paradise, referred to by the local people as 'birds of god', and it has been observed that the early modern history of the bird 'exemplifies the complex relationship between trade, politics, knowledge and the arts'.[5] Small birds were much sought after in Europe. During the fifteenth and sixteenth centuries, as parrots became fashionable pets, a lucrative trade developed. Sailors kept a lookout for them. The Cantino planisphere shows parrots as West African resources, along with enslaved people and timber. They were also considered good eating, and at Madagascar in 1596, Houtman's men killed and ate great numbers of grey parrots.[6] But Pigafetta, in his 1522 account, also related the story of giant birds, so large that they could carry an elephant (Figure 15).

In the same year, Spanish pilot and master of nautical charts Nuño García de Toreno published his Indian Ocean map featuring two giant birds (Figure 16). The birds depicted are chestnut-bellied guans, large turkey-like birds of the genus *Penelope* (Figure 17). Guans belong to an order of ground-feeding birds that includes turkey, grouse, quail, partridge, pheasant, guineafowl and peafowl – commonly known as game fowl.

Chestnut-bellied guans are native only to Brazil, a country claimed for the Portuguese empire in 1500 by explorer Pedro Cabral, who is credited as having been the first European to reach Brazil, and to have led the second European expedition to reach India via

Figure 15. An impression of the Roc, which fed its young on elephants, by Charles Maurice Detmold (1883–1908).

the Cape of Good Hope. The guans on García de Toreno's chart are perched on two phantom islands, southwest of Sumatra, in 10°–12° south – the rough latitude of the Cocos (Keeling) Islands. The islands are labelled 'y[lha]: dos Rocos', Portuguese words suggesting that Polo's Roc birds lived there. The monstrous birds have been seen as a warning to mariners not to approach from the west. The map is thought to have been drawn at least in part by a Portuguese cartographer, and it has placed some of the Indonesian Islands on the Portuguese side of the Tordesillas demarcation line, thereby implicitly claiming rights for Portugal.[7]

The male Chinese Pond Heron is visually the closest eastern hemisphere approximation to the chestnut-bellied guan, but it is just possible that the mapmaker depicted chestnut-bellied guans on islands in the general location of Cocos because he had heard from Indian Ocean islanders, via members of Elcano's crew on the *Victoria*, of palatable, big-footed, ground-feeding, chestnut-bellied birds living on islands in the southern Indian Ocean. North Keeling Island in the Cocos does have the now endangered Cocos Buff-banded Rail (*Rallus philippensis*), a big-footed ground-feeding bird with a brown breast.[8] It was reported in 1836 by Darwin's servant Syms Covington as indigenous to the Cocos (Keeling) Islands, and it shares these superficial aspects of its appearance with the much longer-tailed and larger, chestnut-bellied guan depicted as beautiful guardians of territory on the García de Toreno map.

At the beginning of the eighteenth century, the first English-language version of *One Thousand and One Nights* included 'The Seven Voyages of Sinbad the Sailor', with a fictional hero from Baghdad who, during voyages east of Africa in the eighth and ninth centuries, encountered monsters and witnessed supernatural phenomena.[9] Among the monsters of the southern Indian Ocean today are the world's largest living lizards on Komodo island, lizards classed as endangered on the International Union for Conservation of Nature's (IUCN) Red List of species at risk of extinction. However, it was the flying monsters that received Sinbad's attention. The Roc appears at a tropical island during Sinbad's second voyage.

Figure 16. Detail from the García de Toreno map of 1522 in the Biblioteca Reale di Torino.

Figure 17. The chestnut-bellied guan of Brazil, now on the International Union for Conservation of Nature's Red List of Threatened Species.

During his fifth voyage one of his crew sees, on an island, a gigantic egg that Sinbad recognises as belonging to a Roc (Figure 19). The ship's curious passengers disembarked to examine the egg, only to end up breaking it and having the chick as a meal.

Aspects of the folklore about 'oversized' or very large birds are grounded on solid evidence. When Europeans began to explore the southern Indian Ocean, it was a veritable menagerie of extraordinary birds. As they headed eastward after the Cape of Good Hope, some navigators would read on their charts the words 'land of parrots'.[10] A poem written on a Dutch ship, *Bruin-Vis,* that visited Mauritius in 1602 translates as:

> For food, the seamen hunt the flesh of feathered fowl,
> They tap the palms, and round rump dodos they destroy,
> The parrot's life they spare that he may peep and howl,
> And thus his fellows to imprisonment decoy.[11]

The 1601–03 journal of the Dutch ship *Gelderland*, under the command of Wolphart Harmanzoon, contains a sketch, made during a voyage to Mauritius, of a blue parrot of the genus *Lophopsittacus* (now extinct), with a disproportionately large head and bill.[12]

The Mauritian dodo, *Raphus cucullatus*, was a giant flightless pigeon whose body, as represented in museum exhibitions and the literature, superficially resembles that of a metre-tall chicken, with a beak more like that of a booby. Its close relative, the Rodrigues solitaire, *Pezophaps solitaria*, taller, slenderer and about the size of a swan, was sometimes confused with the Mauritian dodo. The extinction of these birds during the seventeenth century brought attention to the previously unrecognised problem of human involvement in the disappearances of entire species. The dodo achieved widespread recognition from its role in Lewis Carroll's story of *Alice's Adventures in Wonderland*, and it has since become a fixture in popular culture, even generating discussion about the possibility of recreating live dodo specimens from a sequenced genome.

Figure 18. A dodo as painted by Roelant Savery, late 1620s. The long-beaked bird at lower right may be the extinct Red Rail of Mauritius. The two parrots may be the extinct, out-of-place Lesser Antillean Macaw (left) and Martinique Macaw (right).

Substantial evidence has accumulated about much larger southern Indian Ocean birds, found as fossils estimated to be 2,000 BP (years before present) of the elephant-bird family *Aepyornithidae*, in Pleistocene and Holocene deposits on Madagascar. Fossil eggs identified as belonging to these birds have drifted on ocean currents from Madagascar to Western Australia, to be found near Cervantes on the west coast and Scott River on the south coast.[13]

Scientists at the Zoological Society of London's Institute of Zoology have concluded that *Vorombe titan*, of Madagascar, first described in 1894 in a newspaper article by British palaeontologist Charles Andrews as *Aepyornis titan*, reached weights up to 800 kg (heavier than New Zealand's extinct Moa) and a height of 3 metres, making it the world's largest-ever bird.[14]

Les marchands cassèrent l'œuf. (Page 147, col. 1.)

Figure 19. An 1865 artist's impression of the Chrocho egg from Gustave Dore's *One Thousand and One Nights*.

English writer H. G. Wells, often called the 'father of science fiction', studied biology under Thomas Huxley, obtained a degree in zoology, and helped set up the Royal College of Science. It appears that he was inspired by Charles Andrews' account to write his short story *Aepyornis Island*, published in 1894. In this work of fiction, Wells relates a story about a scar-faced, pipe-smoking adventurer named Butcher, who visits Madagascar to collect fossil bones to sell to museums in England. Butcher loads some fresh *Aepyornis vastus* eggs onto his boat. He falls out with, and shoots, his native companions, then drifts eastward for 10 days, before arriving at a coral atoll. Ashore, one of the eggs hatches.

Butcher relates of the hatchling that 'he was a nice friendly little chap at first, about the size of a small hen', and Butcher gives 'him' the name 'Man Friday'.[15] By the end of the second year on the island, Friday is 'about fourteen feet high', and, as Butcher puts it, 'our little paradise went wrong … he began to cock his comb at me and give himself airs'. So Butcher kills Friday and puts him in the lagoon for the fish to pick him clean, before collecting the bones, flagging down a passing yacht and returning to England. He sells the bones to a dealer near the British Museum, and the dealer on-sells them to 'old Havers', apparently a curator at the museum. They are left unattended and forgotten, and someone turns up with an *Aepyornis titan* thigh bone, smaller than that of Friday, but real.

The story is clearly fiction, but it does seem probable that Wells, the zoology graduate, would have bumped into some of the museum's 'outside' collectors, and that Butcher is at least a close representative of some of the gun-toting European rascals who, when beyond the limits of their own jurisdictions, pillaged with impunity the cultural and natural treasures of Indian Ocean islands.

First associations with the Cocos (Keeling) Islands

The Cocos (Keeling) Islands are located 530 nautical miles to the west-southwest of Christmas Island. Linguist Claude Allibert has examined the possible dissemination of the coconut palm, by Austronesians, South Asians and Arabs, from the east to the west of the Indian Ocean.[16] Plant evolutionary botanist Kenneth Olsen has concluded that the Austronesians introduced Pacific coconuts to their Indian Ocean trade routes.[17]

Charles Darwin experimented in his backyard with small seeds soaked in saltwater and, after making observations at sea, he concluded that plants and animals migrate to remote islands by wind, water and wing.[18] On a later occasion he wrote to his friend Joseph Hooker that the seeds from a clod of earth he had removed from the foot of a partridge produced 32 plants after sowing out. When he arrived at the Cocos (Keeling) Islands he observed that, 'As the islands consist entirely of coral, and at one time must have existed as mere water-washed reefs, all their terrestrial productions must have been transported here by the waves of the sea'.[19] He went on to list plant species from the East Indian Archipelago and Australia

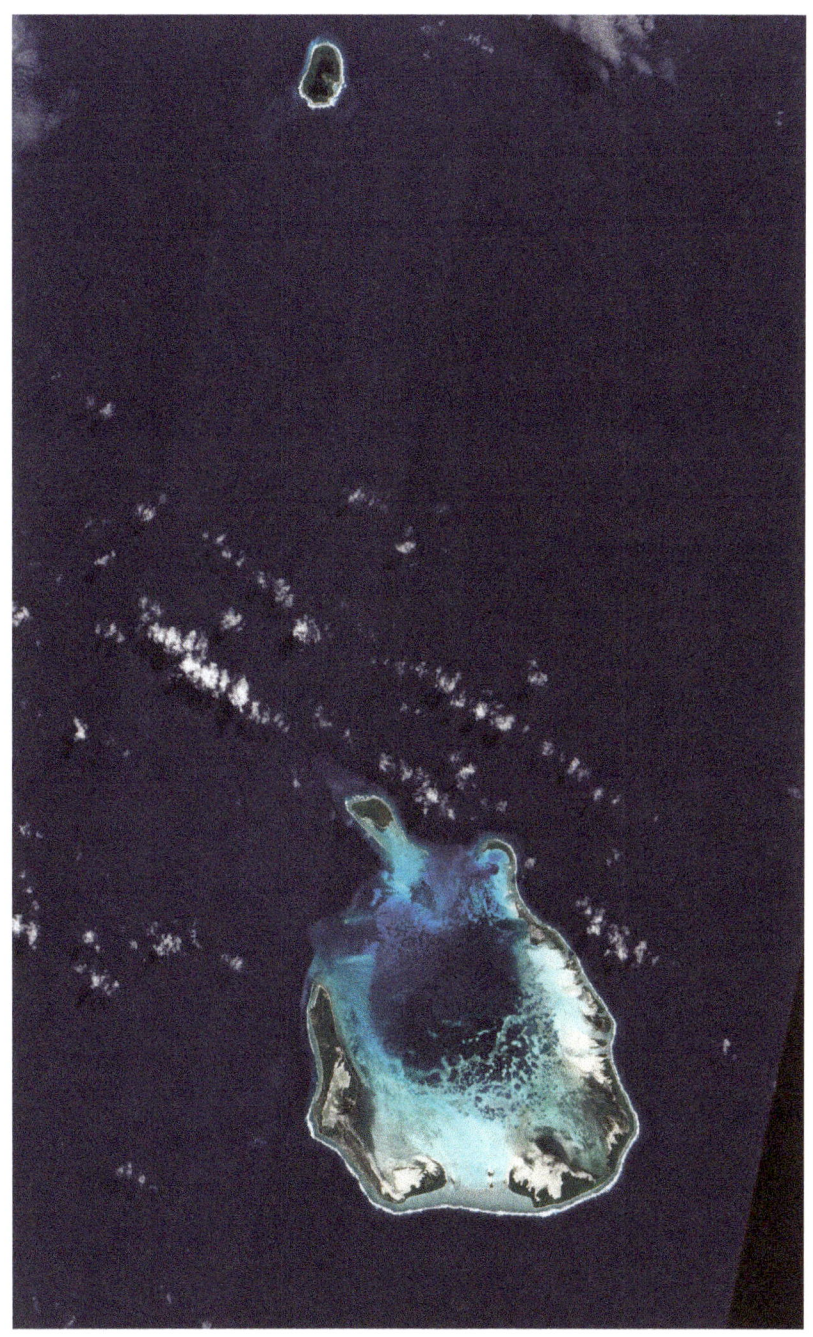

Figure 20. The Cocos (Keeling) Islands. North Keeling is at the top of the image. Image: NASA's Earth Observatory.

that must have drifted, as seeds, between 1,800 and 2,400 miles, but he did not speculate on the origin of the coconut palms, or take any specimens.[20] It would, of course, take much more than a partridge to transport coconuts to remote islands.

In 1890 James Dana, naturalist and President of the American Geological Society, wrote:

> It is doubted whether the ocean is ever successful in planting the cocoanut on coral islands. The nut seems to be well fitted for marine transportation, through its thick husk, which serves both as a float and protection; but there is no known evidence that an island never inhabited has been found supplied with cocoanut trees. The possibility of a successful planting by the waves cannot be denied; but there are so many chances that the floating nut will be kept too long in the water, or be thrown where it cannot germinate, that the probability of a transplanting is extremely small.[21]

Botanist Henry Guppy, also in 1890, took a modified view, writing that, 'In the Keeling Islands many drift seeds and seed vessels cannot be protected from the crabs unless first covered over with sand by the waves in heavy gales, and amongst them, we may include the cocoa-nut'.[22]

If Dana is right, humans must have landed and planted coconuts on the Cocos (Keeling) Islands some years before the publication of Hessel Gerritsz's 1622 'Chart of the Indian Ocean't Amsterdam' on which he marked the islands as Cocos Eylanden. Coconut palms take 20 years to reach full height and a decade or so for the trees to grow to an obvious height for a passing mapmaker to see. For the palms to multiply takes many more years. However, Dana did not seriously consider the impact of cyclones and turtles on these low-lying atolls.

In 2015 visiting Wreck Check members observed parts of wrecked vessels thrown well above the normal tide line of the Cocos (Keeling) Islands, part-buried in a fertile mix of coral fragments, sand and guano, and partly overgrown with foliage. Nesting turtles create chaos equivalent to that of cyclones on sandy beaches by digging holes, depositing their eggs, and then burying them along with beach litter, such as coconuts, in the process. Cocos resident Arthur Keating was quoted in James Holman's 1830s travel account as saying, 'Seeds and plants from Sumatra and Java have been driven up by the surf on the windward side of the islands. Among them have been found ... the cocoa-nut of Balci [Bali], known by its shape and size'.[23] These nuts could have been driven from Bali towards the Western Australian coast by the northwest monsoon, and then back to the Cocos by the southeast trade winds.

Darwin's greenstone

Archaeological research on the Cocos (Keeling) Islands and Christmas Island has revealed no indications of a human settlement history earlier than the period of European exploration, despite

Figure 21. Wreckage of a refugee boat washed ashore and part salvaged, near the West Island airstrip.

these islands lying reasonably close to the theorised Austronesian direct route across the southern Indian Ocean between Asia and Madagascar. It seems likely, if the theories about direct-route Austronesian voyaging across the southern Indian Ocean are correct, that at least one lost mariner would have sighted and visited the islands before the Europeans. To date, however, no artefactual evidence has been found to provide a clear link.

Darwin's notebook entries of 1836
When Charles Darwin visited the Cocos, community leader John Clunies-Ross, who had settled on the Cocos in 1825, was away from the islands, and his apprentice, William Liesk, showed Darwin around. Darwin was given, shown or simply told about a fragment of what he called greenstone, said to have been taken by Clunies-Ross from a boulder found on one of the 'Northern Islands'.[24] Darwin wrote an entry about the sample, whose whereabouts are now unknown, in his little red geological specimens notebook:

> Capt Ross. 3581. From large rounded fragment in Breccia of a compact solid Greenstone.[25]

In the same notebook, he referred to 'Greenstone Rock brought by roots of trees', and to 'Several earthquakes and the Greenstone Rocks [plural] on the Northern Islands [plural]'. If Darwin was writing while on the *Beagle*, anchored inside the South Keeling atoll, then the Northern Islands would have to be Horsburgh and North Keeling, and he must have determined that there were greenstone rocks on both of these islands. An optional interpretation is that he inadvertently penned an s-shaped tail to his hand-written words 'rock' and 'island', and that he meant from the beginning to write of a single rock on a single northern island – North Keeling.

Greenstone and breccia
Darwin was influenced in his interpretation of geological matters by the writings of Scottish geologist Charles Lyell, who defined

greenstone as 'a variety of trap [igneous rock more or less columnar in structure], composed of hornblende and felspar'.[26] Darwin is thought to have used the word greenstone to describe greenish, dark magmatic rocks that are now classified as dolerite-basalt, whereas for modern geologists, it is the name for a metamorphic rock.[27] Greenstone in its several forms is naturally present in many places. Breccia was defined by Lyell as a rock composed of angular fragments connected by lime or other mineral substance. However, it has been observed elsewhere that, 'Few geologic structures so lend themselves to diverse interpretations as the beds of broken rock called breccia'.[28]

In 1845, nine years after making his notebook entry about greenstone, Darwin wrote in his published work, *Journal of Researches*, that:

> A few miles north of Keeling there is another small atoll, the lagoon of which is nearly filled up with coral mud. Captain Ross [John Clunies-Ross] found embedded in the conglomerate on the outer coast [of the small atoll], a well-rounded fragment of greenstone, rather larger than a man's head: he and the men with him were so much surprised at this, that they brought it away and preserved it as a curiosity. The occurrence of this one stone, where every other particle of matter is calcareous, certainly is very puzzling. The island has scarcely ever been visited, nor is it probable that a ship had been wrecked there. From the absence of any better explanation, I came to the conclusion that it must have come entangled in the roots of some large tree ... Stones may often be thus carried; and if the island on which they are stranded is constructed of any other substance besides coral, they would scarcely attract attention.[29]

He also wrote in his *Journal of Researches* that:

> The saucer-shaped summit [of South Keeling] is nearly ten miles across; and every single atom, [171] from the least particle

to the largest fragment of rock ... bears the stamp of having been subjected to organic arrangement. [Footnote 171 reads, 'I exclude, of course ... some small fragments of pumice, drifted here by the waves. The one block of greenstone, moreover, on the northern island must be excepted'].[30]

So, while he appears to have initially written in his notebook in 1836 of a number of greenstone rocks on more than one northern island, in his published work in 1845 he wrote of just one 'block of greenstone' on the (singular) northern island.

Visiting scientists were taking a strong interest in out-of-place rocks found on coral atolls. Darwin had visited the Cocos (Keeling) Islands soon after the occurrence of a severe earthquake on the islands, and soon after leaving Cocos he visited the volcanic South Atlantic island of Ascension, where he referred to 'volcanic bombs' – masses of volcanic lava that had been shot through the air while fluid – 'where there is a shell-like case about the third of an inch in thickness, of compact stone'.[31] Perhaps Darwin reflected upon that shell-like case, and his earlier diagnosis of 'compact solid Greenstone' for fragment 3581, after he saw the volcanic bombs on Ascension.

Henry Guppy wrote, in 1889, of rounded, coconut-sized white pumice from the Krakatoa eruption landing on Cocos beaches, and of black, heavier pumice (scoria, which might contain elements of greenstone) from the eruption of Mount Tambora. Tambora, on Sumbawa Island just east of Java, had suffered the largest and deadliest volcanic eruption in the modern era, in 1815. The island's vegetation was destroyed. Uprooted trees, mixed with pumice, washed into the sea, forming rafts many kilometres wide that drifted long distances.

Guppy also wrote of a huge volcanic bomb (also scoria), composed of a dark reddish cellular lava, which he thought had drifted onto Horsburgh Island. Clunies-Ross had told Guppy that the dome-shaped object, about 4 feet in height, was found 300 yards from the sea, but that in recent years, 'curiosity, perhaps assisted by superstition, had led to the demolition of this so-called thunderbolt'.[32] Pieces from the Horsburgh Island bomb had been taken away by the islanders at various times and for different reasons, so only a few fragments remained when Guppy visited in 1888.

Darwin's 1845 interpretation prompts several questions. On which atoll or island was the greenstone said by Darwin to have been found by Clunies-Ross? Horsburgh Island lies 6 kilometres to the northwest of the Clunies-Ross settlement, while North Keeling Island is 24 kilometres to the north. Was Darwin's fragment 3581 one of the Horsburgh Island pieces taken away by curious islanders? There was room for confusion. Darwin's account came from Liesk while Guppy's account came from Clunies-Ross. However, Darwin's comment, that the island where the single greenstone piece had been found had scarcely ever been visited, makes it clear that he was, by 1845, thinking of North Keeling rather than Horsburgh as the source of the single piece.

Darwin's drifting tree trunk?
Darwin commented that, 'Floating pumice [a light spongy lava according to Lyell] and scoria [volcanic cinders according to Lyell], and occasionally stones transported in the roots of trees … appear the only sources by which foreign matter is brought to coral formations standing in the open ocean'.[33] Darwin had previously been thinking about the possibilities of long-distance dispersal in regard to living plants and animals, an idea intimately linked to evolution. At the Cocos (Keeling) Islands, however, he might have built greenstone into the models of long-distance dispersal he was toying with.[34] Because of North Keeling's isolation he thought it improbable that a ship could have been wrecked there, concluding, 'from the absence of any better explanation', that the greenstone rock had been carried there entangled in the roots of a tree trunk. By such transport it might have been brought on ocean currents from the greenstone present on Java. If the tree trunk speculated by Darwin came from Sumbawa Island, the greenstone may have contained crystals of olivine, a pretty green magnesium iron silicate known to have been ejected from the 1815 Mount Tambora eruption.

There are, however, several possible alternative explanations for its presence on North Keeling Island.

An Austronesian or Chinese visit?
At first glance, archaeological researchers seeing reference to greenstone on North Keeling might reflect on whether its presence points to a visit by Austronesians or Chinese. Austronesian vessels from Java (the ships represented by the Borobudur carvings) might have carried greenstone mined in Java, or obsidian, or other rocks for grinding flour or obtaining flints. Greenstone can imply stone used by early cultures, including the Māori in New Zealand and the Chinese (notably as a source of jade), to fashion carvings such as jewellery, statuettes and ritual tools. Crewmen from whaleships visiting New Zealand collected boulders that had been water-washed and polished in mountain streams. People on Easter Island in the Pacific used scoria to carve the topknots for their moai statues. Such objects are often found far from the rock source, indicating trading networks.[35] Fleets commanded by Chinese Admiral Zheng travelled, between 1405 and 1433, through parts of the northern rim of the Indian Ocean, including Java, and it might be expected that the Chinese obtained any available information there about offshore voyaging routes, from Sunda Strait to Madagascar, that might have taken them past the Cocos.[36]

A European shipwreck?
Darwin concluded that the North Keeling greenstone rock might have come to the atoll entangled in the roots of a large tree, in part because he presumed there had been no shipwrecks there. However, unbeknown to Darwin in 1836, a ship had run aground there in June 1834.[37] The 229-ton, British-registered snow brig *Earl of Liverpool* had left the British colony of Gambia in West Africa, rounded the Cape of Good Hope, and gone on to Singapore.[38] From there it headed south before starting back west, with a cargo including antimony ore, heading for London. It struck the northeast corner of North Keeling Island and the boats were stove in the surf. The hull, or

part of it, was taken to South Keeling, while the crew and some of the salvaged cargo were taken on to Mauritius by the barque *Helen*, which had been discharging cargo at the main atoll.[39] Antimony was sometimes a side product from greenstone-belt gold deposits. Most gold mining in the Gambia before the mid-nineteenth century was alluvial. Miners recovered gold from streams, so some rounded antimony stones might be expected if the ore for the *Earl of Liverpool* was obtained in association with gold mining. The antimony ore could have been loaded either at the mouth of the Gambia River or, more likely, en route to Singapore at an East African port on the coast of Mozambique (an ongoing source of enslaved people), adjacent to the Murchison greenstone belt and now one of the world's largest antimony-producing areas.[40]

Clunies-Ross might have known about the *Earl of Liverpool*'s cargo, including the antimony ore, because he later salvaged the hull and repaired it at Home Island. However, as noted earlier, he was absent when Darwin visited the Cocos, so Darwin's informant was Mr Liesk. Liesk was highly regarded by Darwin for his knowledge of corals, but he probably would not have recognised a greenstone boulder as antimony ore if it was such.[41] Antimony was used for hardening pewter and as an alloy component in bullets and artillery shells. The ore is frequently found as smooth, rounded agglomerates and it usually lacks crystals.[42] So although Clunies-Ross preserved the greenstone boulder as a curiosity, it is doubtful that he would have seen it as something that, like ivory, could be worked into saleable jewellery by members of his island community.

European charts as they relate to Cocos (Keeling) Islands

The Portuguese general Alfonso Albuquerque had Malay sailors guide him through Java and the Lesser Sunda Islands east of Java in 1512. The Portuguese generally approached and left the East Indies from the west or northwest rather than from the south, lessening the likelihood that they would have reached the Cocos (Keeling) Islands during the sixteenth century. However, some charts are marked with islands in locations that could be seen to imply such a discovery.

As discussed in Chapter 2, the Cantino map of 1502 is now interpreted as representing the islands of Java and Ceram much too far to the west. Later in the sixteenth century, however, maps of the Dieppe School of cartographers based in France, who are considered to have sacrificed accuracy for beauty, initially showed islands of the Chagos archipelago too far to the west.[43]

Diego Garcia lies 300 miles south of the Maldives, in 7.2° south, at the southern end of the Chagos archipelago. A 1546 Pierre Desceliers map, produced 12 years before the Portuguese established a presence in the Maldives, shows the Chagos atoll to the west of the Maldives, with 'Grace de Dieu' (Diego Garcia Island) on its south side, shown as an upright rectangle. As if to compensate for the removal of the Chagos Islands and Diego Garcia from the southern end of the Maldives, Desceliers shows on this map another cluster of islands directly south of the Maldives, in 10.5° south according to the scale on the map – close to the latitude of the Cocos (Keeling) Islands.[44] The cluster is marked 'A: defponoada', from the Portuguese word *despovoada* meaning unpopulated or deserted.

The Harleian Mappemonde of 1547, another of the Dieppe School maps, shows the Maldives archipelago with representations of what appear to be three islands of the Addu atoll, and Chagos reinstated at the south end.[45] This map shows Desceliers' A: defponoada triangle as an isolated circle, positioned directly south of the Maldives. Then the 1550 Desceliers map (Figure 22) shows Diego Garcia as 'de dieu grace' in the shape of the boot earlier referred to in regard to the Cantino map. Desceliers shows the detached southernmost island, A: defponoada, as a single island, and takes it considerably further eastward of the Maldives, closer to the location of the Cocos, in 11° south.[46]

By this time, while other European cartographers were getting a clearer understanding of each of the elements of the Maldives and Chagos Islands, they remained unsure of the more remote A: defponoada, which had become a phantom island, alienated by the withdrawal of the Chagos archipelago towards its correct location on the maps. In 1593, Gerard de Jode marked 'Defpopulada', also suggesting 'deserted area', on a triangular cluster of islands in 25° south, 80° east, approximately 900 miles west of where the Cocos lie.

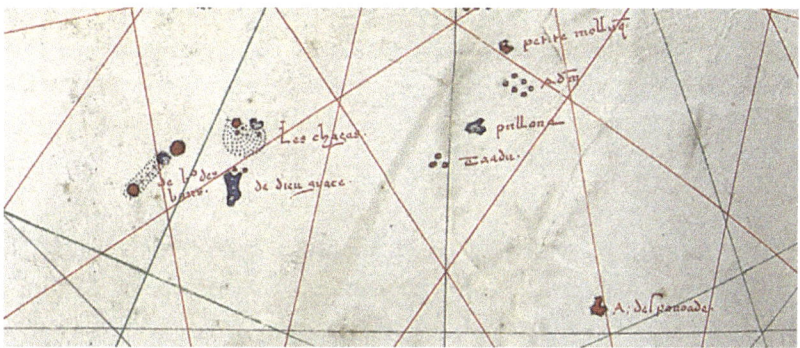

Figure 22. Detail from the 1550 Desceliers map of the world showing Diego Garcia and, to the southeast, 'A: defponoada' as a triangular blob.
See <https://commons.wikimedia.org/wiki/File:Map_of_the_world_-_Pierre_Desceliers,_1550_-_BL_Add_MS_24065.jpg>.

Figure 23. NASA image of Diego Garcia atoll (British Indian Ocean Territory). The profile is similar to a sock or boot.

Defpopulada remained far to the west, but between the sixteenth and eighteenth centuries another phantom version of Diego Garcia appears to have been detached from the southern end of the Chagos archipelago. Its derivatives shifted several hundred miles further south before settling back to a line between 10° and 12° south. Then this phantom island, marked by a succession of evolving toponyms referring to poultry, seems to have 'drifted', like the elephant-bird eggs, 1,450 miles eastward, eventually washing up on the Cocos (Keeling) Islands and integrating with a real island – North Keeling Island.

Gerardus Mercator, on a map of 1569, replaced defponoada with 'pousada', a word meaning a resting place, an inn for eating local produce, or perhaps a roosting place for edible birds. The question arises – had Mercator seen and been impressed by García de Toreno's map with its magnificent guans, or had he obtained information about edible birds such as the Cocos Rail from the natives of islands in the Indian Ocean? Dutch cartographer Abraham Ortelius was recognised both as the creator of the first modern atlas and as the first to speculate that continents might have 'drifted' across the ocean bed. He produced a world map in 1570, now showing 'Poueada' (from *poularde*, or *pollarde*, suggesting pullets or chickens fattened for the table), to the southeast of Diego Garcia in 12° south, the latitude of the Cocos (Keeling) Islands.[47] In March 1596 Cornelis Ceullen, master of the *Duyfken* during the Houtman expedition to the Spice Islands, estimated himself to be 238 Dutch miles from what he termed the 'unproven' island of Polueirija in 11° 50'. On the following page of his journal the island is referred to in shortened forms as Polvera, Polvara, Poluera and Poluara, all of them probably derived from Mercator's Pousada.[48] Then a 1598 map by Linschoten shows, in a similar position, an island replacing Ortelius' Poueada with one named 'I da Poluara'.[49]

All the mapmakers relied in part on pre-existing maps. Mercator family map plates were bought by Jodocus Hondius and his sons. Hessel Gerritsz was apprenticed to future Verenigde Oostindische Compagnie (VOC) hydrographer Willem Blaeu and worked closely with Petrus Plancius. During copying processes, spelling errors crept in, rendering some toponyms meaningless and changing the meaning of others. The word Poluara has no identifiable meaning, but the Latin words *polluc* and *polluere* mean to pollute, as does the Portuguese *poluir*. It may be expected that mariners going ashore or passing downwind of guano islands containing seabird rookeries would regard those places as being polluted. The Italian *polveriera* means a gunpowder store (these were placed in strategic locations through Italy), and the Italian *polverara* means a particularly large Italian chicken breed. As might be expected, each of these toponyms has connotations relating in some way to guano or birds. Several maps of the area show this island with an upright shape, like a boot, heel or sock. Theodor De Bry's 1595/97 chart, showing Cornelis de Houtman's 1597 route, depicts the outward-bound fleet passing to the north of what appears to be Mercator's Pousada.

After Houtman's voyage, homeward-bound Dutch ships leaving Sunda Strait steered a south-westerly course for the Cape of Good Hope, taking many of them through the vicinity of the Cocos (Keeling) Islands. It was inevitable that some of the Europeans would soon report their sightings of this island group.

As will be explained more fully in the following sections, the Hessel Gerritsz 1612 chart shows a basic triangle of islands representing the Cocos (Keeling) Islands to the southwest of Sumatra. In his 1622 chart, Gerritsz has shown Poluara as Polverara, named South Keeling as Cocos Eylanden, and added a small, unnamed, circular island a little to the north that can be construed as North Keeling. Gerritsz has placed his North Keeling too close to his South Keeling, leaving an apparent void in the correct place for North Keeling. Then British chartmaker Robert Dudley has imposed, on the location of Gerritsz's three dots, three impressive triangular islands (Figure 26). Dudley initially named his North Keeling Island 'Riling Island', and on a later chart, 'Killing Island'. In 1780 the English cartographer Samuel Dunn referred to the 'Killing or Coco Islands' in the location of the Cocos (Keeling) Islands. Then in 1787 Alexander Dalrymple was the first to use the Keeling toponym, labelling the southern atoll as 'Keeling or Cocos Islands'.

The Hessel Gerritsz 1612 world map and 1622 chart of the Indian Ocean

During the first two decades of the seventeenth century, marks on charts of the area to the southwest of Sunda Strait show that Europeans had found the Cocos (Keeling) Islands. A 1610 chart by Dutch cartographer Jodocus Hondius, who helped establish Amsterdam as the centre of cartography in Europe in the

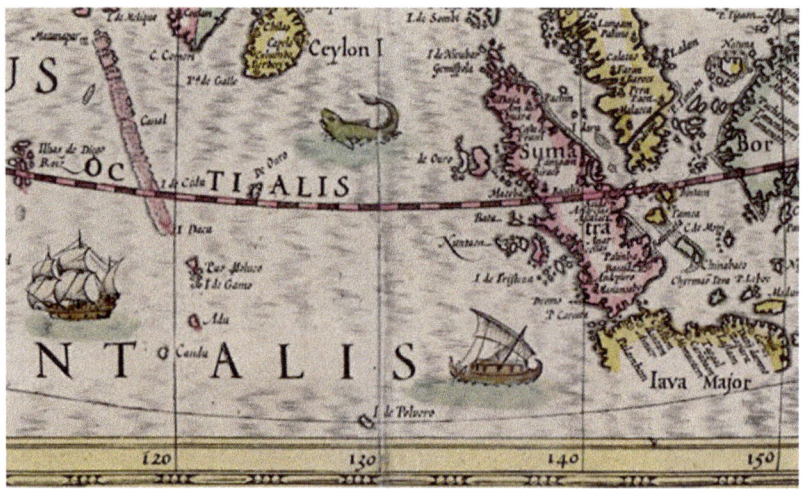

Figure 24. Detail from Hondius' chart of 1610 showing I de Polvero at bottom central in the general location of the Cocos (Keeling) Islands.

Figure 25. Detail of Hondius II chart of 1630, taking 'I da Polvera' back towards the Laccadive-Maldive-Chagos Ridge.

seventeenth century, placed 'I de Polvero' well to the east of the Chagos archipelago, in 10° south, 95° east, roughly the position we now know to be that of the Cocos (Keeling) Islands, situated in 12° south, 97° east.[50] This prompts the questions of which mariner told Hondius of their discovery, and when that discovery was made?

After Dirk Hartog's 'discovery' of the west coast of the Australian continent in 1616, adjustments were made to Hendrick Brouwer's 1611 southern route. Subsequently, during the monsoon period, outward-bound Dutch and English vessels turned northeast towards Sunda Strait soon after reaching Amsterdam Island, and sailed past the Cocos (Keeling) Islands.[51] It may be expected that sightings of these islands then became frequent.

Hessel Gerritsz is considered one of the most important Dutch cartographers of the seventeenth century. He shows on his 1612 world map (see Figure 26), referred to elsewhere as a 'very rare and very important product',[52] several islands along the Sumatran coast. The northernmost is finger shaped and probably represents Siberut, the largest island of the Mentawai Island chain. The island closer to Sunda Strait possibly represents Enggano, while the island shown a little further south is Enggano or, less likely, Christmas Island. More importantly, the triangle of dots shown to the southwest of Sunda Strait represents West Island, South Island and Home Island of the South Keeling Islands, rather than the solitary Christmas Island or the inshore Mentawai Islands.

The Gerritsz 1612 world map is the earliest clear evidence that the South Keeling Islands had been discovered. Because of the small scale of the map, the islands lack a bold outline, but the fact that Gerritsz has marked the three largest islands of South Keeling indicates that the reporting navigator had inspected the group rather than obtaining a mere distant sighting.[53]

The navigator who reported to Gerritsz his sighting of the three largest islets of South Keeling would, if outward bound, have taken a good year to continue on to the East Indies, conduct trade and return to the Netherlands with his report. It can be expected that

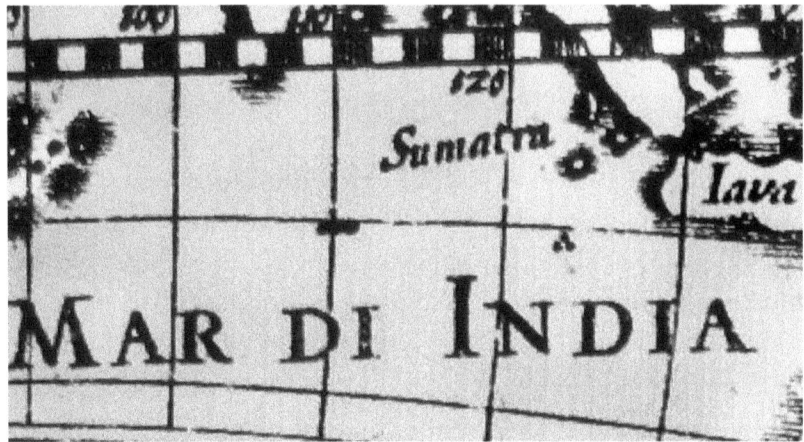

Figure 26. Detail of the Hessel Gerritsz world map of 1612 showing Cocos as a triangle of dots in 12° south.

Gerritsz would not have rushed to the publication of his 1612 chart based on a report of three small islands southwest of Java — such a report could wait. His schedule would surely have been determined by more important developments. So Gerritsz's reporting navigator might well have sighted them before 1609 when English merchant William Keeling's fleet sailed homeward across the Indian Ocean. Hartog's 1616 'discovery' of the west coast of Australia was kept secret for a decade before Hessel Gerritsz's 1626 publication of the first edition of a map depicting 'Land Eendracht'.[54]

The first use of the toponym 'Cocos' for the Cocos (Keeling) Islands appears to have been on the Gerritsz 1622 'Chart of the Indian Ocean 't Amsterdam', showing 'Cocos Eylanden' southwest of Sunda Strait.[55] The use by Gerritsz of this toponym indicates that coconut palms were already well established there, planted previously by humans or, more likely, brought ashore by ocean currents. The Gerritsz 1622 map also depicts, for the first time, what are probably both the northern and the southern atolls of the Cocos (Keeling) Islands, showing that the two atolls had been found.[56] On this map, Gerritsz has interpreted Linschoten's Poluara, shown well to the east of the Chagos atoll, as Polverara.

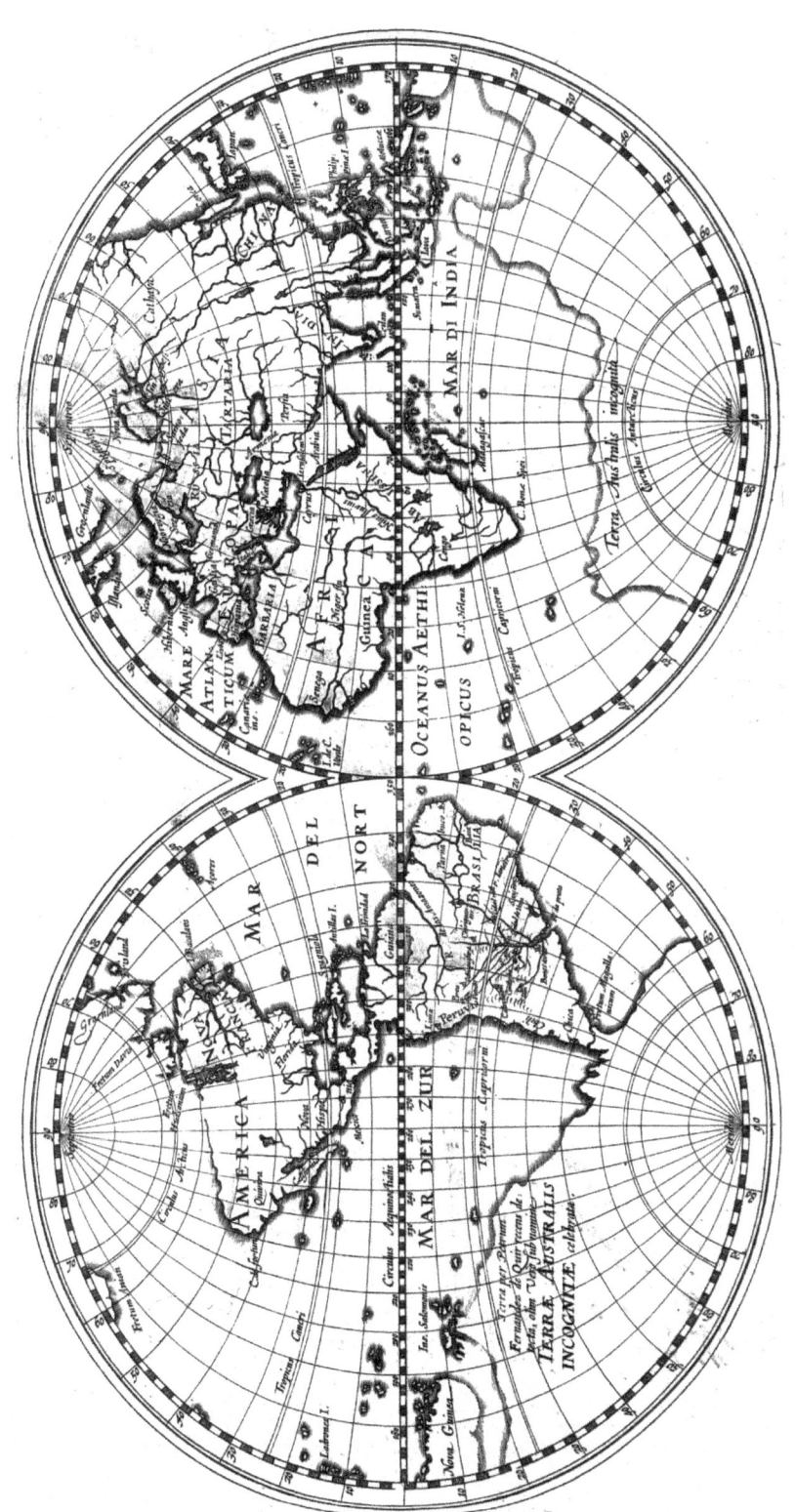

Figure 27. The Hessel Gerritsz 1612 world map.

It is useful to examine the several meanings of this word. Polverara (sometimes spelled 'Polveriera') is a municipality 30 kilometres southwest of Venice in the Italian province of Padua. It is a natural oasis, with nesting wild birds of many types, cared for by an environmental association.[57] In the early sixteenth century the area was famous for the abundance of a breed of sometimes black, sometimes white, domestic chickens of remarkable size, especially in Polverara, a village within the municipality, described in 1622 as 'the kingdom of the roosters'.[58] The polverara chickens (Figure 28), tasty birds with darker flesh than other chickens, were difficult to contain and, like the wild birds, preferred to roost in branches of trees.

Of the birds roosting on islands in the southern Indian Ocean, once the dodo, last recorded in 1681, had become extinct, the branch-roosting red-footed booby (*Sula sula*, Figure 29) was the bird most likely to conjure, for mariners, images of polverara chickens. It had similarities in colour, size and roosting habit, had a tasty flavour, was numerous and was easy to capture. North Keeling Island, the only seabird-breeding colony within a radius of 900 kilometres, is today possibly the world's largest colony of red-footed boobies. Boobies had a habit of landing on sailing ships, where they were easily captured and eaten. William Bligh ate them during his boat voyage after the *Bounty* mutiny. The red-footed boobies are by far the most numerous seabirds on North Keeling atoll, and they have been regularly harvested for eating by the Cocos Malay people of Home Island over the last century.[59] It is unlikely that any other Indian Ocean island rivals North Keeling's range of seabird species, although 1,500 nautical miles west-northwest, in 7.3° south, Diego Garcia also has a large colony of red-footed boobies, and guano has been exported commercially from that island.[60] The presence of boobies on both Diego Garcia and North Keeling was reason for confusion by mapmakers who named islands after edible birds.

The European mariner who introduced the toponym Polverara to Gerritsz would have been aware of the supposed dangers presented by giant birds such as Marco Polo's 'Roc' to the eastward of Madagascar and, perhaps, of García de Toreno's 'dos Rocos' islands, southwest of Sumatra. At the same time, he would have been interested in potential island resources, such as tasty edible birds as an alternative to the daily ration of salted beef or pork carried in barrels below deck, and, apparently, he was impressed by the similarity between the big-chicken rookeries at Polverara (in Padua) and the booby rookery on North Keeling Island.

Figure 28 (above left). A Polverara chicken.

Figure 29 (above right). A red-footed booby.

Figure 30. Alice's dodo, by Karl Beutel, 2011, following earlier depictions. Resemblances between chickens, boobies and dodos influenced the mythology of the southern Indian Ocean.

Other mapmakers varied the spelling of the toponym for this phantom island. The Italian word *polveriera* means gunpowder, and the sites of several historic gunpowder deposits in Italy are so named. The Latin *polluere* means pollution, possibly an oblique reference to bird droppings. Guano from bird and bat droppings was used for fertiliser, but also for saltpetre, an ingredient of gunpowder. The use of gunpowder spread from China through the Middle East to Europe in the late-thirteenth century.[61]

In 1675 the young William Dampier, of about 23 years, was a keen observer of collectable resources. He noted that the Spanish collected soil from cisterns at Cape Catoch on the Yukatan Peninsula in Central America, to make saltpetre.[62] At Tonquin (Vietnam) in 1688 he discussed with a French priest his method of making gunpowder. Then Dampier obtained sulphur, saltpetre and coals, and, 'having drunk a Glass or two of Wine with him I went to work', making eight barrels of 'very good powder before I went from thence'.[63]

Mariners in the Indian Ocean, reading Dampier's works, could not fail to notice the presence of guano on atolls such as the Cocos (Keeling) Islands. A later chart by Pierre Mortier shows the toponym 'Cago I' beside North Keeling Island.[64] The word 'cago' comes from the Old Portuguese *cagar* meaning 'to defecate', a clear reference to the roosting sea birds on North Keeling.

As the European presence extended through much of the Indian Ocean, many of the native myths disappeared and the Europeans introduced their own. Both the popular literature and the historical sources attribute to English sea captain William Keeling the first sighting of the Cocos (Keeling) Islands. The following section shows, step by step, how this myth – in this case a widely held but false belief or idea – was initiated and developed.

William Keeling's 1609 voyage from Java to the Cape of Good Hope

William Keeling's third English East India Company (EIC) spice-trade voyage from 1607–10 on the ships *Dragon* and *Hector* was highly successful, with the cargo of nutmegs, mace and pepper realising 234 per cent on the subscribed capital back in England.[65] The original journal for his 1609–10 homeward voyage on *Hector* has not survived. Samuel Purchas, who published part of it, wrote that it had been 'very voluminous in a hundred sheets of paper' and that he had been so bold as to shorten it for publication.[66] Others, including historian Robert Kerr, have criticised both Purchas and Keeling:

> The editor of Astley's Collection [of Voyages and Travels] observes, 'That this narrative is written very obscurely, in an abrupt, uncouth style, which he thinks Purchas ought to have reformed when abridging it'. The author [Keeling] seems to have kept no regular journal, but only to have entered such things from time to time as seemed most material. In many places, it consists only of loose imperfect hints, thrown together without connection, and often referring to things not mentioned before. Possibly these defects may have been owing to Purchas, in order to abbreviate the journal; and indeed, whether from want of care or judgment, he spoiled almost everything he abridged. It contains, however, many valuable nautical remarks.[67]

Some writers have stated that Keeling was a cultured individual, so concerned about the moral fibre of his men that he had them perform 'Hamlet' and 'Richard II' at Sierra Leone and Socotra to prevent idleness and unlawful games, these being the first recorded amateur performances of Shakespeare.[68] However, it appears probable that a forger added the part about Keeling's Shakespeare performances.[69]

Figure 31. Woodcut of the *Dragon*, or *Red Dragon*, as it was sometimes referred to.

William Keeling's journal shows that, in 1608, during his outward voyage to the East Indies, he sailed nowhere near the Cocos (Keeling) Islands. Having rounded the Cape of Good Hope he sailed north to the island of Socotra in the Arabian Sea, and then eastward across the northern Indian Ocean. Like other navigators of the time, he would have seen along the way many islands covered with coconut palms, a source of refreshment for his crew. He passed the Maldives, south of India, where there was a Cocoa Island, and continued to Sumatra (where Marco Polo had developed a liking for the coconuts), and Sunda Strait, Bantam and Banda. At Banda, he complained about the behaviour of natives, who killed some of his crew who had walked into the woods to gather 'Cocus Nuts'.[70]

While in Bantam, Keeling met with the EIC's chief factor, John Saris, who, in his diary, had expressed interest in exploration, discovery and Keeling's activities. Saris also wrote that Dutch captain Willem Jansz had, in November 1605, set out in the *Duyfken* to explore the land called 'Nova ginnea', said to produce a great abundance of gold, and returned to Banda, having found the island. Jansz had found Australia![71] Saris accompanied Keeling in 1609 when he set out homeward from Bantam for England in the

300-ton *Hector*. Saris was interested in exploration, and it is easy to imagine that during the voyage to England the two would have discussed and commented upon any notable discoveries.

During both his outward and homeward voyages, Keeling would have seen hundreds of Indian Ocean islands, but he had no reason to be interested in a small uninhabited atoll such as North Keeling that offered no prospect of trade. The records (the Gerritsz 1622 chart with the toponym 'Cocos') indicate that coconut palms were already present on the islands in 1609. However, Keeling had resupplied his vessel with food and water in the East Indies, so it is doubtful that he would have paid any attention to the Cocos (Keeling) Islands, even if he had sighted them.

The Purchas concise edition of Keeling's homeward journal reads blandly for the Indian Ocean return voyage:

> The second of October, 1609. I went and tooke my leave of the Governour ... The third, betimes I came aboord for adue, having visited all my friends. The first of November, 1609. About the distance fixe hundred and fiftie [leagues] from Bantam, wee were in five and twenty degrees South Latitude having foure and twenty degrees variation and foure and twenty days running it.[72]

How should the Purchas edition of Keeling's homeward voyage be interpreted? A direct 650 leagues (1,950 nautical miles) course through Sunda Strait from Bantam to a position 25° south might have taken Keeling close to or even through the 16-mile gap between the North Keeling and the South Keeling Islands. Using the southeast trade winds, a direct course was achievable. If there was 24° of variation (not all ships experienced such variation) throughout that leg of the voyage, and Keeling did not adjust his course accordingly, then the *Hector* would have passed to the north of the Cocos (Keeling) Islands. However, the vessel would have had to pass within 12 miles for the atolls to be visible. Samuel Dunn later stated that the South Keeling Islands were 'not to be seen above 4 leagues [12 nautical miles]'.[73] Alexander Dalrymple described them as being 'all very low'.[74] There is nothing in the Purchas edition of Keeling's journal (or in any other known source of that time) to indicate that Keeling had sighted, or claimed to have sighted, any part of the Cocos (Keeling) Islands.

With minor diversions from the direct route, if he had any interest in noting the presence of coconut palms, Keeling could have sighted Deli Island (previously named 'Cocoa Island' and 'Clappers Eylanden') just southeast of Sunda Strait and close to the homeward route from Bantam, or 'Cocos Eylanden' off the south coast of Sumatra, or 'Cocos Eyl' off the southwest coast of Sumatra.[75] If he followed the Houtman 1597 course speculated in the early eighteenth century by Dutch cartographer Pieter van der Aa,[76] he would have passed close to Rodrigues Island, on the north side of which lies 'Cocos Islet'.

William Dampier, during his two homeward voyages from the Spice Islands to the Cape of Good Hope, had his routes shown on one contemporary chart as passing to the south of the Cocos (Keeling) atolls, and on another chart as passing between the two atolls, but in neither case has it been suggested that Dampier saw these islands. Keeling appears to have been credited with the sighting for two reasons.[77] Firstly, mapmakers had a predisposition to attribute discoveries to their countrymen. Secondly, in the absence of alternative interpretations, the family name Keeling would have appeared similar to the toponym Killing, given to those islands by Sir Robert Dudley in one of his 1646 series of Indian Ocean charts. This last supposition would have been encouraged by later British cartographers studying Keeling's homeward course and calculating that his route, as described in the journal, placed him within a hundred miles of North Keeling Island.

There is no evidence that Keeling observed or recorded the small, low, isolated, coral encircled Cocos (Keeling) Islands. He did not need to make note of the thousands of small, uninhabited islands with no trade value dotted across the Indian Ocean, and he is not relevant to the question of discovery. He was not a cartographer, and he did not keep a regular journal on his homeward voyage – just sheets of paper, the details of which might later be slotted in on maps. Nevertheless, because the English explorer and cartographer Sir Robert Dudley's charts caused others much later to conclude that William Keeling discovered the Cocos (Keeling) Islands in 1609, it is necessary to analyse those charts further.

Sir Robert Dudley's 1646 charts of the Indian Ocean

Dudley wrote his memoirs of navigation and seamanship between 1610 and 1620, soon after William Keeling's return to England. He incorporated his notes in his six-volume *Dell' Arcano del Mare* (The Secret of the Sea), an atlas of sea charts published in Florence when he was in his 70s.[78] It is possible that Dudley, whose father had been a close friend of Queen Elizabeth, would have met with Keeling, the celebrated trading voyager. Keeling may have told Dudley that he had seen islands in the Indian Ocean, and even if he did not, it seems certain, given his cartographic interest, that Dudley would have heard some rough details about Keeling's voyage through the Spice Islands.

On his *Asia Carta III*, Dudley, or his Italian baroque engraver Antonio Lucini, who signed the charts and gave them their distinctive character, inserted a group of islands representing the southern atoll of the Cocos (Keeling) Islands, labelled 'I Triangolare' Scoperte' dall Inglesi' (Figure 33). Beside an upright-sock-shaped island immediately north of them, he has inserted

Figure 32. Cabinet miniature of Sir Robert Dudley (1574–1649).

the toponym 'Riling Island'. His northern island is located southwest of Sunda Strait in approximately 12° south, the latitude of North Keeling Island. On his later *Asia Carta XIIII*, Dudley named the sock-shaped island Killing Island, rather than Riling Island.

Analysis of Dudley's charts
The Dutch cartographers during the first decades of the seventeenth century had marked islands progressively eastward of the location of the Cocos (Keeling) islands, but the English cartographer, Robert Dudley, in the middle of the seventeenth century, appears to have moved other islands westward from Indonesia to overlay the Hessel Gerritsz triangle of islands in the location of the Cocos, and in effect to claim them for England. Several questions arise from the Indian Ocean charts in Dudley's atlas.

First: What does the terminology 'I Triangolare' mean, and why has Dudley placed a triangle of islands on his 1646 chart in the locality of the Cocos (Keeling) Islands?
The words on Dudley's *Asia Carta III* chart could read either as 'group of islands forming a triangle' or as 'group of triangular islands'.[79] It appears that Dudley has lifted a detail from Gerard de Jode's 1593 map (Figure 10) showing the finger-shaped Augama island above three Sondur islands south of Sumatra, and superimposed it on Gerritsz's 1612 tight triangle of dots representing the Cocos. In doing so he has effectively transformed Augama (now Siberut) into North Keeling, and other islands from the south side of Sunda Strait (smaller Mentawai Islands and Enggano) into South Keeling.

There are other possible interpretations of Dudley's triangle of islands, with an upright finger located to their north.[80] He may have reinterpreted the Gerritsz 1612 chart showing an unnamed triangle of islands representing the South Keeling Islands. The 1622 Gerritsz chart shows Cocos Eylanden as three or four tightly packed islands with a circular atoll to their north – a reasonable representation of the two atolls of the Cocos (Keeling) Islands – and

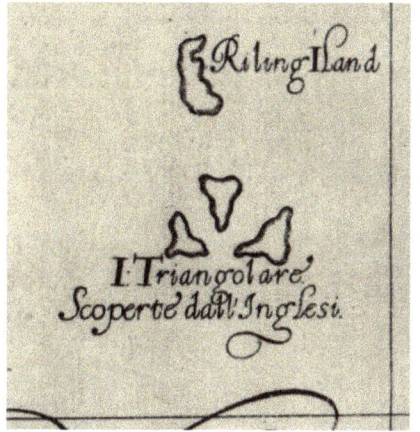 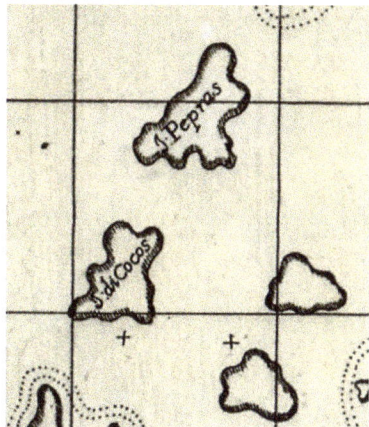

Figure 33. Dudley's Cocos (Keeling) Islands.　　Figure 34. Dudley's Coco Islands in the Bay of Bengal.

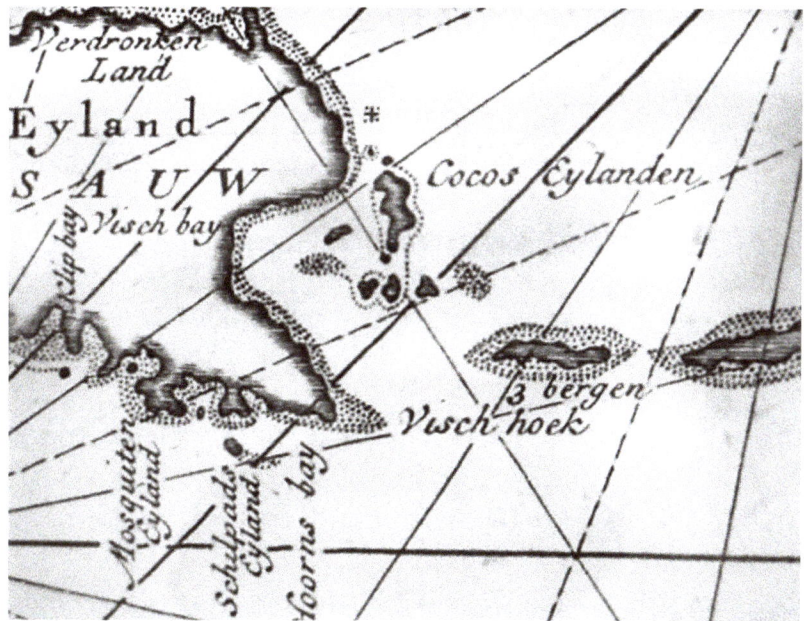

Figure 35. Detail from van Keulen's 1753 chart showing Cocos Eylanden off the south coast of Sumatra in 2° S, 100° E.

the phantom island Polverara in a similar latitude to his North Keeling Island.[81]

Dudley may have merely elaborated upon the Gerritsz triangle and incorporated the Gerritsz island of Polverara. Dudley's *Asia Carta III* chart has an equivalent to Gerritsz' tightly packed islands of South Keeling, but instead of the small 1622 circle drawn by Gerritsz a little north of South Keeling atoll to represent the North Keeling atoll, Dudley has inserted an impressive upright-sock-shaped island, nothing like the shape of the North Keeling atoll. It may be that Dudley had become aware that a real bird-roosting island existed in a similar latitude to the phantom island Polverara, so he has duplicated Gerritsz' Polverara, leaving one in its earlier position and imposing another one further eastward, in a position north of the South Keeling Islands, to become his Riling Island (North Keeling Island).

Second: Why did Dudley mark the triangular islands of the Cocos as 'discovered by the English'?

The inaccurate longitude measurement of the period may be the reason for Dudley's comment. As mentioned above, the Cocos (Keeling) Islands were frequently shown lying too close to the longitude of Sunda Strait, and some mapmakers confused the Cocos (Keeling) Islands with islands along the Sumatran coast and even Christmas Island. As will be discussed in Chapter 5, in 1615 an Englishman named John Milward discovered Christmas Island to the south of Sunda Strait. Christmas Island is a single peak – not a triangle of islands – but its location, in the same corner of the Indian Ocean as Dudley's Cocos Islands triangle, likely encouraged Dudley to presume that the English (that is, Milward) had discovered his triangle of islands.

During the late sixteenth and early seventeenth centuries, the English, Dutch and French established their overseas empires in direct competition with each other. Dudley marked many islands as having been discovered by the English, presumably to impress atlas customers on the imperialistic basis that English discovery implied prestige, with rights to trade and resources.[82]

There are numerous examples of him wrongly attributing English discovery of the places in his atlas, including Greenland ('terra scoperta d' Inglesi'; see Dudley's *Europa Carta XXXXVIIII*) – Icelandic sources show that Eric the Red had founded the first settlement there some time between 950 and 1003 CE. To the east of Mauritius (see his *Africa Carta XIII*) Dudley has placed an island labelled 'England's Forest Scoperta d'Inglesi' (England's Forest discovered by the English). Here, he appears to be mistakenly referring to the native forests on Diego Garcia, 'discovered' by the Portuguese during the sixteenth century, or the hardwood forests of Mahe in Seychelles, 1,700 miles north of Mauritius, which were also discovered before the English arrived. To the southeast of Mauritius, Dudley has placed another upright-sock-shaped island and labelled it 'I Scoperti d'Inglesi' (Island discovered by the English). Yet there are no islands to the southeast of Mauritius. It is another phantom island: a purported island (likely derived from Diego Garcia) that appeared on maps for some time, but that was removed after it was proven not to exist or shifted eastward to become Dudley's Riling Island in the location of North Keeling Island.

Dudley marked a large 'island' (North West Cape, a part of the northwest coast of Australia seen by survivors of the English *Trial* wreck in 1622) as 'I Scoperta da Inglesi' (island discovered by the English). Yet the Dutch had previously been the first Europeans to discover the northwest coast of Australia, and John Brookes, master of the *Trial*, had reported that it was the 'island' formerly seen by the Flemings.[83] Willem Jansz of the VOC ship *Mauritius* had landed there on the Australian coast in 1618. Dutch mapmaker Hessel Gerritsz later placed the words 'Hier ist Engels Schip de *Trial* vergaen Iunius, A°1622' (Here the English ship *Trial* was wrecked in June 1622) on his 1627 Chart of the Land of *Eendracht*.[84]

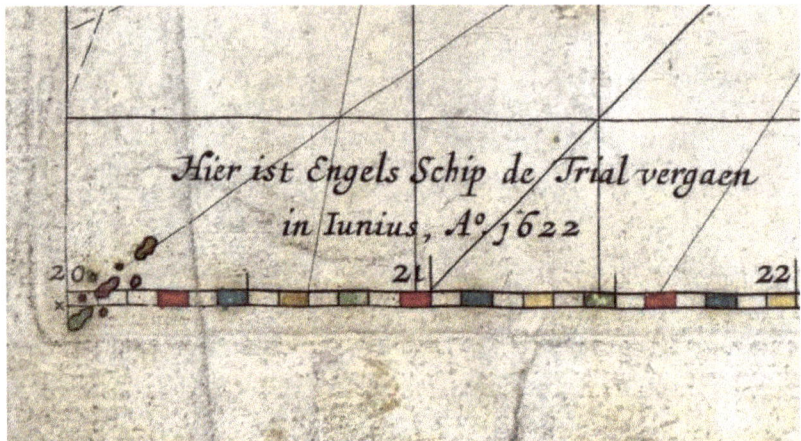

Figure 36. Detail from the bottom left corner of Hessel Gerritsz's 1627 'Chart of the Land of Eendracht'.

Third: Why did Dudley initially call the northern atoll Riling Island, and later change it to Killing Island?
Consideration will be given here to the meaning of the words Riling and Killing as used by Dudley and others.

The meaning of 'Riling' and 'Killing'
The etymology of these two words does not fit well with 'Keeling'. Connotations that might be drawn from the term 'riling' and its variations include turbid water, channels in coral or rock surfaces, and the availability of a water source. The *Oxford Dictionary* defines the noun 'rile' as 'a turbid or muddy condition of liquid'. Charles Darwin, whose ideas were influenced by those of Prussian polymath Alexander von Humboldt and Scottish geologist Charles Lyell, referred to the lagoon of the North Keeling atoll as being 'nearly filled up with coral mud',[85] so the report received by Dudley might have also referred to the tidal outflow of a turbid liquid.

The more commonly used terms, and most probable explanation of Dudley's Riling, are 'rill', and 'rilling' as the formation process of a rill. The term 'rilling' means the formation of small narrow channels, furrows, trenches, cracks, ditches or rivulets, formed in rock and coral by tidal ebb and subsequent fossilisation. Features of this description can be seen on the North Keeling atoll. Darwin visited the Cocos (Keeling) Islands in 1836, soon after having developed his coral atoll theory in the Pacific, so he paid particular attention to the form of the Cocos (Keeling) Islands.[86] Island residents reported to Darwin that the atoll had been shaken by a severe earthquake just two years before his visit, and Darwin referred to the fissures that earthquakes can cause in the Earth's crust. However, Darwin dwelt more fully on other more obvious channel-producing processes. In a chapter titled 'Keeling Island Coral Formations', he wrote that sediment washed outward by receding tides killed the coral along the way, thus forming channels over time:

> In barrier-reefs it has long been remarked with surprise, that the passages through the reef exactly face valleys in the included land, even in cases where the reef is separated from the land by a lagoon-channel so wide and so much deeper than the actual passage itself, that it seems hardly possible that the very small quantity of water or sediment brought down could injure the corals on the reef. Now, every reef of the fringing-class is breached by a narrow gateway in front of the smallest rivulet, even if dry during the greater part of the year, for the mud, sand, or gravel, occasionally washed down, kills the corals on which it is deposited. Consequently, when an island thus fringed subsides, though most of the narrow gateways will probably become closed by the outward and upward growth of the corals, yet any that are not closed (and some must always be kept open by the sediment and impure water flowing out of the lagoon-channel) will still continue to front exactly the upper parts of those valleys, at the mouths of which the original basal fringing-reef was breached.[87]

Coral atolls can change relatively quickly. Aerial photographs of North Keeling Island, taken in 1976 (Figure 37), show a channel leading from the 'lake' to the ocean. In 1990, reef scientist J. (Charlie) Veron wrote of North Keeling atoll that:

> In the longer term (tens to hundreds of years) there appears to have been a progressive closing of the lagoon by sand accretion on the island arc. Habitat diversity has thus been gradually decreasing and it is likely that the coral death of 1983 was the most recent (and perhaps final) of a series of catastrophic events resulting from closure of the lagoon.[88]

The channel entrance has silted up, but underwater there is a gap (natural or man-made) in the island's coral fringe in line with the above-water channel.[89]

If Dudley's informant was particularly perceptive, he might have had in mind not the geological feature of a rill, but the optional implication in the word – 'fresh drinking water from a small rivulet' – a kind of public benefit announcement to other seafarers, akin to referring to islands as having coconuts. Fresh water could be found from such a source on the Cocos (Keeling) Islands, as Darwin observed:

> On this island [Home Island] the wells are situated, from which ships obtain water. At first sight, it appears not a little remarkable that the freshwater should regularly ebb and flow with the tides; and it has even been imagined, that sand has the power of filtering the salt from the sea-water. These ebbing wells are common on some of the low islands in the West Indies. The compressed sand, or porous coral rock, is permeated with the saltwater; but the rain which falls on the surface must sink to the level of the surrounding sea, and must accumulate there, displacing an equal bulk of the saltwater. As the water in the lower part of the great sponge-like coral mass rises and falls with the tides, so will the water near the surface; and this will keep fresh if the mass be

Figure 37. Aerial view of North Keeling Island in 1976, showing a white sand channel to the ocean.

Figure 38. North Keeling Island in 2012, showing the channel permanently blocked and overgrown.

sufficiently compact to prevent much mechanical admixture; but where the land consists of great loose blocks of coral with open interstices, if a well be dug, the water, as I have seen, is brackish.[90]

Dudley's *Africa Carta XIII* has an island in 21° south (the location of Réunion Island) named 'I S Appolonia', and marked 'Per Fav Aqua', close to his Mascarene Islands. This could imply that Dudley has shifted his Mascarene Islands, including the water-producing Appolonia (Apolonia), eastward to the location of the Cocos (Keeling) Islands.[91]

The *Oxford Dictionary* definition of a rill sits most comfortably with the North Keeling atoll interpretation. Dudley's Riling appears to have been derived from *ril* or *rill*, which are Dutch, East Friesian or Low German words for a small rivulet or brook, or long narrow trenches formed in the soil after rain or preserved in rock. Dudley's initial use of the term 'riling' implies that he derived the information for his chart from a Dutch source. A Dutch source, in turn, implies that Dudley's rill information relates to the Cocos (Keeling) Islands rather than to the Portuguese-influenced Coco Islands in the Bay of Bengal.

There is no reason to assume that Dudley intended his Riling to mean Keeling. If he had, then he would have insisted upon using the word 'Keeling', rather than replacing his Riling with Killing on the second version of his chart. Nor is there any indication that the word related in Dudley's mind to a murder.[92]

There is an obvious explanation for Dudley's 'Killing'. The *Oxford Dictionary* defines a 'kill' as 'a stream, a creek, a tributary river' and explains the etymology as 'Dutch *kil*, Middle Dutch *kille* riverbed, channel'.[93] 'Ril' and 'kil' are both words of Dutch origin with implications of channels and tidal flows. It is clear that Dudley had these geological concepts in mind – not 'William Keeling' – and that he swapped from Riling to Killing without much thought.

Several remarks are necessary to conclude this chapter. Some researchers have sought to establish when and by whom islands in the southern Indian Ocean were discovered and settled. Studies have been made involving linguistic evidence of colonisation, global wind and ocean current systems, wind and current system changes over time, ship technology and ancient shipping routes. These studies have led to the development of simulation patterns for hypothetical voyages between the Sunda Strait and Madagascar by the Austronesians, before the arrival of Europeans in the Indian Ocean.

If the simulations are an accurate representation of early Austronesian voyaging, they might be taken to suggest that some of these vessels would have sailed close to, or visited, Christmas Island (in 10° south) and the Cocos (Keeling) Islands (in 11.8° and 12.2° south) during their westward passage in the monsoon trade winds belt (north of 30° south) to Madagascar. However, the computer simulations and replica ship voyages have not entirely convinced some researchers, including Atholl Anderson, who comments:

> There is no evidence of Austronesian sailing directly across the Indian Ocean, at least not before the second millennium AD. The evidence suggests, rather, Austronesian travelling along the well-known trading route from Indonesia to east Africa, via Sri Lanka/Maldives and India/Arabia to the Horn of Africa.[94]

The question arises as to whether the coconut was introduced to the Cocos (Keeling) Islands by the Austronesians. Archaeological research has not revealed indications of human settlement before the period of European exploration. On the other hand, by 1622 coconut palms had spread across the islands in sufficient number and size for a mapmaker to title the islands 'Cocos'. That title suggests that there had been many generations of palms by 1622, taking the hundreds of years required for them to develop into a forest after the generation of the first seed that was planted or washed ashore. Some researchers have been sceptical about the chances of a nut drifting from Indonesia, remaining viable during its ocean voyage, being deposited in soil amenable to the generation of growth, and avoiding destruction by crabs before developing. However, there is now growing recognition that the nuts can remain viable for long periods, perhaps travelling as long as 110 days, or 3,000 miles by sea, and still be viable for germination.[95]

The coconuts now present on the Cocos (Keeling) Islands are of the ridged, triangular-shaped 'Indo-Atlantic' group rather than the round 'Pacific group' nuts that have been linked with Austronesian voyages. This suggests that the nuts would have drifted to the Cocos (Keeling) Islands from Indonesia rather than having been brought by Austronesian voyagers. The expansion of Arab shipping from the tenth century is thought to have ended the Austronesian voyaging.

The mapmakers who constructed the sixteenth-century Dieppe School maps in France were heavily reliant upon Indian Ocean informants for information about the southeastern part of that ocean, informants who might have been aware of the 6° south parallel route mentioned above. The 1546 Desceliers map shows the Chagos archipelago in 5°–6° south, and the isolated tight triangle of islands – A: defponoada – considerably further south, in approximately 10.5° south. The 1547 Harleian map shows an atoll of the same name a similar distance south of the Maldives. Then a 1550 Desceliers map depicts the same tight triangle of islands further to the east, in 11° south. The phantom island A: defponoada moved between the east and the west on successive European charts, hovering through the sixteenth century in 10°–12° south in its search for a permanent place on the planet. It is possible that Indian Ocean informants told Dieppe School cartographers that mariners who travelled the trading route between Sunda Strait and Madagascar had seen the Cocos or Christmas islands in approximately 11° south during their voyages, but there is no record of any such discoveries.

The 1610 chart by Jodocus Hondius marking 'I de Polvero' (implying poultry or bird droppings) in 10° south, 95° east, roughly the position we now know to be that of the Cocos (Keeling) Islands, situated in 12° south, 97° east, indicates that the Dutch were aware of these islands during the first decade of the seventeenth century. The 1612 and 1622 charts of Hessel Gerritsz are clear evidence of Dutch discovery and probable evidence of close examination.

Chapter 4

Exploration of the Cocos (Keeling) Islands

Timeline

1724 The Dutch ship '*s-Graveland* reported floating wreckage in the latitude of the Cocos.

1724 The Dutch ship *Windhond* mapped the Cocos after the *Fortuyn* failed to arrive in Batavia.

1724 The Dutch mapmaker Godlob Silo surveyed both Cocos (Keeling) atolls.

1726 A Dutch map by J. van Braam showed Cocos Eylanden southwest of Sunda Strait.

1726 Satirist Jonathan Swift showed the mythical islands of Lilliput and Blefuscu in the location of the Cocos.

1747 An Emanuel Bowen chart showed islands named 'Cocos' in the latitude of the *Trial* wreck.

1749 North Keeling Island was sketched by Swedish captain Charles Eckeberg.

1794 Cartographer Samuel Dunn showed atolls as 'Keeling's or Cocos Id', implicitly claiming British discovery.

1805 Hydrographer James Horsburgh referred to 'Cocos-Keeling Islands' in his *Sailing Directory*.

1807 The *Slave Trade Act* prohibited the slave trade in the British Empire.

1825 The brig *Mauritius* was wrecked at or near Direction Island, Cocos.

1825 Merchant John Clunies-Ross surveyed the Cocos, dug wells and prepared for settlement.

1826 English merchant Alexander Hare arrived on the *Hippomenes* in June and established his settlement.

1826 The brig *Sir Francis Nicholas Burton* was wrecked at West Island, Cocos.

1827 John Clunies-Ross raised the British flag over his settlement.

1829 Alexander Hare exported the first coconut oil from the Cocos to England.

1829 John Clunies-Ross stated that William Keeling had discovered the Cocos Islands.

1831 Disputes led to Hare leaving and John Clunies-Ross assuming control.

1834 The *Slavery Abolition* Act abolished slavery in most British colonies.

1834 The snow brig *Earl of Liverpool* was wrecked on North Keeling atoll.

1836 British commander and scientist Robert Fitzroy marked 'North Keeling' and 'South Keeling' on his chart.

1857 Captain Stephen Fremantle mistakenly annexed the Cocos (Keeling) Islands instead of Coco Islands.

1857 Fremantle specified that William Keeling passed to the north of North Keeling Island.

1889 Henry Guppy saw Dudley's 1646 toponym 'scoperta d'Inglesi' as evidence of Keeling's discovery.

1889 Guppy replaced Dalrymple's 'Northern I.' with 'North Keeling Island'.

1941 The Dutch flag was flown at the Cocos (Keeling) Islands for a short time.

For many years after its discovery – indeed up to the present – writers have continued to presume that the English captain, William Keeling, discovered the Cocos (Keeling) Islands. This chapter introduces some of the early European and American literature about the southern Indian Ocean, explains the processes of exploration and planning for island settlement, and examines the ongoing mythologising of William Keeling's voyage, with its influence on the settlement outcomes.

A poet, a satirist, a master of the macabre, cartographers and natural scientists

For centuries after Aristotle postulated a large southern hemisphere landmass to balance the northern hemisphere, cartographers obliged by placing Terra Australis Incognita, a fearful land of weird monsters, in the space between the eastern end of the Indian Ocean and the western end of the South Pacific. Poets and other writers told even more fearful stories about the southern part of the Indian Ocean. Dutch navigators partially outlined the west coast of New Holland in the seventeenth century, but by the early eighteenth century New Holland and Antarctica were the only extensive parts of the world that could be said to be almost entirely unknown to the outside world.

As shipping traffic through the central-eastern part of the Indian Ocean – the waters south of Indonesia and west of Australia – grew during the years following the publication of Robert Dudley's atlas in 1646, so too did the confusing state of the charts. English cartographers followed Dudley's terminology, and some elaborated upon their predecessors' spelling mistakes. For example, a chart of 1700 by John Thornton titled 'A New Map of the World' showed 'Kelling' island in the vicinity of the Cocos (Keeling) Islands.[1]

John Milton, the poet
Italian artist Lorenzo Ghiberti created the iconic relief panels on main gates of the Florence Baptistery between 1425 and 1452, gates referred to by Michelangelo as fit to be the Gates of Paradise. The Florence Baptistery is also the church where the thirteenth-century poet, Dante Alighieri, was baptised, and the Baptistery doors inspired part of the imagery in his epic poem, *The Divine Comedy*, describing his journey through Hell, Purgatory and Paradise.

Dante's hell consists of nine circles of wickedness, culminating at the centre of the earth, where Satan is held in bondage.

Paradise Lost, a masterpiece of blank verse, widely considered one of the greatest works of literature, was written by the blind English poet, John Milton. One of the most scrutinised texts in the Western canon, it is relevant to our present story because it places the Gates of Hell (Figure 39) in the general vicinity of the Cocos (Keeling) Islands and Christmas Island. Milton begins his story with Satan as a fallen angel, cast out by God from heaven to hell.

Unlike Dante and other poets of the classical and medieval worlds of the Mediterranean, Milton, writing in the second half of the seventeenth century, was able to include in his epic story the European mariners who were by then braving the wider world of the Indian Ocean. The text of Milton's *Paradise Lost* must have given literate mariners of the time cause for great concern as they headed south. His phraseology indicates that he is sending both the flying Satan and the returning East Indiamen sailing ships down to the Gates of Hell, located south of India and the Spice Islands, in the southern Indian Ocean. Inside the Gates of Hell he has placed (as a parody of the most magnificent European churches) Pandaemonium, a temple occupied by hundreds of thousands of devils who shrink from giants into dwarfs for their assembly. He writes:

> Mean while the Adversary of God and Man,
> *Satan* with thoughts inflam'd of highest design,
> Puts on swift wings, and towards the Gates of Hell
> Explores his solitary flight; som times
> He scours the right hand coast, som times the left,
> Now shaves with level wing the Deep, then soares
> Up to the fiery Concave touring high.
> As when farr off at Sea a Fleet descri'd
> Hangs in the Clouds, by *Aequinoctial* Winds
> Close sailing from *Bengala*, or the Iles
> Of *Ternate* and *Tidore*, whence Merchants bring

> Thir spicie Drugs: they on the Trading Flood
> Through the wide *Ethiopian* to the Cape
> Ply stemming nightly toward the Pole. So seem'd
> Farr off the flying Fiend: at last appeer
> Hell bounds high reaching to the horrid Roof,
> And thrice threefold the Gates; three folds were Brass,
> Three Iron, three of Adamantine Rock,
> Impenitrable, impal'd with circling fire,
> Yet unconsum'd. Before the Gates there sat
> On either side a formidable shape;
> The one seem'd Woman to the waste, and fair,
> But ended foul in many a scaly fould
> Voluminous and vast, a Serpent arm'd
> With mortal sting: about her middle round ....[2]

European navigators, crossing the incompletely charted waters of the Indian Ocean, would have felt even more ill at ease on reading Milton's later lines about the Gates of Hell, and what lay within:

> ... So wide they stood, and like a Furnace mouth
> Cast forth redounding smoak and ruddy flame.
> Before thir eyes in sudden view appear
> The secrets of the hoarie deep, a dark
> Illimitable Ocean without bound,
> Without dimension, where length, breadth, and highth,
> And time and place are lost; where eldest Night
> And *Chaos*. Ancestors of Nature, hold
> Eternal *Anarchie*, amidst the noise.

Figure 39. Satan enters the Gates of Hell to be challenged by his incestuous offspring Death. Satan's daughter, Sin, interposes herself between father and son. From William Blake's 1807 Illustration 2 to Milton's *Paradise Lost*.

Jonathan Swift, the satirist, and Edgar Allan Poe, the master of the macabre

In 1679, five years after the publication of the second version of Milton's *Paradise Lost*, William Dampier joined the crew of the buccaneer captain Bartholomew Sharp on the Spanish Main of Central America. Dampier has rightly been credited with 'stripping away myth, uncertainty and prejudice and describing faraway lands objectively'.[3] However, his recollection of his unsuccessful attempt in 1688 to reach the Cocos (Keeling) Islands (see Chapter 6) was somewhat confusing. He wrote in circumstances of divided command – the buccaneers' democratic code of conduct. His travel accounts, of voyages to unknown lands inhabited by unfamiliar people, influenced such writers as novelist Daniel Defoe in his *Robinson Crusoe,* and satirist Jonathan Swift in his *Gulliver's Travels*, published in 1726.[4]

Gulliver's Travels depends upon parody, imitating the language used in the travel-writing genre, with a traveller describing his adventures in ever more exotic and undiscovered locations. Swift, who hailed from the island of the leprechaun legend, sends his narrator, the naive and unsophisticated Gulliver, to increasingly bizarre territories, beginning with Lilliput, the island of little people, continuing on to the flying or floating island of Laputa, and ending off the southwest coast of Australia on an island ruled by High-Dutch speaking horses called Houyhnhms.[5]

Satire requires the reader to translate the ideas from the parody to a different and more significant meaning. As Gulliver describes the political systems of the Lilliputians and their neighbours, it soon becomes clear that Swift is describing the political systems of England and France at the time. However, it is not Swift's satire that is relevant to our story, but his chosen geographical context.

Swift explicitly mentioned Dampier as a mariner comparable to his gentleman traveller character, Lemuel Gulliver, who had attended Cambridge, studied physics at Leyden (Leiden, in South Holland, was the residence of the Pilgrim Fathers before they sailed for America in 1620) and gained a smattering of High and Low

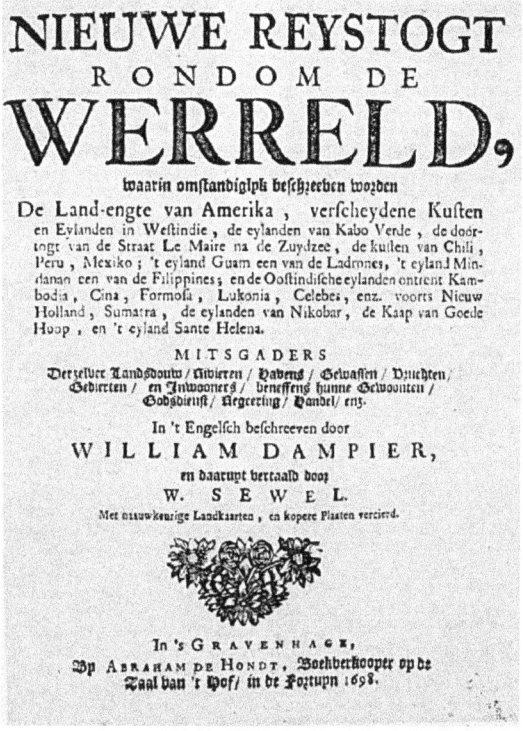

Figure 40. Frontispiece to the Dutch version of Dampier's book.

Dutch. When Swift wanted a faraway, alien setting for his critique of European society, there was no better place on Earth than one of Dampier's old sailing grounds – that poorly charted, mysterious region south of Sunda Strait where the Dutch had lost their East Indiamen the *Fortuyn* in 1724 and the *Aagtekerke* in 1726. So Swift wrecked Gulliver's ship, the *Antelope*, there, near his mythical island of Lilliput.

As an aside, in 1831 American writer Edgar Allan Poe, known for his tales of mystery and the macabre, constructed a short story titled 'Ms found in a bottle'. It was a story built on the legend of the Flying Dutchman, a legendary ghost ship that can never make port and is doomed to hover continually upon the brink of eternity, without taking a final plunge into the abyss. It is tempting to think that Poe had in mind Milton's fleet hanging in the clouds, or Swift's flying island further east: in both cases, from the scientific point of view, probably a mirage – an optical illusion caused by the refraction of light in heated air. And Poe may even have heard of certain Dutch East Indiamen being wrecked in that area south of Sunda Strait. Poe's narrator, the author of the message in the bottle, wrote that he was heading southward from Batavia, on a voyage to the 'Sunda Islands', when his ship was disabled by an 'ungovernable hurricane' and that he was swept down past the coast of New Holland. His disabled ship collided with another vessel, and he wrote:

> Casting my eyes upwards, I beheld a spectacle which froze the current of my blood. At a terrific height directly above us, and upon the very verge of the precipitous descent, hovered a gigantic ship of perhaps four thousand tons. Although upreared upon the summit of a wave more than a hundred times her own altitude, her apparent size still exceeded that of any ship of the line or East Indiaman in existence.[6]

Poe's message-in-a-bottle narrator fell onto the deck of the giant ghost ship, but he found that the crew seemed unconscious of his presence, that their knees trembled with infirmity, their shoulders were bent double with decrepitude, and their shrivelled skins rattled in the wind. Concluding, he wrote that, 'we are plunging within the grasp of the whirlpool – and amid a roaring, and bellowing, and thundering of ocean and of tempest, the ship is quivering – Oh God! And – going down!'.[7] It was then that he threw overboard his message in the bottle.

Jonathan Swift exchanged ideas with English cartographer Herman Moll, who knew William Dampier socially, had access to data and observations from Dampier's voyages, had a reputation for mapping according to modern scientific discoveries, and had created a map of the world showing Dampier's voyage around it (see Figure 54). Moll created for Swift the 'Map of Lilliput and Blefuscu', which appeared in the first part of the 1726 novel and shows Lilliput in the location later reserved by mapmakers for the Cocos (Keeling) Islands.[8] A previous 1701 chart by Moll titled 'The Principal Islands of the East Indies' shows a similar outline of Sumatra, but Gulliver's islands to the southwest of Sunda Strait are more akin to those of Robert Dudley in his *Il Mare Del Indie Orientales*. It is tempting to think that Swift was also influenced by the maps of the Dieppe School. The Harleian Mappemonde of 1547 had shown an island named 'Zanzibar Isle des Giants' to the south of the area he has placed his Lilliput, rather than his 'Brobdingnag' (his island of giants in the North Pacific).

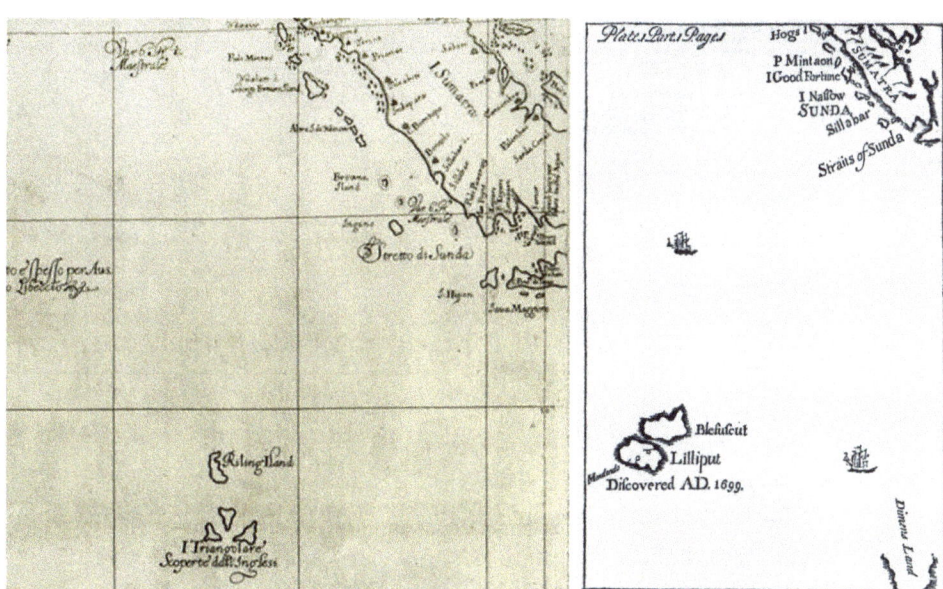

Figure 41. Left: Dudley's 1661 map portraying North Keeling and South Keeling. Right: Gulliver's Lilliput, shown on Swift's map as southwest of Sunda Strait in the general location of the Cocos (Keeling) Islands.

It appears that Swift was also influenced by the words of Magellan's crewman Antonio Pigafetta who, while travelling through Indonesia, had written that:

> Our old pilot from Maluco told us that there was an island nearby called Arucheto, the men and women of which are not taller than one cubit [the length of the forearm, possibly longer in the medieval Islamic world], but have ears as long as themselves. With one of them, they make their bed and with the other they cover themselves. They go shaven close and quite naked, run swiftly, and have shrill voices.[9]

Swift described his Lilliputians as human creatures less than six inches high, with a shrill but distinct voice. Perhaps not coincidentally, in 2004, fossils discovered on Flores Island, in the Indonesian archipelago, were classified controversially as *Homo floresiensis*, a new species of human approximately three feet tall, and estimated to date back at least 50,000 years.[10]

The cartographers and British Navy captains
Cartography is the art, science and technology of making maps, but maps serve both practical and political ends.[11] For example, during the Age of Imperialism, beginning around 1760, European nations heightened their engagement in colonising and annexing other parts of the world, and one of the main tools of the imperialists was cartography. Blank spaces on maps denoted potentially available, unknown or unexplored territory.

Early toponyms on the islands marked in the southern Indian Ocean frequently indicated danger – avoid these latitudes! As confidence grew, however, this was reflected in helpful, altruistic toponyms indicating to chart viewers where refreshing water, coconuts and edible birds could be found, where geological features could be recognised by passing mariners as 'marker buoys', and where marketable items such as cowrie shells could be collected. The toponyms referring to guano imply some interest in gunpowder.

Then, a little later, there was a shift away from altruism, towards the use of the names of discoverers – cartographic propaganda suggesting rights to possession by nation-states.

Dutch cartographers were confused about the locations of many islands, but from the time of the Gerritsz charts early in the seventeenth century, it is clear that the Dutch had a better idea than other Europeans about the existence and location of the Cocos (Keeling) Islands and that, like the French, they did not generally accept the Keeling toponym.

Shipping losses stimulated attention to both search expeditions and surveys of obstacles along shipping routes. Early in the eighteenth century, the VOC lost several outward-bound ships in the eastern Indian Ocean, including the *Fortuyn* in 1724 and the *Aagtekerke* in 1726. The circumstances of these shipwrecks are outlined in Chapter 7. The skipper of the fluyt (Dutch cargo vessel) *'s-Graveland*, which left the Cape of Good Hope for Batavia a fortnight after the *Fortuyn*, reported that on 6 April he had come across floating wreckage of a Dutch ship in latitude 13° 20' south, the approximate latitude of the Cocos (Keeling) Islands. The VOC sent the *Windhond* to investigate, and the crew examined and mapped the islands soon after. The crew saw no wreckage, but they stayed in the vicinity for four days, sailing around the islands, firing a cannon several times to draw any survivors to the beach, and trying unsuccessfully to land in a small boat.

The 'Compass chart of the Kokos Islands' by mapmaker Godlob Silo (Figure 42) is evidence that the Dutch entered the Cocos (Keeling) Islands lagoon for a detailed survey in the 1720s,[12] and that they visited North Keeling Island – the 'Norder Eyland'. Catalogue information on the chart in the Dutch National Archives gives a date of circa 1724. So Godlob Silo was probably the mapmaker on the *Windhond* when its crew spent four days examining the Cocos (Keeling) Islands, finding no sign of the *Fortuyn* or any other lost ship.[13]

Associated information suggests that subsequent interest in the Cocos (Keeling) Islands by the VOC was part of an extension through

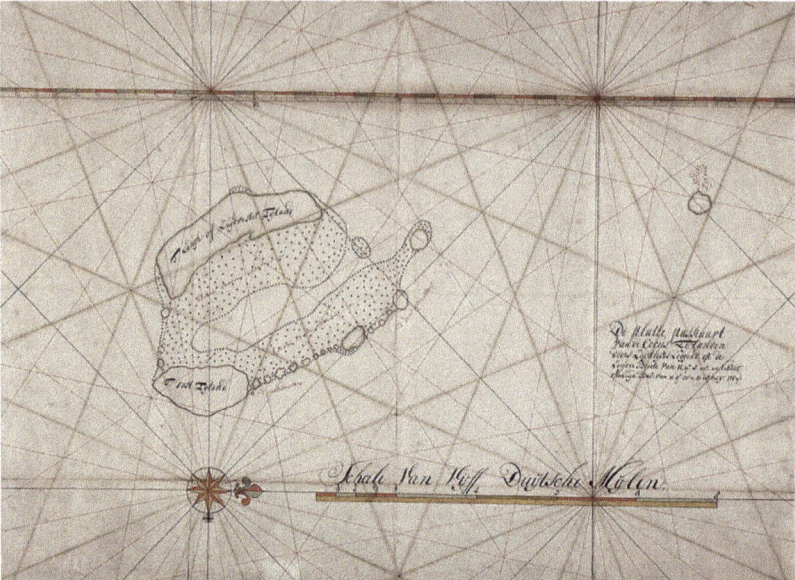

Figure 42. Godlob Silo's 'Compass chart of the Kokos Islands', circa 1724. North is at right.

the Indian Ocean of the European trade in African enslaved people. Silo sailed to the Cape of Good Hope in October 1752 as skipper or master of the VOC's Amsterdam chamber ship *Drie Heuvelen*.[14] He was at the Cape for part of 1753–54, during which time he made a trip to Batavia[15] and a slaving trip to Madagascar.[16] He made another slaving trip to Madagascar in 1755, before setting up as a merchant in Amsterdam. Also attributed to Silo are surveys of Amsterdam Island, Saint Paul Island and Madagascar, all in the Indian Ocean.[17] So it appears that the VOC was examining prospects at various Indian Ocean islands, including the Cocos (Keeling) Islands, with a view to involvement in slave-labour-based settlements on those islands, some 76 years before the arrival at the Cocos (Keeling) Islands of Shetland merchant entrepreneur John Clunies-Ross and English merchant and 'apprentice' owner Alexander Hare. The 1834 *Slavery Abolition Act* had provided for enslaved people in the British colonies to be redesignated as apprentices.[18]

In 1749, at the Cocos (Keeling) Islands, Swedish captain and mapmaker Charles G. Eckeberg, travelling on the ship *Gotha Lion* under Captain Axboom, kept a journal that was translated into English by Captain Charles Chapman in 1760. It is cited on a chart published by Alexander Dalrymple in 1787. Eckeberg's journal, the earliest description of North Keeling Island and South Keeling Islands, reads:

> On the E side of the Island could see no landing-place, being full of Breakers from a Reef stretching 1' toward the SE, where we saw five rocks above-water as high as a Ship's Boat, about which were many white-Birds & Mews. At the N. End there stretched out a Reef on which the water broke: Within the NE most Breakers saw a plain Beach of reddish sand: On the W. side of the Island saw a long flat Bank, on which the water was smooth, with the appearance of good-landing. The whole Strand was full of Coco-nut trees, of which were many Nuts: It is unknown if there be other refreshments. The Island was full of Trees, This was the Northmost of the Cocos; it is 5' or 6' long and 3' or 4' broad: we saw two other Islands; which lay from this Island one S¼E 4 or 5 lea.s, the other SbW 3 or 3½ leagues, they did not look to be so large as this Island. We soon lost sight of it & were followed by a Flock of Men of War Birds (frigate birds). Lat.11°59' S. MC [Meridian Canaries?]. From Java Head 6°47'. W. Var.n 2°.40' W.[19]

Johannes van Keulen's 'Chart of Cocos Eylanden' (Figure 43) comes from the six-volume sea-pilot book *De Nieuwe Groote Lichtende Zee-Fakkel* (the Great New Shining Sea Torch), brought together between 1681 and 1753 by Johannes II van Keulen,[20] with data for the sixth volume by the VOC's Amsterdam chamber examiner Jan de Marre. A Jan de Marre is listed as skipper of the *Heesburg*, arriving at Batavia 21 December 1728.[21] However, it appears that the chamber examiner of the same name acquired the data and that the plan views have been derived from the Silo chart,

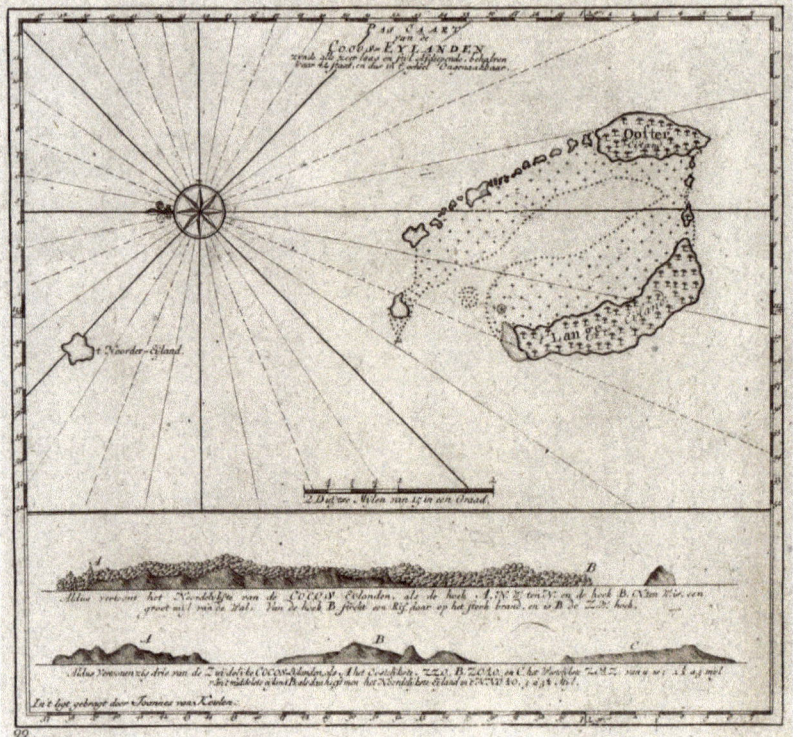

Figure 43. Johannes van Keulen's 1753 chart of the Cocos Islands. North is at left.

with the elevation views, coconut palms, and toponyms 'Ooster Eyland' (East Island) and 'Lange Eyland' (Long Island) added later. North Keeling Island is titled 'Noorder Eyland', and the South Keeling Islands are marked 'Cocos Eylanden'.

In 1780, in his *A New Directory for the East Indies*, Samuel Dunn referred to the Cocos (Keeling) Islands as the 'Killing or Coco Islands'. His reference to 'Coco', a Portuguese word, continued the descriptive terminology more appropriate to the Coco Islands in the Andaman Archipelago.[22]

As previously mentioned, a chart (Figure 44) was published in 1787 by the hydrographer and propagandist Alexander Dalrymple, whose biographer wrote of him, 'That he should be remembered as

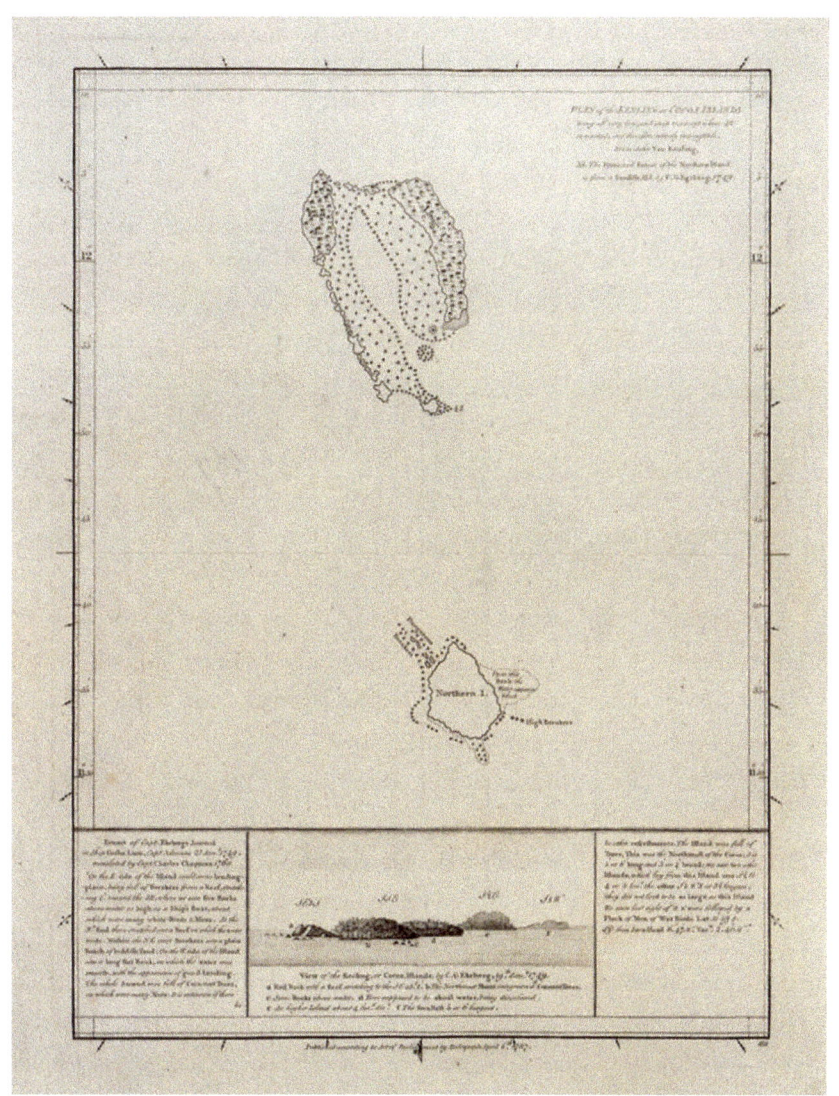

Figure 44. Alexander Dalrymple's 1787 'Plan of the Keeling and Cocos Islands'. North is at bottom.

one who ... supported erroneous geographical theories is perhaps inevitable'.[23] Dalrymple was an acting-hydrographer to the English East India Company (EIC).[24] His 1787 chart is a copy of Dutch cartographer van Keulen's 'Cocos Eylanden' (South Keeling Islands) with the Dutch toponym removed. It includes a larger scale chart of North Keeling Island labelled 'Northern I.', with a text borrowed from Eckeberg's journal, and elevation views of the South Keeling Islands titled 'View of the Keeling, or Cocos, Islands'.[25]

So, Dalrymple, 178 years after William Keeling's homeward voyage between Java and the Cape of Good Hope, appears to have been the first to attach Keeling's name to a chart of these islands, and thus implicitly to claim British discovery. He applied his toponym, 'Keeling, or Cocos, Islands', to the entire group, and he named North Keeling Island 'Northern I'. Dalrymple's replacement of Dutch toponyms with British ones would doubtless have made a positive impression on the British Government during a period of political instability in the Dutch Republic. In 1795 they appointed him as the first Royal Navy Hydrographer.

Dalrymple had made plates of his charts available to Samuel Dunn for the 1780 publication of *A New Directory for the East Indies*, which Dunn edited. Dunn was influenced by Dalrymple. When Dunn published his 'General Map of the World' in 1794 he changed his previous toponym of 'Killing or Coco Islands' to 'Keeling's or Cocos Id', going beyond Dalrymple's inference. Dunn's use of the possessive apostrophe meant that he overtly claimed, for the first time, that the Englishman, William Keeling, had discovered the islands, and so indicated that Great Britain had rights to them.[26]

Between 1646 and 1794 English hydrographers had changed Dudley's 'Riling' and 'Killing' to 'Kelling', then to 'North Keeling' and 'Keeling's or Cocos'. Dunn, like Dalrymple, would have had access to the editions of William Keeling's voyage, studied them intelligently and concluded correctly, given that Keeling's course was across the Indian Ocean, that it was possible (although highly unlikely) that Keeling had both seen and recorded having seen the Cocos (Keeling) Islands.

In 1805, EIC hydrographer James Horsburgh followed Dunn when he used the words 'Cocos-Keeling Islands' in his *Sailing Directory*. In turn, HMS *Beagle*'s commander, Robert Fitzroy – a fourth great-grandson of England's King Charles II, a friend of Francis Beaufort, Hydrographer to the British Admiralty, and a natural-history enthusiast – extended upon Horsburgh's supposition about Keeling. Fitzroy titled the two atolls 'North Keeling' and 'South Keeling' on his 1836 chart. He wrote, 'These lonely islands (also called Cocos) were discovered in 1608–9 by Captain William Keeling, who was in the East India Company's service, and held a commission from King James I'. Fitzroy added a rambling full-page footnote, partly about the superiority of the British in their contests with the duplicitous Dutch in the East Indies, commencing with the words, 'Of these facts, I was credibly informed, on the authority of the late Captain Horsburgh, and presumptive evidence of their reality is afforded by the following extract...'.[27] Lacking a substantive historical record of discoveries, these two men (Fitzroy and Horsburgh) cited each other as 'authorities' in historical matters.

Circumstantial evidence is indirect evidence, distinguished from direct evidence which, if believed, proves a particular fact without inference or presumption being required. Someone offering circumstantial evidence argues that a series of facts, by reason and experience, is so closely associated with the fact to be proved that the fact to be proved may be inferred simply from the existence of the circumstantial evidence. Much historical and scientific evidence is circumstantial because it requires one to make a connection between the circumstance and the fact in issue. In many situations, direct evidence does not exist, and circumstantial evidence is the only evidence available to support a conclusion. A jury, for example, may have only circumstantial evidence to consider in determining whether to convict or acquit, and the United States Supreme Court has stated that 'circumstantial evidence is intrinsically no different from testimonial [direct] evidence (*Holland v. United States*, 1954)'. So the distinction between direct and circumstantial evidence has little practical effect on the presentation or admissibility of evidence in trials.[28] To test the historical evidence, the reader must ask whether it is more likely than not, to interpret the balance of probabilities.

The above logic is pertinent to the claim by many writers that William Keeling discovered the Cocos (Keeling) Islands. There is the fact he sailed across the Indian Ocean from Java to the Cape of Good Hope that might, perhaps, be taken as circumstantial evidence that he sighted either of the small, low atolls of South Keeling (being 13.1 km²) and North Keeling (just 1.1 km²), lying in a vast ocean. Our alternative interpretation of Dudley's 'riling' and 'killing' as derived from observed geological associations, presented in Chapter 3, is a more credible explanation than the 'Keeling' association.

In 1857, a very confused Royal Navy captain, Stephen Fremantle, added several new elements to the discovery story, including his statement that William Keeling had passed to the north of what is now North Keeling Island. Fremantle wrote, while visiting the Cocos (Keeling) Islands:

> The Cocos was discovered some 50 years before Captain Keeling passed to the Northward of the single Northern Isle (1608–9) by a Portuguese who named them the Cocos. Previous also to Captain Keeling's time these islands had been discovered by the crew of a Dutch East India Company's ship which had been burnt to the southeastward. They landed and lived on the islands while they fitted their boats for going to Padang, which place they reached in safety. These islands are also known by the name of Cocos to the Buccaneers of South America.[29]

The directors of the EIC had, in 1856, required Captain Fremantle, the Senior Naval Officer for Australia at the time, to take possession of, and occupy, 'the derelict Cocos islands', meaning the Coco Islands in the Bay of Bengal, some 1,540 nautical miles north of the Cocos (Keeling) Islands.[30] The EIC directors did not specify which 'Cocos' Islands they wanted, or even which hemisphere, and their use of the wrong toponym had significant consequences: Captain Fremantle took possession of the wrong island group. He later conceded:

> ... it appears that some misapprehension has arisen as to the islands which the Court of Directors were desirous to obtain possession of; that instead of the group situated within the limits of the Australian Station (the possession of which I have just effected by command of their Lordships) the Court of Directors intended the Great and Little Coco Islands to the Northward of the Andaman Islands in the Bay of Bengal, not more than 600 miles from Calcutta.[31]

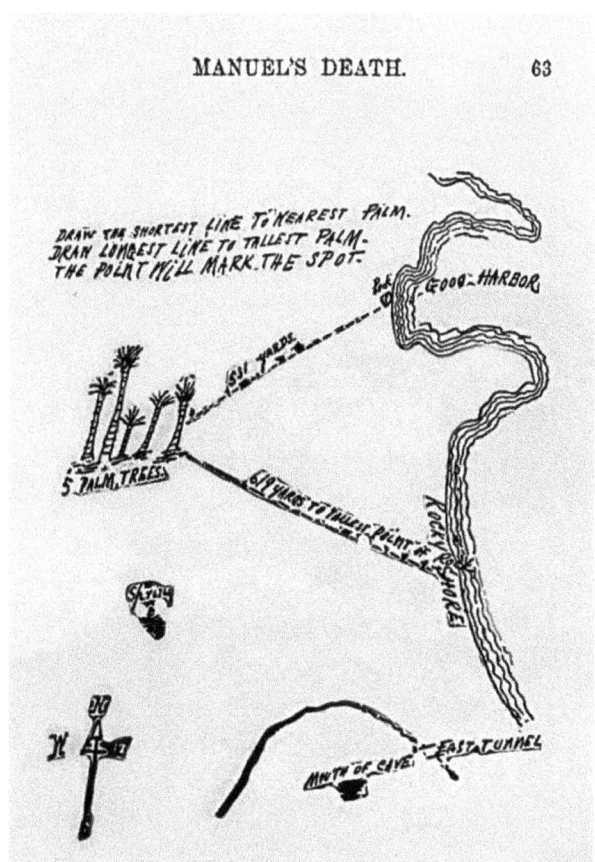

Figure 45. Fiction writer James Otis switched a buried Inca treasure story from Central America to the Cocos (Keeling) Islands.

Captain Fremantle had probably read Dampier's confusing account about the locations of the Cocos (Keeling) Islands and the Coco Islands in the Bay of Bengal, and if so, he learned nothing from it. Fremantle's comment that Keeling had passed to the northward of North Keeling Island was not a direct assertion that Keeling had seen it, but later commentators have assumed that was what he meant, and they specified a North Keeling Island discovery by William Keeling.

Role of the early natural scientists in mythologising William Keeling
Charles Darwin's visit to the Cocos (Keeling) Islands in 1836 was a stimulus for other natural scientists to visit. However, the lack of attention given by historians to the pre-settlement history of the islands is reflected in the historical commentary by the natural scientists, which has generally been limited to one-paragraph notes in the introductions to their scientific accounts.

In 1889 Henry Guppy, British surgeon, geologist, botanist and photographer, set the historical scene for later natural scientists, writing in a guarded fashion that:

> The discovery of these islands is usually attributed to Captain William Keeling during his return from Bantam in 1609; but I have failed to find any reference to such a discovery in the narrative of the voyage given by Purchas, Prevost, and other compilers of the early voyages. It is, however, evident from the accounts there given that his homeward track lay in the vicinity of these islands. That the discovery was made by the English, and probably by Keeling, is shown in the circumstance that these islands are laid down in Dudley's *Arcano del Mare*, published in 1646–47, where it is expressly stated that they were discovered by the English. In the maps of this atlas their size is much exaggerated, but their position, about 500 miles SW. of the Sunda Strait on the 11th and 12th parallels, leaves no doubt as to their identity.[32]

In essence, Guppy stated that there is no evidence that Keeling discovered the islands in 1609, but that Dudley's toponym 'scoperta d'Inglesi' (discovered by the English) in 1646 makes Keeling's discovery probable. However, the apparent lack of any reference in the Keeling archives to a 1609 discovery leaves Guppy with a very weak case. One could more justifiably claim that crew from one of the earliest Dutch fleets, on the route established by the Dutch, first saw the Cocos (Keeling) Islands but lost the report of the sighting, simply did not bother to tell any Dutch cartographers about it, or kept it secret. As pointed out in Chapter 3, any use of Dudley's words 'scoperta d'Inglesi' to argue for English discovery of the Cocos (Keeling) Islands is also weak: Dudley placed similar words on several other places that were definitely not discovered by the English.[33]

Guppy published an altered version of Dalrymple's North Keeling Island chart, replacing Dalrymple's 'Northern I.' with 'North Keeling Island'. On it, he compared the content of the 1749 Eckeberg chart with that of an 1836 chart of North Keeling Island, produced by Captain Robert Fitzroy, in the light of some of Charles Darwin's observations about coral reef formation. Guppy located the remarks that Eckeberg had made in 1749 when developing his sketch plan.

The British anatomist, naturalist and anthropologist Frederic Wood-Jones was influenced by Dudley's charts and Guppy's argument and was convinced about English discovery, despite also conceding the lack of any evidence. He further extended the claim of English discovery from just the northern atoll (as stated by Captain Fremantle) to include the southern atoll:

> There is no doubt that the islands were discovered by the early English navigators, and there seems most reason to assign to Captain William Keeling – after whom the northern atollon is named – the honour of their first finding. In 1609 Captain Keeling, who was a captain in the service of the East India Company, sailed home from Bantam, and on this voyage, it is supposed that

he sighted the islands, and it is certain that his course must have lain close in their neighbourhood. And yet the actual record of their sighting does not appear to be forthcoming, for no reference was found to it in the account of his voyages: and no more direct evidence than the date of the first charting of the islands, and their name, associates Keeling with their discovery. In any case, it is probable that Keeling only saw the northern island that today bears his name, and the southern atoll – the Cocos Islands – were the independent discovery of another English navigator, and was made soon after Keeling's finding of the northern atollon.[34]

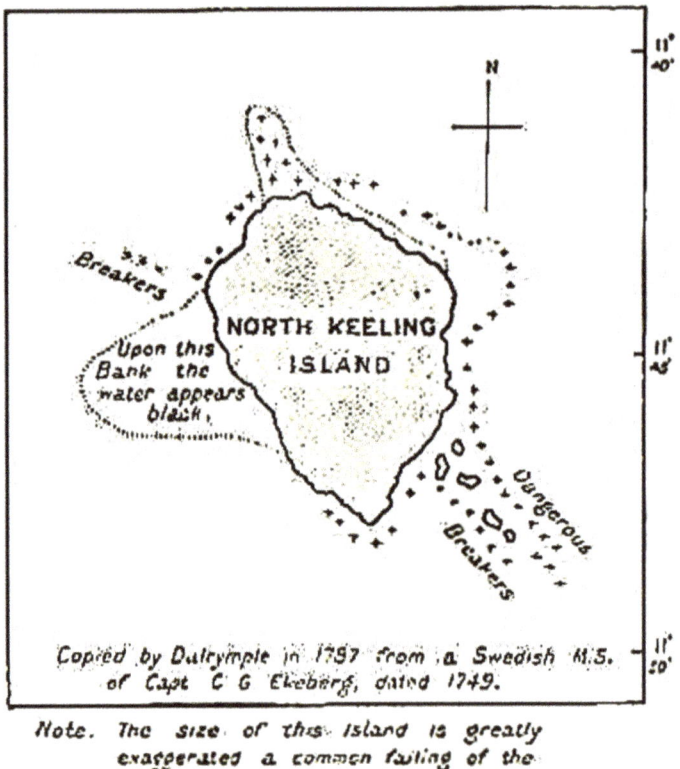

Figure 46. 'Eckeberg's Island of 1749', with Dalrymple's modification and Guppy's 1889 comments

In the absence of contrary information, later researchers repeated the nineteenth-century natural scientists' reliance on the belief that Keeling was the first European to sight the islands. However, there is no evidence, in either Keeling's journal or the Dudley atlas, that William Keeling discovered any part of the Cocos (Keeling) Islands, or that he ever claimed to have discovered them. Given Keeling's role as an English trader, he had no reason to have taken any notice of the small, isolated, unoccupied North Keeling Island even if he had seen it. His men collected coconuts when they landed on Banda, but they would also have collected food supplies before departing on the homeward voyage, and so would have had no reason to be interested in yet another small atoll if they passed in the vicinity of North Keeling Island. Keeling's onboard discussions with merchant John Saris would have been about more lucrative or inspiring topics, and if Keeling did ever meet with Dudley in England, he would have had more notable islands to talk about. Any word-pictures conjuring Keeling in the crows-nest with a telescope trained on the Cocos horizon (the earliest known telescope appeared in 1608 in the Netherlands) would be ludicrous.

What then of the Hessel Gerritsz maps? The small triangle of islands shown to the southwest of Sunda Strait on his 1612 world map represents the Cocos (Keeling) Islands, making this the earliest clear cartographic evidence that the South Keeling Islands had been discovered, by the Dutch, in 1611 or before. The 1622 Gerritsz map of the Indian Ocean, showing Cocos Eylanden, is the first use of the toponym Cocos for these islands and the first probable depiction of North Keeling Island, and this reinforces the idea of the Dutch being the first discoverers of the Cocos (Keeling) Islands. In 1889 Henry Guppy commented, 'Strange to say, the Dutch, doubtless for good reasons, have never accepted the name of Keeling for these islands'.[35] A renaming of the islands as the 'Cocos (Gerritsz) Islands' would more accurately reflect their history.

Events leading to permanent settlement

Captain Le Gour's brig Mauritius was wrecked on the Cocos (Keeling) Islands in 1825

John Clunies-Ross, in his various reports, made no mention of landings on the Cocos (Keeling) Islands before his first landing in 1825.[36] Nevertheless, given his claim that he had in 1820 ascertained that the islands had a safe anchorage,[37] he may have been made aware that Godlob Silo had done soundings inside the lagoon about 100 years previously.

Carl Alexander Gibson-Hill, a British medical doctor, naturalist, ornithologist, curator of zoology and later director of Singapore's Raffles Museum, published research on the natural, geographical and cultural history of Christmas Island and the Cocos (Keeling) Islands, where he served as resident medical officer for several years.[38] Gibson-Hill noted the statement made by Cocos settler Arthur Keating that the islands 'were first inhabited in 1825, by Capt. Le Cour [sic], of the brig *Mauritius*, the fact having been recorded on the cocoa-nut trees, on which the names of himself, crew and vessel are cut'. Keating added that:

> On Captain R's arrival, he found the remains of the huts, which had been occupied by the crew of the brig *Mauritius*, and the several pits which they had dug for water. Some characters, apparently Arabic, were discovered on the trees.[39]

In 1952 Gibson-Hill analysed Keating's quoted remarks, and became confused:

> It seems likely that Le Cour's landing was due to shipwreck, and not of deliberate intent, but it is nevertheless odd that Ross makes no mention of it. A wreck was also reported by Capt. Driscoll of the barque *Lonach*, from Port Jack-son, bound for Bombay. He hove-to off the atoll on 24 November 1825 [12 days before Clunies-Ross arrived there], and put a boat's crew ashore,

the men landing 'on a fine sandy beach, covered with crabs, and aquatic birds.' Ashore they discovered 'a large mast, with a bowsprit, and a teak carline, the remains of a wreck.' They also saw several snakes, and as in the case of the men who landed on Christmas Island and found limes and wild boars, one may wonder if they ever got ashore at all: but assuming that they did, it seems likely that they are describing Le Cour's ship.[40]

Gibson-Hill went on to cast further doubt on Keating's association of the brig *Mauritius* with the Cocos (Keeling) Islands, referring to the 'Klapper or Cocoa Islands', on the south coast of Java, being 'greatly infested with enormous snakes'. He asked, 'was this same confusion also the origin of the snakes which the men from the barque *Lonach* saw on Cocos in November 1825?'[41]

The 391-ton British convict ship *Lonach*, after offloading its 143 male prisoners at Port Jackson, New South Wales, had set off for Bombay under the command of William Driscoll. Gibson-Hill had derived his information about Driscoll's visit from a paragraph in James Horsburgh's 1843 edition of *The India Directory*, stating that while passing the Cocos (Keeling) Islands on 24 November 1825 Captain Driscoll had:

> ... sent a boat to that [island] called by Captain Ross Horsburgh Island, which Captain Driscoll made in lat. 12° 3' S., by noon observation taken two hours previously, and he made it in lon. 97° 2½' E. by observations of sun and moon, which agrees with the position assigned to these islands in the first volume of this work. The *Lonach*'s boat landed on a fine sandy beach, covered with crabs and aquatic birds, and a path was perceived where the branches were parted and the leaves trodden down, leading into the jungle; several snakes were also seen; and a large mast with a bowsprit and teak carline, the remains of a wreck.[42]

Observations can be made about the *Mauritius*, Le Gour and Gibson-Hill's analysis. The *Mauritius* did exist. The vessel was first registered in 1823, as a 90-ton brig, built on Mauritius at Grand Port, where the slave-trading brig *Le Courier* was built.[43] The *Mauritius* did go to the Cocos (Keeling) Islands. In December 1823 it sailed for Madras with a cargo of sundries, under the command of Louis Le Gour. Then in August 1824, it sailed for 'Diego' with 'sundries', a term sometimes used by slave traders as an alternative to enslaved people. After that, the trail is not entirely clear.

The British abolished slavery on Mauritius in 1835. The master of the brig *Mauritius* initially sailed for Diego Garcia in the Chagos archipelago, at that time a staging post for slave ships between Sumatra, the Seychelles and Bourbon, or Diego Suarez on the northern tip of Madagascar, where the population included Arabs. Arthur Keating's statement about the next leg of the voyage of the *Mauritius* commenced with the words: 'This group of islands is situated in the southern Indian Ocean, nearly 600 miles to the s.w. of Java Head'.[44] This shows that Le Gour indeed took the *Mauritius* to the Cocos (Keeling) Islands rather than the Klapper or Cocoa Islands situated near the south coast of Java. In turn, this indicates either that Le Gour established the first, albeit temporary, settlement on Cocos, building huts and digging wells, or that Le Gour used wells dug by previous visitors. These visitors might have been Austronesians from South-East Asia, crew from East Indiamen, or more likely crew from the English, American or French whalers who had frequented the area since the 1790s.

The records do not state whether in August 1824 the brig *Mauritius* was carrying enslaved people rather than 'sundries', or whether Le Gour, like English merchant Alexander Hare soon after, had decided to try the Cocos (Keeling) Islands as a base. There Le Gour could, with slave labour perhaps from 'Diego', establish a coconut-product export and ship victualling business without being harassed by abolitionists. John Clunies-Ross, implying that Le Gour must have been wrecked mid-journey because of longitude errors while on route to 'Diego', stated that two other ships (*Sir Francis Nicholas Burton* in 1826 and *Earl of Liverpool* in 1834) had been wrecked at the Cocos (Keeling) Islands for similar reasons.

However, it is clear that Le Gour intended to head southeast from Madras to the Cocos (Keeling) Islands, either to establish a settlement or to consider the prospect of doing so, rather than southwest to Diego Garcia, 1,500 nautical miles from Cocos.

Had the *Earl of Liverpool*'s captain also been contemplating involvement in the slave trade or similar labour force arrangements before it was wrecked at North Keeling? En route to the Cocos in 1834 he had visited Gambia, traditionally the source of many enslaved people, but that was the year that Britain's *Slavery Abolition Act* took effect. He likely continued on from Gambia to Mozambique, an ongoing source of antimony ore and enslaved people. Opportunity-seeking shipowners would have seen advantage in taking enslaved people from East African countries such as Mozambique to more remote places in the Indian Ocean, or at least scouting those islands to prepare for such opportunities.

Charles Darwin, during his visit to Cocos in 1836, wrote that the brig *Mauritius* was the source of the wreckage reported by Captain Driscoll in 1825. However, the description given by Driscoll does not match the *Mauritius*. The *Mauritius* disappeared from the register after 1824, so it probably was wrecked on the Cocos (Keeling) Islands. However, Driscoll was master of a 391-ton vessel. His description of an assemblage of structural wreckage – a large mast, bowsprit and carling (framing beams supporting the deck) – rather than isolated pieces of flotsam, indicates not the small brig *Mauritius*, but a large ship, a second shipwreck, close by on the atoll. The *Mauritius* was only 90 tons, so it may be expected that in Driscoll's mind it would have had a small mast. A large mast implies an East Indiaman. Horsburgh Island, part of the South Keeling Islands, does have the fine sandy beach and thick foliage, as described by Captain Driscoll.

The 'several snakes' that Driscoll's men saw are also consistent with Horsburgh Island. With no jetties, the men would have had to wade ashore, through the shallow water. James Holman, visiting the Cocos (Keeling) Islands in January 1831, wrote:

There are two species of water-snakes, which are generally from four to five feet long, and from six to nine inches in circumference. The colour of one is silver-grey, and of the other, which is the larger one, a reddish grey. They live on the small crabs which abound especially on the beach. Their bite is very severe, and they are consequently much dreaded in shallow water among the coral reefs.[45]

The National Park Management Plan lists two species of sea snakes recorded at the southern atoll, these being the yellow-bellied sea snake, *Pelamis platurus*, and the banded sea krait, *Laticauda colubrina*.[46]

Holman, the travel writer, has been described as 'history's most prolific explorer',[47] but he, like the poet John Milton, was blind, so the question arises as to whether his written observations are credible. He explains:

> I am constantly asked, and I may as well answer the question once and for all, what is the use of travelling to one who cannot see? I answer, does every traveller see all that he describes? And is not every traveller obliged to depend on others for a great proportion of the information he collects? ... freed from the hazard of being misled by appearances, I am the less likely to adopt hasty and erroneous conclusions.[48]

John Clunies-Ross landed on the South Keeling Islands and took formal possession in December 1825

In 1823 the Doctrine of Discovery was expounded as a concept of public international law in a series of United States Supreme Court decisions. The Chief Justice stated that title to lands lay with the government whose subjects travelled to and occupied a territory whose inhabitants were not subjects of a European Christian monarch. In that same year, Scottish merchant seaman John Clunies-Ross decided that the profession of master of a merchant

Figure 47. James Holman, the blind travel writer, by George Chinnery, 1830.

vessel could not be relied on to bring him a sufficient income. He made up his mind to emigrate and determined to settle on an island. Among those he considered were Melville Island off the coast of the Northern Territory of Australia, Kerguelen Island in the Southern Ocean, Saint Paul Island in the southern Indian Ocean, the Pagi Islands off the west coast of Sumatra, Christmas Island, and the Cocos (Keeling) Islands.[49]

The 1724 Treaty of London had meant the surrender of some British possessions in the East Indies to the Netherlands, so John Clunies-Ross abandoned his initial idea of settling in the Pagi Islands. He left Bencoolen, Sumatra, on the ship *Borneo* in November 1825, searching for a possible new place to reside for his employer, English merchant Alexander Hare. John Clunies-Ross intended to examine Christmas Island to form a settlement there for himself, but adverse winds caused him to bear away towards the Cocos (Keeling) Islands, where he arrived on 6 December. As Godlob Silo must have done, he entered the lagoon by the main channel, and he anchored for four days, examining the islets surrounding the lagoon. The advantage of the Cocos over the other islands would have been immediately apparent to Clunies-Ross, as it was to others. When lone sailor Joshua Slocum (the first person to sail single-handedly around the world) called there in 1897, he remarked that, 'If there is a paradise on this earth it is Keeling'.[50]

However, Clunies-Ross wrote blandly that:

> On concluding the examination, I found reasons for deciding on adopting the place for settlement, and in commencement proceeded to take formal possession and to clear a space at each of the entrance-bounding isles, wherein I placed the seeds, roots and plants which I had provided at Sumatra for the purpose.[51]

He also stated that when he first arrived, in 1825, the islands had the appearance of having been previously uninhabited.[52] He might not have seen evidence of Le Gour's camp or the *Mauritius* wreck during his four days on the multitude of islets, and even if he did, he was canny enough a Scotsman to have realised the legal implications of stating that he was not the first to make a landing, claim possession and establish a settlement.

Alexander Hare established the first permanent settlement in June 1826
The Dutch had evicted Alexander Hare from Batavia, along with his household slaves, when they took over Java in 1819.[53] He was banned from residence in the Dutch territories in the East Indies and took his people to South Africa, where he settled temporarily on a farm 20 kilometres from Cape Town. He asked John Clunies-Ross to help him find a new home, but John Clunies-Ross, in his travels,

Figure 48. A chart of the Cocos (Keeling) Islands, 1840.

visited the uninhabited Cocos (Keeling) Islands in December 1825 and claimed them for himself.

Unaware of the John Clunies-Ross claim, in January 1826 Hare left South Africa to sail eastward and settle on the Cocos (Keeling) Islands with his harem and other enslaved people.[54] He arrived at the islands in June 1826 on *Hippomenes*, skippered by Robert Clunies-Ross, a brother of John. After establishing the first permanent settlement on Home Island, Hare commenced the harvesting of coconuts and the production of coconut oil.

The brig Sir Francis Nicholas Burton was wrecked on West Island in December 1826

In his description of the Cocos (Keeling) Islands, Dutch naval officer H. van der Jagt referred to:

> ... the English ship *Sir Francis Nicholas Burton* which was wrecked during the night of 15 December 1826 on the south corner of West or Hare Island. This vessel sailed from London on 14 July 1826 and was bound for Calcutta.[55]

James Holman's account reads:

> ... the *Sir Francis Nicholas Burton*, a large brig from London to Calcutta, was totally wrecked on the SW point of Hare Island, and part of the crew drowned. They were some degrees out in their longitude, and the night on which the wreck took place was dark and stormy.[56]

Lloyds Register of Shipping listed a 410-ton barque named *Sir Francis Burton* as sailing for Bombay, but *The Times* of 2 October 1832 shows a *Francis Burton* as having arrived back at Liverpool from Bombay, so that was not the vessel stranded at the Cocos (Keeling) Islands. Another vessel, the 124-ton snow brig *Sir Francis Nicholas Burton*, was listed in Lloyds during the late 1820s as sailing from London to Vera Cruz. The information given is of a copper-fastened vessel, equipped with three chain cables and having a draft when loaded of 13 feet, sailing under the command, at different times, of W. Hare and J. Clibborn. Lloyds does not say that this vessel was wrecked, but the association with a member of the Hare family makes it reasonably certain that this was the vessel wrecked on the southwest corner of West Island in 1826.

John Clunies-Ross wrote that the captain was not intending to stop (that is, he was unaware of there being an anchorage, settlement, or atoll), that the vessel ran onshore in fine clear weather with all sails set because of errors in reckoning and lookout negligence, that the ship's boats had been lost in the surf, and that he (Clunies-Ross) had taken the crew to Batavia.[57] However, given that the vessel had come from Vera Cruz, a location with a high population of African enslaved people, and was listed in *Lloyds Register* as being under the command of a W. Hare, it was probably intending to engage in business with Alexander Hare at the Cocos (Keeling) Islands.

Clunies-Ross again took formal possession, in the name of King George IV, in February 1827
John Clunies-Ross started another settlement when he reached the atoll in the *Borneo* on 16 February 1827, bringing with him to the island then known as Burial Island his wife, children and a small number of European colonists. He referred to the islands as 'Cocos or Keeling's Isles', using the possessive to emphasise a British claim to ownership through discovery. In 1829 he applied to the British Government, in a petition through the Governor of Mauritius, for the incorporation of the islands into the British Empire,[58] with the inference of government protection of British nationality settlers – the Clunies-Ross family.

In the 1829 petition, he set out his logic: that the islands were first discovered by the English captain William Keeling; that they were, previous to the visit by Clunies-Ross, considered destitute of anchorage; that he had discovered and explored a convenient harbour where he had settled his family; that a map showing the location and extent of the islands was attached; that the islands could be a depot for commodities, refreshment and the establishment of a naval force in times of war; that his Majesty's rights of sovereignty arose from the islands having been first explored and settled by subjects of his Majesty; and that, in the hands of an enemy, incalculable mischief might be done to commerce in the Indian Ocean. In support of his petition, Clunies-Ross stated that on 6 December 1825 he had made a plan, taken possession in the name of the king, hoisted the British flag, cleared a space of ground, and planted roots, vegetables and fruit trees.[59]

His reference to an enemy was perhaps a prescient warning if considered in the light of the geopolitics of the twenty-first century. However, the Lords Commissioners of the Admiralty were not convinced, the Colonial Department stating that:

> They do not think that any advantage will result either to the British Navy or to British commerce by the formation of an establishment on those Islands. Sir G. Murray concurs in the opinion expressed by their Lordships, and he does not therefore consider it expedient to guarantee the possession of those islands by making a grant of them to Mr Ross, or to any other British subjects.[60]

Clunies-Ross was more successful in dissuading the Dutch, who were not much interested anyway, from any ambitions regarding the Cocos (Keeling) Islands. Dutch naval officer H. van der Jagt examined the islands on behalf of the Netherlands East Indies Government, and in his 1829 report, stated that:

> The Cocos or Keeling Islands, which were probably discovered in 1609 by an English Captain called Keeling, whose name they bear, are not of great interest in appearance or in natural products.[61]

Meanwhile, the relationship between John Clunies-Ross and Hare quickly deteriorated, and many of Hare's followers left him to join the Clunies-Ross camp. Hare finally abandoned the islands and his flock in March 1831, taking up residence in Batavia. Clunies-Ross then made appeals to both British and Dutch authorities to annex the islands.[62] For some years he flew Dutch colours on his trading schooner, and for a short period on the island itself in 1841. But the Dutch government did not support this action and Clunies-Ross had to haul the flag down. The islands were annexed as a British territory during Captain Stephen Fremantle's confused visit on HMS *Juno* on 31 March 1857.

Chapter 5

Discovery of Christmas Island

Timeline

1615 English merchant John Milward reported an island (Christmas Island) at 10° south.

1618–28 A chart by Dutch cartographer Hessel Gerritsz showed 'Monij Island'.

1643 Englishman William Mynors in the *Royal Mary* named Christmas Island.

1665 An English chart by Nicholas Comberford showed Christmas Island.

1666 A Pieter Goos chart showed Mony Island southwest of Sunda Strait.

1667 Nicholas Comberford showed three islands in the general vicinity of Christmas Island.

1688 William Dampier gave the first descriptive account of Christmas Island.

1711 A Samuel Thornton map showed triangles for both Christmas and the Cocos (Keeling) islands.

It might be expected that Christmas Island, 265 nautical miles south of Sunda Strait, would have been first sighted by Europeans before the more remote Cocos (Keeling) Islands, another 500 nautical miles west-southwest of Christmas Island. On the face of it, the wording of several English-language documents emanating from the account by Bernardt Langhenez of the Dutch first fleet (to the East Indies) voyage raises the possibility that men on one of Houtman's ships saw Christmas Island on their approach to Sunda Strait in 1596. Under scrutiny, however, such an interpretation does not hold water.

In April 1595 the *Mauritius*, *Amsterdam*, *Hollandia* and *Duyfken* left Amsterdam to pioneer a new sea route to Indonesia, beginning the Dutch spice trade and leading to the formation, in 1602, of the charter company Vereinigde Oostindische Compagnie (VOC). The 1595 fleet was commanded by Cornelis de Houtman, the chief merchant on the *Mauritius*, who, with his brother Frederik, had previously been imprisoned by the Portuguese for attempting to steal their secret charts of East Indian sailing routes.

Houtman's fleet rounded the Cape of Good Hope and sailed to Madagascar, guided by Portuguese sea cards – compass cards and ocean charts containing navigational information.

From the northeast coast of Madagascar, the fleet sailed eastward towards Java in February 1596.[1] Portuguese traders controlled the

Figure 49. Cornelis de Houtman.

Figure 50. Cornelis de Houtman's fleet.

Malacca Strait, and they had been approaching the East Indies from the northwest, avoiding the south coasts of Sumatra and Java. However, Jan Huygen van Linschoten suggested that Houtman approach the East Indies along the south side of Sumatra and through Sunda Strait to avoid the Portuguese.[2] After leaving Madagascar, Houtman's fleet experienced compass variation, ocean currents and lack of wind. Around 6 June, the ships came together at Enggano Island, off the coast of Sumatra, a little to the west of Sunda Strait. Coincidentally the word 'engano', in Portuguese, means 'mistake', 'deception' or 'deceit'.

The Dutch-language account of the voyage by Bernardt Langhenez was translated into English in 1597 by William Phillip and printed by John Wolfe in 1598. It then read:

> The 1st of July we saw the Island of Emgano ... whereat we much rejoiced, because of the great thirst we endured in our ship; and when we made nearer to it, we perceived it to be an island lying before the straights of *Sonda*, under 9 degrees on the south side of the line, and 16 leagues from the island of Sumatra.[3]

On the same page, the Langhenez account reads, correctly, 'The 14th of June ... Java beginneth under seven degrees on the south side', showing that he was aware of the actual latitudes of the islands. The above statements have what appear to be internal contradictions. An island situated in 9° south would fit more easily with Langhenez and his companions seeing Christmas Island, lying between 10° 25' and 10° 34', rather than Enggano Island, which is at 5° 17' to 5° 30' south.

It may be expected that the English translator, Phillip, saw the contradiction of the Langhenez reference to 9° because he has provided a footnote to the text, where he explains 'Sumatra or Taprobana'. At that time many cartographers equated the island of Taprobana (Figure 51), a concept developed by Ptolemy, with an ill-defined Sumatra. However, some saw it as being quite vast. Phillip refers to this:

Some writers affirm it is 700 leagues in circumference, and 200 in breadth. Others say it is but 170 *German* leagues long, and 60 broad. Those that dwell in the middle of this island, are directly under the equinoctial line; so that one half reaching to the south, and the other half to the north, the whole reaches from the 16th degree of south latitude, to the latitude of five degrees north.[4]

It is not entirely clear why Phillip has added this footnote about the position and size of Ptolemy's Taprobana. If it is interpreted as meaning that Sumatra extended 8° south of the equator, with Enggano another 60 miles further south at 9°, it would, despite being incorrect, make sense. However, if Langhenez knew the latitude of the southwest corner of Java to be 7°, he surely knew the latitude of Enggano to be around 5° 20′, so the reason for the reference in the main body of the Langhenez text to men seeing an island in 9° remains not fully answered. Edgar Marchant wrote in his entry in the *Dictionary of National Biography* that Phillip's translations were not very accurate.

The Dutch-language accounts given by the masters of the Houtman ships *Duyfken* and *Hollandia*, recorded in the 1915 Rouffaer and Ijzerman book, make it clear that those ships approached Enggano not from the south but from the west, along the south side of Sumatra, and on this route they did not approach the more southerly Christmas Island.[5] The journal information regarding the routes of the *Amsterdam* and the *Mauritius* is less specific but contains no reference to an island at 9°, so it is not conceivable that they saw Christmas Island.

Life was short for these early adventurers. Of the 249 men who had embarked on the voyage a year previously, fewer than half were still alive when the ships reached Bantam. The high death rates were not confined to men of the lower decks. In 1599 Cornelis de Houtman, at the age of 33, was killed during battles with the Achehnese Navy after he had insulted the Sultan. Lambert Biesman was a 22-year-old gentleman volunteer when he sailed in

Figure 51. Detail of Sebastian Munster's Tabula Orientalis, 1580.

the *Hollandia* on the Dutch first fleet voyage. In December 1600, Biesman, serving his first command as captain of the jacht *Eendracht*, was captured and imprisoned at Manila by the Spanish. Refusing to renounce the reformed religion, he was taken to the garrotting post and executed at the age of 28.[6]

In 1611 Pieter Both, the first governor-general of the Dutch East Indies, established a post at Jacatre, to the east of Bantam on Java, giving it the name Batavia. In 1619 the fourth governor, Jan Pieterszoon Coen, transferred his residence to this site, which became the capital of the Dutch possessions.[7]

Hendrik Brouwer, of the Dutch East India Company (Verenigde Oostindische Compagnie, VOC), had pioneered a new southern 'roaring forties' route to the East Indies in 1611, turning north in the longitude of Sunda Strait. Then it was inevitable that outward-bound Dutch ships would encounter Christmas Island, situated just 265 nautical miles south of Sunda Strait in the same longitude.

However, the earliest clear documentation of a European sighting of Christmas Island was by John Milward of the English East India Company (EIC), formed in 1599 under an original charter granted by Queen Elizabeth. In 1615 he reported having fortuitously discovered Christmas Island during his outward voyage. Milward had been a jeweller by vocation. Sir James Lancaster had opened a

Figure 52. Hendrick Brouwer (1581–1643), explorer and governor-general of the Dutch East Indies.

trading factory in Bantam in 1601 during the EIC's first East Indies voyage, and the English were interested in widening the variety of their East Indies trade items, as merchant John Saris observed from Bantam:

> Soocodanna is a Town situate upone Borneo … To this place is a great trade in Iunkes and Prawes, for it yeeldeth great store of Diamonds, the which are accounted the best in the world. There is store to be had at all times … They are brought downe the river called Lave by Prawe. The manner of getting them is as you dive for Pearle.[8]

The EIC had recruited Milward as the head merchant for their trading post at Bantam, thinking his knowledge of jewellery would progress their increasing trade in diamonds from Borneo. Milward left Plymouth on 23 May 1614 on the *Thomas*, commanded by Richard Rowe, in a fleet commanded by General David Middleton. The fleet stopped for refreshment at Soldanha Bay, near the Cape of Good Hope, and then set out across the Indian Ocean for Sunda Strait. Rowe overshot his easting and missed sighting Sumatra. Then, after making landfall on the south coast of Java, the *Thomas* was pushed southward by the summer northwest monsoon winds. In tacking back to Sunda Strait, Milward wrote:

> On the three and twentieth [January 1615] … we bore in with the land, and anchored in a bay … some fiftie leagues to the East of the North end of Java … The second of February we were in tenne degrees twelve minutes. We saw the next day a small Iland, fortie leagues to the South of Java major, in tenne degrees, about five leagues broad, eight long … On the fifth we had nine degrees sixteen minutes … On the thirteenth we were in the straights of Sunda, having on our Larboord Sumatra and Java on our Starboord. The foureteenth at night we anchored within three leagues of Bantam Road.[9]

Milward, discoverer of Christmas Island, did not last long, dying at Tiku, West Sumatra, in July 1617, of poison thought to have been administered by the native people.[10]

After news of Houtman's homeward-bound route in 1597 spread, other Dutch navigators realised that by initially heading south from Sunda Strait, the northwest or northeast monsoon enabled them to reach the latitudes 10° to 30° south, where the southeast trade wind prevailed. With this continuous wind, a south-westerly course could be held to the Cape.[11] It was inevitable that some of the many Dutch vessels following this homeward route would sight Christmas Island.

In 1620 English captain Humfrey Fitzherbert, in the *Royal Exchange*, successfully followed the Dutch southern Indian Ocean outward-bound route. The new route brought subsequent English ships close to Christmas Island, which was then in the path of both outward and homeward-bound Dutch and English ships. Soon after Milward's 1615 report, the island appeared on charts, represented in various locations and nomenclature.

Dutch cartographer Hessel Gerritsz showed 'Monij' (Christmas Island) as a single island southwest of Sunda Strait on a 1618–28 chart,[12] initiating some confusion between representations of Christmas and the Cocos, which lay a more distant west-southwest. Blaeu showed Christmas Island in 1664 as three islands, and on later charts the island appeared considerably south of Sunda Strait with names that included 'Moni', 'Mony', 'Selam', 'Selan' and 'Celan'. Jan Tent has concluded that these maps show languages from Javanese, Dutch, Portuguese or Sanskrit origins.[13] His candidates for Monij include the Sanskrit word *muni* (sage, holy man, monk, silent) and the Portuguese word *múni* (a pious or wise Indian man), and for Selam, his candidates are the Arabic word *selam* (peace, greeting) and the Javanese word *sela* (from the Sanskrit *śilā*, meaning 'a rock'). The word *molshoop* is Dutch for a molehill or a conical mound, and the Greek *monos* means 'solitary one', but it also seems logical that Mony might come from the Latin *Mons*, meaning 'a mountain, or great rock'.

Captain William Mynors, of the EIC ship *Royal Mary,* sighted Christmas Island on Christmas Day in 1643 and named it thus. He wrote:

> The 25th ditto in the morning I saw an island, of which I cannot find any mention either in English, Dutch, or Portugall plaits. It lves in lattytude 10d. 27; S. ½ E. from the head of Java, distance 75 leagus; and longitude from the said head 00d. 31 E. To see to, tis a fine smooth island of 7 leaugs longe. I came not neerer it then 6 leaugs, but caus'd the lead to be hove but found noe ground. There I lay becalm'd two dayes; which did heartily greeve me, in regard of the many sicke men I had then aboard, beinge noe less than 20. But the 29th ditto it pleas'd God to send a fresh gale.[14]

The log of the *Royal Mary* reads:

> [At] 3 howers morne had sight of an iland bearing, the body of it, S.W. b. W. about 7 lea. Of; and because it was Christmas Day, we called it by the name of Christmas iland.[15]

A 1665 English chart of the East Indies by Nicholas Comberford shows 'Christmas Island', and his 1667 chart, like that of Gerard de Jode in 1593, shows three islands (in this case named Christmas, Mony, and Selam) in the approximate location of Christmas Island.[16] EIC hydrographer Samuel Thornton continued the conflation into the eighteenth century, showing three islands in the location of Christmas Island.[17] It was a case of having two bob each way, a common strategy for map makers of that era.

Chapter 6

Exploration of Christmas Island

Timeline

1688 William Dampier visited the island to collect boobies and water.

1697 Willem de Vlamingh visited the island searching for shipwreck survivors.

1718 English captain Daniel Beekman sketched the island from the sea.

1811 Survivors from the American China Trader *Rapid* visited the island en route to Bantam.

1826 Alexander Hare went ashore at Christmas Island but was discouraged by landing difficulties.

1852 Survivors of the Dutch ship *Vice Admiraal Rijk* spent 57 days on the island before rescue.

1852 The account of a *Vice Admiraal Rijk* survivor referred to 'Indians' previously resident.

1857 Crew of the British ship HMS *Amethyst* attempted to explore the island.

1872–6 Scottish naturalist John Murray conducted surveys during an HMS *Challenger* expedition.

1886 Captain Maclear of HMS *Flying Fish* found an anchorage on the north coast.

1887 HMS *Egeria* crew collected samples from beds of phosphate lime.

1888 HMS *Imperieuse* crew formally annexed the island for Britain.

1888 George Clunies-Ross initiated a settlement at Flying Fish Cove.

1890 George Clunies-Ross established his family with wells, palms and coffee plants.

1891 John Murray and George Clunies-Ross obtained a mining lease for phosphate mining.

This chapter outlines the early visits, intentional and accidental, to Christmas Island. The island initially lacked obvious resources, had no easy access and had no native population for trading activities or labour supply. So both the Asian and European powers showed little interest until the discovery of phosphate lime in the 1880s.

William Dampier's visit in 1688

The first recorded visit to Christmas Island was by William Dampier during his first circumnavigation voyage while in the *Cygnet*, under the command of Captain Charles Swan (Figure 54). The crew careened the *Cygnet* at King Sound, on the coast of Western Australia, in 16° 30' south. Then, Dampier wrote, his crewmates threatened to maroon him if he did not agree to go to 'island Cocos which lies in latitude 12° 12' north, by our charts, hoping there to find that fruit, the island having its name from thence'.[1] At 'island Cocos', in the northern hemisphere, they intended to collect coconuts, and then sail on to Cape Comorin in southern India.

Why would the men want to sail some 2,590 nautical miles (as the crow flies) from King Sound to 'island Cocos' (usually called Coco Island), in 14° north (not south) of the equator in the Bay of Bengal, to collect coconuts? Many islands were named Coco, Cocos, Cocoa, Clapper and Klapper, all referring to the presence of coconuts, a source of refreshment for passing ships. Marco Polo had observed that fresh coconut juice has a better taste than wine, and Dampier waxed lyrical about coconuts, describing them as a 'vegetable which is possibly of all others the most generally serviceable to the conveniences as well as the necessities of human life'.[2]

The husk of the coconut shell could be used to make coir ships' cables, oakum for caulking ships' hulls, and coarse cloth for sails. Dampier saw great profit in both the nut and the shell. The kernel was used to make oil for burning or frying, or to make a savoury broth for boiling meat. The shell was used in the East Indies for cups, dishes, ladles, spoons and drinking vessels. Arabs used it for the hubble-bubble, the shell of the coconut serving as a container for the water through which smoke from the tobacco bowl is sucked. Dampier wrote that besides its 'sweet, delicate, wholesome and refreshing water', a sweet and pleasant wine could be made

Figure 53. English explorer, buccaneer, navigator and naturalist William Dampier, by Thomas Murray (1663–1734).

from the sap of the tree, for drinking within 24 hours, or distilling to make a spirit called arak – 'But it must have a dash of Brandy to hearten it because this arak is not strong enough to make good punch of itself'. Dampier pointed out how easy it was to grow the coconut palms on low sandy islands, indicating that it was his custom to do so.

By Dampier's time, there was a general acceptance that fruit and vegetables cured scurvy. Dutchman Johann Bachstrom deduced in 1734 that scurvy was a deficiency disease. But was the men's clamouring for coconuts, and Dampier's ongoing keen interest, an indication that they thought that fruit more than simply wholesome and refreshing? Did they think that it might prevent, delay or cure scurvy? Coconut water has 2.4 milligrams of vitamin C per 100 grams, which does not compare well with lemon juice, which has 39 milligrams of vitamin C per 100 grams. Nevertheless, Fred Swart wrote that 'While coconuts are not a rich source of vitamin C, a single coconut, eaten every day, is sufficient to prevent symptoms of scurvy to develop, even though a deficiency exists', and other reports suggest that even such a low level would delay the onset of the disease, providing more time for other interventions to be put in place.[3]

Accepting that coconuts were an attraction to Dampier's fellows, the question nevertheless arises as to why they should want to sail past the many palm-covered islands between King Sound and the Bay of Bengal to get themselves to Coco Island in the northern hemisphere. Dampier wrote that they wanted to sail northward from the Australian coast (that is, towards Coco Island) but that the winds forced them on a more easterly course than they wanted. The Cocos (Keeling) Islands, lying in latitude 12° south, are approximately 1,565 nautical miles west-northwest from King Sound. Dampier had written that from early in the voyage the men were so tired of the voyaging that they did not care what they did or where they went. They left King Sound on 12 March, and Dampier hoped that he might leave the ship at one of the islands on the west side of Sumatra, but 14 days later, with winds from

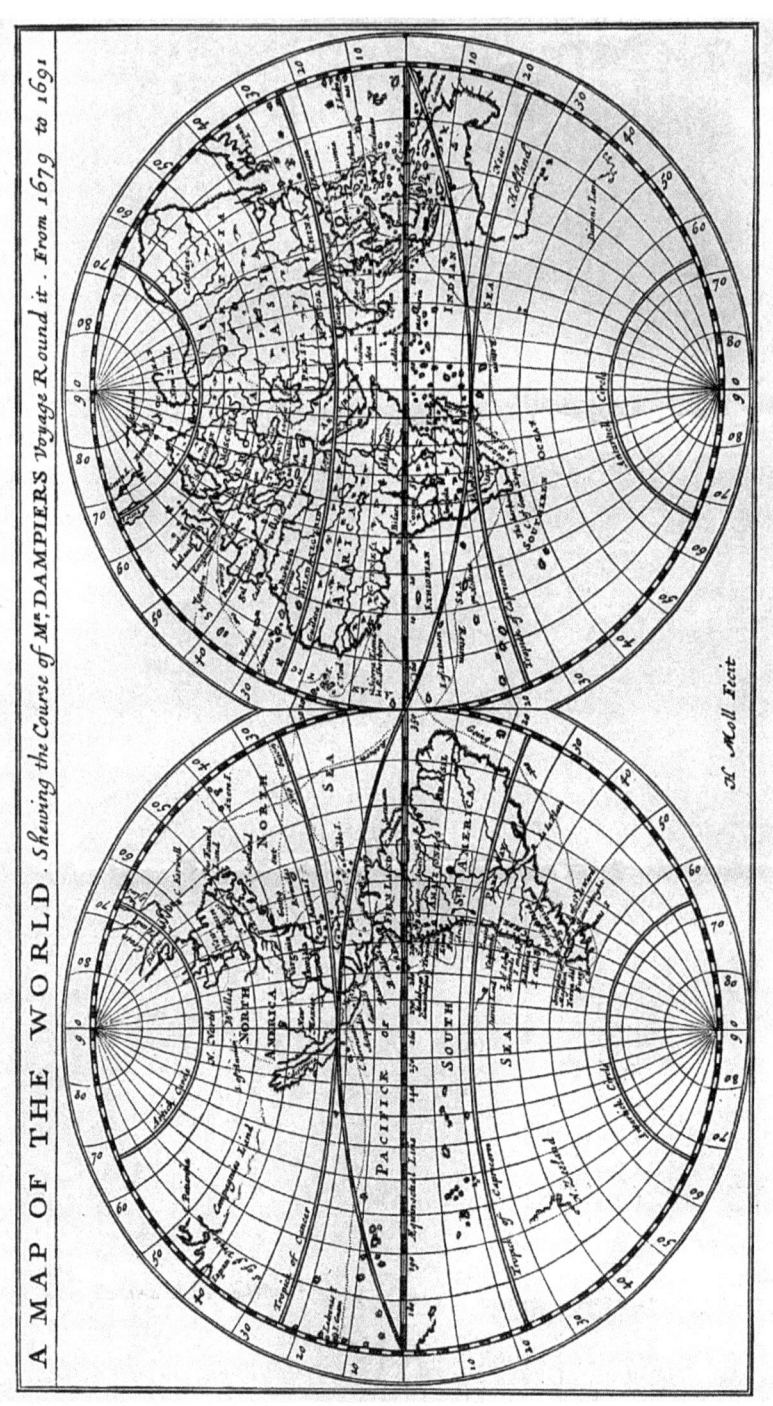

Figure 54. A map of the world showing Dampier's course.

the north, they judged themselves 40 or 50 leagues east of 'island Cocos' – this time apparently meaning the Cocos (Keeling) Islands. Then, Dampier wrote:

> ... we fell in with a small woody island [Christmas Island] in latitude 10 degrees 20 minutes ... It was deep water about the island, and therefore no anchoring, but we sent two canoes ashore; one of them with the carpenters to cut a tree to make another pump; the other canoe went to search for freshwater and found a fine small brook near the southwest point of the island, but there the sea fell in on the shore so high that they could not get it off. At noon both our canoes returned aboard; and the carpenters brought aboard a good tree which they afterwards made a pump with, such a one as they made at Mindanao. The other canoe brought aboard as many boobies and men-of-war birds as sufficed all the ship's company when they were boiled ... This island is of a good height, with steep cliffs against the south and southwest, and a sandy bay on the north side; but very deep water steep to the shore.[4]

Dampier went on with the *Cygnet* to Nassau Island, now named Siberut Island, in the Mentawai Islands near the Sumatran coast. The crew replenished their stock with four boatloads of coconuts at the small low island situated off the east end of Nassau Island and shown as 'Cocos Eylanden' on a chart by van Keulen (see Figure 35).

The *Cygnet* continued toward the Coco Islands and Cape Comorin in the northern hemisphere. However, after onboard dissension at the Nicobar Islands, Dampier left the ship and the *Cygnet* sailed to the east coast of India, ignoring the Coco Islands. Dampier's reference to the 'island Cocos' lying in the northern hemisphere, and his statement that the men directed their course to the north (rather than west) to reach the 'island Cocos', may have been just a simple editing error, but it is confusing. Given the great popularity of his account, this must have contributed to the subsequent bizarre confusion among some mapmakers

Figure 55. The outflow of a stream into the ocean on the northwest coast of Christmas Island.

Figure 56. Dolly Beach on Christmas Island's southeast coast is now covered with coconut palms.

and mariners between the southern hemisphere Cocos (Keeling) Islands, the northern hemisphere Coco Islands in the Bay of Bengal, Cocos Eylanden off the south coast of Sumatra, and other similarly named islands.

Willem de Vlamingh's visit in 1697

Dutch sea captain Willem de Vlamingh set out in 1696 on an Indian Ocean voyage of exploration with orders that included searching for the wrecks of the VOC ships *Ridderschap van Holland*, lost in 1694, and *Vergulde Draeck*, lost in 1656. He sighted Christmas Island on 5 March 1697, and his *Geelvinck* journal entry for the following day reads:

> In the afternoon, eight [sand timer] glasses having passed saw land which was an island … the 6th Wednesday in the morning after breakfast the wind ESE, topgallant breeze. Our upper-steersman went ashore to examine how the bottom was and to see if there was any possibility to land since as far as we could see from the ship the shore was altogether steep and sounded no bottom a cannon-shot from shore. In the forenoon sent our third mate with the other boat to another place. At noon the estimated course and distance in 24 hours was N½W 12½ miles, according to which the position by dead reckoning was 10 deg. 13 min. S lat. and 124 deg. 2 min. long. In the afternoon got our boats on board, reported thus: that the under-steersman and third mate, having a carpenter with them, found some trees which were suitable for making masts from, and also many palmite-trees, some of which they brought on board; braced round again and made sail … [we had] found the island which we were confident to be Mony [Christmas Island].[5]

Figure 57. In 1718 Captain Daniel Beekman sketched Christmas Island from the sea.

Visit by survivors of the wreck of the American China Trader *Rapid* in 1811

The American China Trader *Rapid*, commanded by Henry Dorr, was wrecked at Point Cloates on the northwest coast of Australia in 1811, while on a voyage from Boston to Canton, carrying ballast and US$280,000 in coin for buying goods in China.[6] Five of the survivors sailed a boat to Bantam, seeking help. En route, they stopped at Christmas Island. The newspaper account of their visit reads:

> On the 22nd [January] they landed on the NW side and found no fresh water, but then it rained heavily on the next day, and they could catch a considerable amount of water with the sails. They found nothing to eat but beautiful large rats and land crabs, of which they cooked a supply for two days, before setting sail again.[7]

Figure 58. Christmas Island robber crabs and red crabs.

The beautiful large rats were Bulldog Rats, last recorded in 1903.[8] The land crabs (robber crabs) had been described earlier by Dampier as:

> ... resembling a large crawfish without its great claws. These creatures lived in holes in the dry sandy ground like rabbits ... They were very good sweet meat and so large that two of them were more than a man could eat; being almost as thick as one's leg. Their shells were of a dark brown but red when boiled.[9]

Account given by Roelof Bennet, a survivor of the *Vice Admiraal Rijk* in 1852

The 496-ton Dutch barque *Vice Admiraal Rijk* was built by Cornelis Gips & Sons, shipbuilding masters at wharf De Merwede, located at the Lijnbaan in Dordrecht (South Holland). The vessel was launched on 25 June 1846 with a length of 34.33 metres, a beam of 6.33 metres and depth of 5.14 metres.[10] It had two decks, three masts, a wooden hull and copper sheathing attached with copper nails, to protect the hull from shipworm, barnacles and various marine weeds. During its lifetime it was in use as a cargo vessel owned by A. Ahlers Jr, a shipping company located in Amsterdam.[11]

On 7 March 1852, the *Vice Admiraal Rijk* left Ramsgate in East Kent, England, heading for Batavia with a general cargo apparently including military clothing.[12] However, the vessel got into difficulties and was wrecked as it headed past Christmas Island towards Sunda Strait. It was lost on Egeria Point, the southwest extremity of Christmas Island, on 28 June. The crew of the *Vice Admiraal Rijk* consisted of: J. Bakker (master), Pieter Graat (first mate, rescued), F. Schelkes (second helmsman), H. Vuijk (third helmsman), M. Zeilstra (boatswain), Monson (sails), Matzen (carpenter), R. Hollander (cook), Carel Kipping (sailor, rescued), P. Visser (sailor), P. van der Wal (sailor), L. Ringsma (sailor), M. Zwensen (sailor), E. Hansen (sailor), J. Booij (ordinary seaman),

Figure 59. The Dutch barque *Vice Admiraal Rijk*.

J. Terhagen (ordinary seaman), W. Bakker (ordinary seaman), J. Valkema (ordinary seaman), P. Engelhart (ordinary seaman), and Roelof Arnold Herman Tollius Bennet (passenger, rescued).

Of the 20 men on board, only three survived the wrecking event. They managed to scale the cliffs and live ashore, eating raw seabirds for 57 days before being rescued by the passing ship *Amicitia*. Roelof Bennet, one of the survivors, left a detailed account of the wrecking event and his experience on the island. The title page of the book containing Bennet's account translates as:

> Historic and literary curiosities, descriptions of nature, geographical particularities (features/curiosities), historical and romantic stories. Collected from the pen of several famous and anonymous writers as well as 'scholarly' and skilled translators from the best pieces of foreign periodic and other works.[13]

Despite the book's title, the Bennet account generally matches the geographical features of the island and the other sources regarding the loss of the vessel, and it can be regarded as a historical rather than a romantic account.

Bennet would have celebrated his 40th birthday aboard the *Vice Admiraal Rijk* on 10 March, three days after they left Ramsgate. He was born in Velthausen, Germany, in 1812 and appears to have lived for a time in Ede, Netherlands, as an officer (lieutenant at sea 2nd class) of the Royal Netherlands Navy, before departing for Batavia.[14]

After his rescue, Bennet returned to the Netherlands, and on 27 April 1854, he married Adele Douin in Amsterdam. Together they had three daughters, all born on Banda Neira in Indonesia. Bennet's wife died there on 13 July 1864, but it is not known when Bennet died. He wrote the following account of his shipwreck experience:

> The Christmas, or Kerstijds, Island is at 105° gr. 33′ longitude [of Greenwich] and 10°32′ south latitude, about 55 miles from Java. It

is three and a half hours wide and four hours long [presumably he meant minutes of angular measurement rather than hours]. It consists of coral rocks, with trees whose crowns are occupied and it is only approachable on the north-western side. On all the other sides it is surrounded by steep cliffs, and it provides no ground to anchor, because within a few fathoms of the island, the sea is so deep that a sounding lead cannot reach the bottom. There were never residents other than some Indians who, however, after spending nine months said goodbye again to this inhospitable land.

On the 27 June 1852, at noon, we were, according to observations, 15 [Dutch] miles south of Christmas Island, to which we set sail in hopes of getting it in sight before nightfall. The wind was southeast and east southeast.

Unfortunately, the weather changed in the evening and heavy rain, in the direction of the island, forced us out of caution to sail away from it. After they moved the bow to the south, we moved, with reduced sail, to sea. At 9.30 pm the sky brightened and we could see the island, approximately three and a half geographical miles from us; at about 10 pm we turned the prow towards the north, to sail around the island at a distance of seven or eight miles. At 12 pm, when we had the island at two and a half miles north-northeast, the chief mate De Groot gave his watch to the captain and went to bed, like the men who had been on watch with him; as a passenger, I went to rest at 11.30 pm and dreamed that the next day, after a voyage of 113 days, I saw the coast of Java. Therefore, none of the three of us who were saved can report on what was happening after 12 pm until the moment when we were awakened by the cries of the second steersman.

'The tiller to starboard'. From this and other commands, it appeared to us that they had discovered a surf in front of the bow. At the same moment, a dreadful shock made me jump out of my army bed: the ship had stranded! I rushed to the deck and saw that it had crashed onto the island because, despite the darkness, we could distinguish its trees, and the sea, which was whipped up to a height of 40 feet. Since the ship had been pushed back when

Figure 60. Swell conditions on the southwest coast of Christmas Island.

it crashed, the prow was turned to the west and the helm and the square rear yards moved us away from the wind to the sea.

Unfortunately, the leak that the ship experienced from the impact on the sharp rocks underwater was so large that the ship sank rapidly. We knew that all hope was gone and that the sloops urgently needed to be deployed. Everyone rushed for the big sloop, which stood on the deck, but the ship, whose bow sank first, gave us no time to reach her, and the crew were forced to seek refuge in the gig, which hung on the side of the ship. The captain and I were in already, but the sinking was faster than we could handle and we lost our last hope.

Death looked so inevitable to us that there was no attempt made to rescue the ship anymore. Following the rage and excitement just a moment before, silence followed, as the herald of eternal silence! The splashing of the waves was the only sound that could be heard. The bow was already engulfed by the waves and the whole deck was submerged. Then the second mate De Groot and the sailor Kipping saw that the waves had knocked loose the hut from the stern. They hastened to go there.

Then the waves flowed over us. The ship sank with full sails. When I came back above water, with great difficulty, I saw nothing more of the ship or its high masts. People either! While I tried to orientate myself, I discovered something white floating. I swam there, followed by a greyhound, which died a few moments later. The object I approached was the roof of the hut that had come loose. Riding on the roof were the second mate De Groot, the sailor Kipping and cook Hollander. So I was the fourth person who joined them.

That terrible night, which we spent that way, I will not attempt to describe. We stood up to our chests in the water and we could hardly stand up straight because of the movement. Finally, the day came and we saw that our vessel seemed stranded to the southwest corner of the island, from where we were rather far because the wind was going northwest.

We immediately went to work to rid our raft of superfluous ballast and using the wood boards, which we broke off, as oars, and with a small flag as a sail, we reached at about 4 pm the northwesterly corner of the island, the only place where we could land. Cast on a rather low coast, three of us had the luck to cling to the sharp parts of a coral reef without the receding waves pulling us back. Only the cook was not so lucky; after he smashed his head against the rocks, he was carried off by the wave again, uttering faint cries, as if to ask for impossible assistance. When we came to breathe only a piece of his blue shirt, which hung on the cliff, was evidence he had lived!

We rushed up the steep coral reef before another wave there could drag us off again. When we were out of danger, we saw our raft being shattered. After climbing down with unbelievable effort, we succeeded in saving our three pieces of wood and the flag, which later became our salvation. Seventeen people had died!

When we climbed the rock for the second time, we found some holes with water from the rain of the previous night. This served to quench our burning thirst. All around us we saw distinctive birds on the small trees, which in no way were scared by the presence of men, whom they did not know. We could approach them near enough with a tree branch, killing two. We ate them raw before sunset.

After we had found a place where the ground permitted us to stretch, we fell asleep, overwhelmed by fatigue, in a hurriedly built cover of leaves. When we awoke the next morning, the saddest ideas arose within us. What would we do on this desolate island? How long would we have to stay? Would we die here?

Tormented by hunger and thirst, we proceeded into the forest in the hope of finding some fruits, like coconuts, bananas, or any other, which could serve us for food. We found nothing but a few bitter fruits, which were not edible. There was no other option than to eat the raw birds again.

After some effort, we succeeded in fixing our flag high at one branch, which was stripped of its leaves and still arose above the highest tree of this part of the island. We hoped that this would be noticed by any passing sailing vessel. Close by we manufactured a kind of roof to shelter us as much as possible from rain and the inclement weather during the night.

The first day we had a knife in our possession, which was lost, and a clock, whose spring we used, just like the knife, to try to make fire. But the coral, which is a sponge-like stone, gave no spark. Knowing that the Indians make fire by rubbing bamboos against each other, we went through the whole forest to find it, but it was in vain. We tried it with any other type of wood without better results and after a few days of sustained efforts, we were forced to give up hope.

Two or three days later, the water in the potholes around our hut was dry, so we had to track down another source. For our wanderings we had made wooden soles from the three planks salvaged out of the wreckage, which we tied to our feet with tree fibres, making it possible for us to go on the sharp points of the coral. Despite this precaution, we still tumbled off often, wrenching our clothes, consisting of a pair of trousers and a shirt, and resulting in our whole bodies being covered with wounds.

Finally, we found, at a half-hour distance, very good and plentiful water, but to reach it we had to pass through an inlet of the sea or to take a fair detour through the forest. Several young trees, which we uprooted and laid down on the cove, formed a bridge over which we could go on all fours.

The second day after our arrival on the island (the 29th) we saw a ship sailing past, which did not notice our flag. The next Sunday, 3 July, we saw two ships behind each other, but with no better result! Only hope kept us still standing! But after 14 days and seeing ships sailing past only at a great distance while we felt our strength diminish daily, a gloomy despondency came upon us. Death seemed almost inevitable for us!

Already we had spent 30 days on the island; 16 ships had sailed past without noticing our signal, though near enough to see the southwestern tip of the island; but as the shipping route then ran northward, they moved away again. We decided to make our way to that point, but the first ship that we saw again sailed past without coming to help. On Sunday, the 35th day after our shipwreck, a brig sailed close by, without giving any sign that she had noticed us. Then we immediately took the decision, and after we slashed the only plank that was left to make a couple of new soles, and picked up our flag from the branch, we went that same afternoon on our way.

We passed the source from which we had refreshed ourselves for so many days, and struggled with great difficulty through the forest, using the sun as our guide, not removing ourselves too far from the coast, where we spent the night. The depth of the recesses and crevices in the rocks prevented us from following the coast in our march. In the middle of the island, we came across a bight [Smithson Bight] which was half as much again deep [than the indent between the northwest point and the southwest point]. In making the detour, which this forced upon us, we had to overcome the biggest trouble, like climbing heights and climbing down again, and such lofty and thickly grown plants that only with the greatest difficulty could we wade through. All this meant we often needed an hour to make a hundred paces of progress.

So, by the 8th day, we came with incredible difficulties and objections, with torn clothes, and covered with wounds, to the southeastern tip. Fortunately, we found a lot of water over there, and in the evening, when we came out of the forest, a sufficient number of birds to collect stock for the next day. We built our new hut in the vicinity of water sources and, with great difficulty,

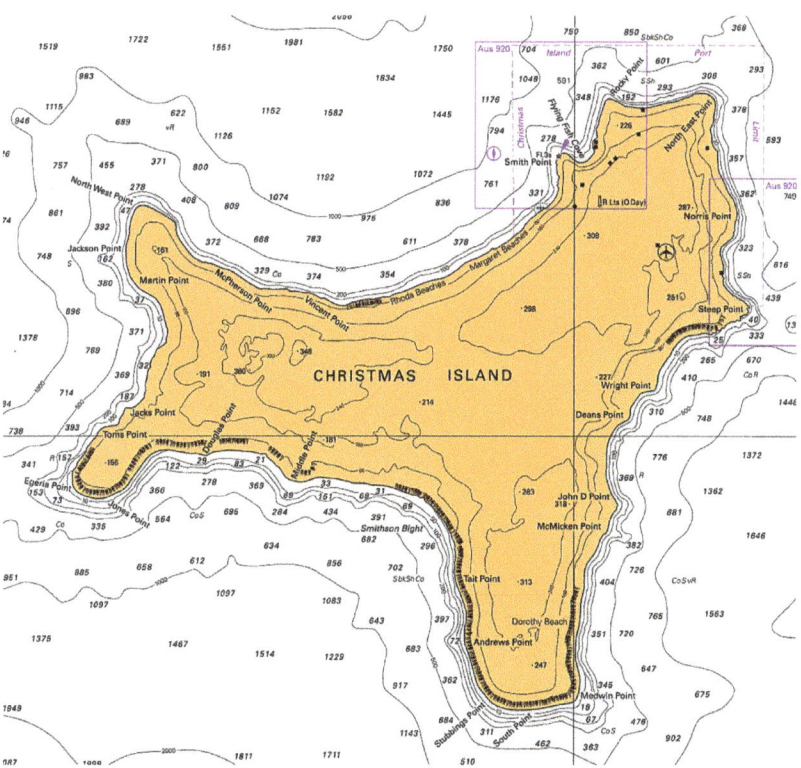

Figure 61. Christmas Island showing water depths. Source AUS 00608 Australian Hydrographic Service. Not to be used for navigation.

we hoisted our flag again on top of the cliff, from where she was well marked. So we waited patiently for our liberation.

We had suffered on the other side of the island from the rats and big land crabs that emerged from the forest in the evening. Here they were more numerous and more difficult. The crabs pinched us in the feet. Always armed with our sticks, we beat them often half-dead, and they took to flight but were immediately attacked by rats that ate them half alive. Finally, on the 23rd August, being the 57th day after our arrival on the island, the day came for our salvation. The three-masted ship *Amicitia* that sailed past the island noticed our flag, turned and unloaded one of the boats to the water, and the boat set sail to the island.

I was in the cabin busy making a fishing line of plant fibres. The mate and the deckhand were on the hunt. Encouraged by thirst, I went to the source on the beach. I could not believe my

Figure 62. The *Amicitia* rescue ship.

eyes! A ship lay turned bow into the wind!! While I could hardly keep standing out of joy, I went to the bank, while I waved my shirt up on my stick. But I saw nothing showing up. No sloop was unloaded and I became overwhelmed by acute anxiety. Weren't we noticed?

But suddenly I saw a boat circumnavigate the projecting corner of the island. My two companions were sitting there in the boat already! One of them called out to me that I had to jump into the sea because the boat could not land. I did this at once and a few moments later we felt a ship's deck beneath our feet. Then, for the first time, we became aware of our weakness. Captain Crap-Hellingman, the passengers and crew tried to make us forget that by doing their care.

On the 28th of August, we arrived in Batavia, where we encountered the most unequivocal evidence of interest. When I visited Mr P. van Rees, a resident of Batavia, I had the opportunity to acknowledge how his reputation as a philanthropist and supporter of unfortunates is deserved. His generous hospitality did everything possible to erase my past calamities from my memory.

A few days after our arrival, they told us of a merchant ship, in Batavia at anchor, that had seen a large fire on the island where we had so long resided, which gave rise to the idea that other castaways could have reached the island. As a result, the steamship *Semarang* was sent there to keep the island in sight for two days, while unloading gunshots. But there arose no trace of living! It is unfortunately indisputable that the remaining crew died in the night of the 27th![15]

Bennet's reference to 'Indians' denotes natives of the East Indies. His wording, that they had spent nine months on the island, suggests survivors of a shipwrecked vessel from Indonesia, and that he had been told about them on arrival in Batavia, rather than personally seeing evidence of them on Christmas Island.

Figure 63. Two views of a Dutch gin bottle collected from near the number two Dale waterfall.

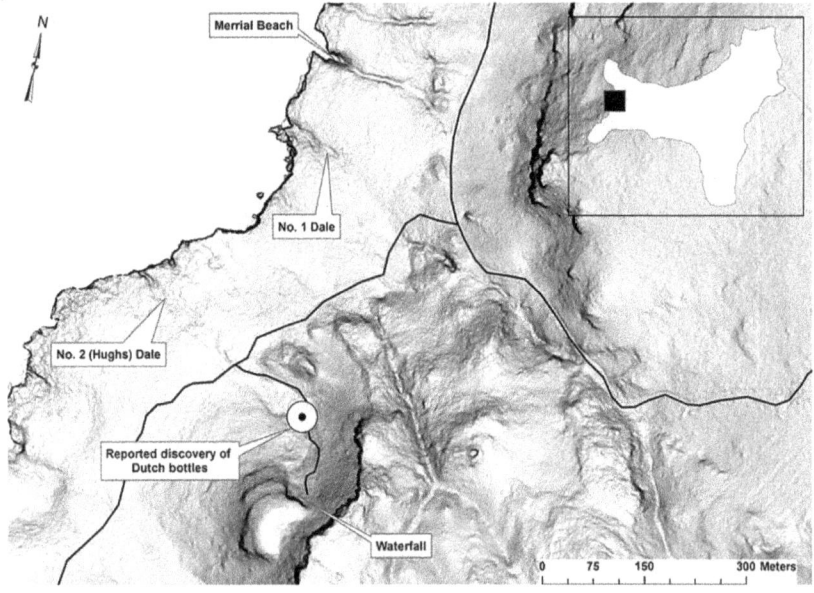

Figure 64. The location of the bottle find.

Figure 65. The medal awarded to Boatswain Gerd Addicks of the *Amicitia*.

During the 2015 Wreck Check expedition to Christmas Island, Mieko Scholes told us about her family's finding of a Dutch gin bottle near a hill where people had been getting water, in the area of Bennet's water source. The bottle is of the type made after 1876 for the Hoboken family of gin distillers and shipowners.[16] Coincidentally, Anthony van Hoboken was the owner of the ship *Arinus Marinus*, wrecked in 1821 to the north of Christmas Island (see Chapter 7). Curiously, Bennet makes no mention of flotsam coming ashore from the wreck of the *Vice Admiraal Rijk,* other than the three planks from their raft. The fire, reported as seen by another vessel, was presumably on a different island.

Interest in colonisation

Government officials visited Christmas Island frequently during the second half of the nineteenth century, the English showing more interest than the Dutch. In 1857 Captain Sidney Grenfell, of HMS *Amethyst*, tried to cut his way to the summit.[17] In 1866 Dutch scholar Robide van der Aa commented that:

It is surely strange that so little is known of this apparently uninhabited island. Of all the geographic works that I have examined during my lifetime, both old and new travel narratives, I cannot remember that I have ever read that it was visited or even sighted. Therefore, without remotely pressing for annexation, I think it, nevertheless, appropriate, that this land lying adjacent Java's west point be officially surveyed.[18]

During visits by HMS *Challenger* between 1872 and 1876, the British naturalist John Murray carried out surveys and predicted phosphate deposits.[19] The hydrographic survey ship HMS *Flying Fish* found an anchorage westward of the north point of the island and the crew collected natural science specimens. Captain John Maclear reported in 1887 that:

> One very large tree had something like the letters WW cut inside a scroll, and nearly illegible from time; this was the only sign of the island having been visited before. One of our officers heard at Batavia that a Dutch vessel was wrecked on the southeast point of the island in a calm about fifteen years ago and that the crew escaped and lived many months before they were taken off, but I have no other details about the affair.[20]

There is no indication that the letters on the tree were made by a *Vice Admiraal Rijk* survivor. Bennet's report indicates that he and his companions did not walk to Flying Fish Cove. The Dutch vessel referred to by Maclear was, notwithstanding the location disparity, clearly the *Vice Admiraal Rijk*, wrecked on the southwest side of the island 35 years previously.

Maclear wrote that there were numerous rat holes and that there appeared to be banana palms at a small beach on the eastern side, although they looked withered and showed no signs of fruit. The men landed cocks and hens but doubted that they would survive because the crabs immediately began to chase them.

Charles Andrews also referred to letters cut on trees by whalers. He wrote that, 'A few ships, probably whalers, seemed to have touched at Flying Fish Cove, for some of the large trees had letters cut on them'.[21] Andrews was right in presuming visits by the whalers – French, American and British whaleships first entered the western New Holland grounds between Christmas Island, Timor and the west coast of Australia during the 1790s. In 1790 the French whaler *Caroline du Sud* of Dunkirk, under the command of James Whippey, sailed north from Dirk Hartog Island and took sperm whales off Christmas Island.[22] Perhaps Captain Whippey had marked the tree with what appeared to be 'WW', 97 years before Maclear's visit. William Whitecar, a keen observer of island signboards, sailed whaling voyages on American ships between 1855 and 1859, spending time in the area between the whaling grounds off Western Australia and Bali. He saw a name on a headboard on Middle Island in the Abrolhos, and wrote that, 'I found a number of trees covered with the names of ships that had visited Balli, with date and country attached'. It seems most likely that it was he who carved his initials on the Christmas Island tree.[23]

Captain Pelham Aldrich of HMS *Egeria* reported on the island in 1887, providing a coastal chart. He found no evidence that it had ever been occupied.[24]

Beginning of settlement

In 1888 Britain annexed Christmas Island to claim the phosphate deposits. Phosphates are mined to obtain phosphorus for agriculture and industry. Captain William May of the British warship HMS *Imperieuse* formally annexed the island, placing it under the Straits Settlement government. During the same year, a settlement was established at Flying Fish Cove by George Clunies-Ross of the Cocos (Keeling) Islands. After that date, George's brother Andrew, together with his family and a few Cocos Malays, resided there almost continuously. They built houses, dug wells and made small clearings for planting coffee.²⁵ John Murray and George Clunies-Ross were provided with a lease and they set up the Christmas Island Phosphate Company, making their first shipment of phosphate in 1900.

Figure 66. George Clunies-Ross of Christmas Island.

Chapter 7

Casualties along the spice-trade route

Timeline

1694 The VOC's *Ridderschap van Holland* was lost after leaving the Cape of Good Hope for Batavia.

1724 The VOC's *Fortuyn* was reported wrecked south of Christmas Island while en route to Batavia.

1726 The VOC's *Aagtekerke* was reported wrecked between Cape Town and Batavia.

1744 The derelict VOC ship *De Lis* was reported as offloading cargo near Cocos but may have been damaged near Coco Island in the Bay of Bengal.

1745 or before The journal *Neptune Oriental* referred to a Dutch ship thought wrecked at Christmas Island.

1821 The Dutch ship *Arinus Marinus* wrecked north of Christmas Island en route from Batavia to the Netherlands.

1825 The French brig *Mauritius* was wrecked near Direction Island, Cocos.

1825 The captain of the ship *Lonach* reported wreckage (an East Indiaman?) on Horsburgh Island.

1826 The British brig *Francis Nicholas Burton* was wrecked at West Island, Cocos (Keeling) Islands.

1834 The British brig *Earl of Liverpool* was wrecked on North Keeling Island.

1852 The Dutch barque *Vice Admiraal Rijk* was wrecked at Christmas Island.

There was a long interval between the discoveries of Christmas and the Cocos (Keeling) islands and their first settlements, because of the difficult access and lack of easily accessible commodities. The attention given to the islands during the interval was limited to brief visits to stock up on water; to collect edible birds and refreshing coconuts; to reduce the risk of shipwrecks by mapping hazards; to search for ships that had gone missing; and to ascertain any potential for settlements based on slave labour or manumitted-slave labour, manumission being the conferring of freedom on the enslaved by their enslavers before the end of the slave-labour system. This chapter reviews the historical information about shipwrecks on, or near, the islands before their first settlements. We also look at how Wreck Check members and our collaborators have employed artefact analysis and other scientific approaches to expand upon the historical record.

Historical background to the spice-trade shipwrecks

The Dutch were the largest competitors in the spice trade between Europe and Asia. Verenigde Oostindische Compagnie (VOC) ships undertook some 4,800 voyages to Asia, and at least 19 of these ships were lost in the Indian Ocean during their outward voyages.[1] Of those 19 ships, three were captured by enemy ships, one sank after a battle off Mozambique, two sank at sea after catching fire, and five were stranded while following a northern Indian Ocean route to Asia. Just eight were lost while following, or thought to have been following, the southern Indian Ocean route.

The wrecks of the *Batavia*, *Vergulde Draeck*, *Zuytdorp* and *Zeewijk* have been found on the Western Australian coast. The *Ridderschap van Holland* was probably lost in the western Indian Ocean on its outward voyage to Batavia, while the *Fortuyn* and *Aagtekerke* were probably lost further to the east. Consideration is given here as to the locations of these last three vessels. It is doubtful that they followed Brouwer's original route, across the southern Indian Ocean to the longitude of Sunda Strait before turning north to Batavia. After Hartog's 'discovery' of Eendrachtsland in 1616, the prescribed route was modified. Skippers travelling the Cape-to-Batavia route between October and March had to sail northeast after passing the mid-ocean islands of Saint Paul and Amsterdam, head up to 30° south, and then sail north-northeast to bring themselves west of Sunda Strait.[2]

Most ships that get wrecked do so on reefs along major trade routes.[3] On the shorter, modified Dutch route, ships would pass much closer to the Australian territories of the Cocos (Keeling) Islands and Christmas Island than to the Australian mainland – some 1,350 nautical miles further to the east. This circumstantial and archival evidence points to the *Fortuyn* and *Aagtekerke* having been lost on or near the Cocos (Keeling) Islands or Christmas Island, rather than the Houtman Abrolhos Islands off Western Australia. If these ships struck either Christmas or Cocos en route to Batavia, it may be expected that they would have encountered the south or southwest coasts of those islands.

The risk of shipwreck for vessels sailing on the homeward route from Batavia to the Cape of Good Hope was greater than on the outward voyage because of the greater frequency of cyclones along the homeward route. The wind systems generally allowed homeward-bound vessels to follow a more direct south-westerly route across the Indian Ocean, bringing them reasonably close to Christmas Island or the Cocos (Keeling) Islands. However, the records indicate that most of the homeward-bound wrecks occurred around Mauritius and Madagascar,[4] far away from Australia's islands, so more detailed attention will now be given to the vessels lost on the outward route.

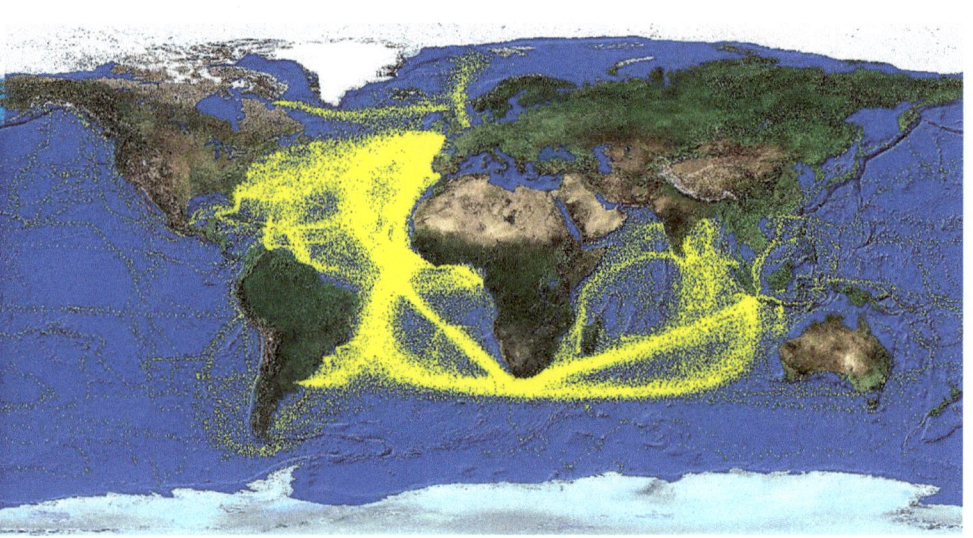

Figure 67. Climatological Database of the World's Oceans (CLIWOC) ships' position plots 1750–1850, showing evidence from logs of the shipping route to and from the East Indies.

Ridderschap van Holland

The return-ship *Ridderschap van Holland* sailed eastward from the Cape in February 1694, but it never reached Batavia and was most likely captured by pirates or wrecked at Madagascar.[5] However, the VOC was not aware of such ideas when in 1696–97 they decided to send a fleet consisting of the *Nijptangh*, *Weseltje* and *Geelvinck*, under the command of Willem de Vlamingh, to search for the wrecks of the *Ridderschap van Holland*, the *Vergulde Draeck* and any other wrecks at the islands of St Paul and Amsterdam and the Southland (Australia as known to the Dutch at that time). The de Vlamingh fleet also approached Christmas Island, and the ships' boats were used to search there for mast-making timber. Subsequently, de Vlamingh sent his son back from Batavia to further investigate the island, but the stated reason for the continued interest was the investigation of timber for ships' masts, rather than persevering with shipwreck searches.

Fortuyn

The 800-ton, 145-foot East Indiaman *Fortuyn*, built in 1722 for the Amsterdam chamber of the VOC, departed from Texel on 27 September 1723 on its maiden voyage. Under the command of Pieter Westrik, with a crew of 225, it anchored in Table Bay on 2 January 1724. Having taken on fresh provisions, the *Fortuyn* sailed eastward from the Cape on 18 January 1724, but it never reached Batavia.

In October 1728 the Dutch governor-general and councils in Batavia wrote to the Netherlands that survivors of the *Zeewijk*, wrecked on the Houtman Abrolhos in 1727, had seen 'some signs of a Dutch ship that has probably been shattered at the aforementioned reef. This could have been the *fortuyn* or *aagtekerk*'.[6] However, the analysis and report on possible locations of VOC shipwrecks off the Western Australian coast by the Centre for International Heritage Activities rightly casts doubt on the veracity of this secondary source – it is the only contemporary mention of the presumption that these two wrecks occurred on the Abrolhos, and there is no indication of VOC plans for a search party to the Abrolhos to look for the money and survivors.

The records indicate that the *Fortuyn* was wrecked at or near Christmas Island. In 1966 Chris Halls, a researcher at the Western Australian Museum, found a report stating that men on the VOC ship *'s-Graveland*, sailing two weeks behind the *Fortuyn* in the same fleet, had seen floating wreckage, which they recognised as having come from the *Fortuyn,* in the latitude of the Cocos (Keeling) Islands. Halls presumed that it must have been wrecked at Cocos.[7] However, another floating wreckage report, in the VOC's *Daily Journal of Batavia*, is more specific:

> Towards the evening there arrived here the previously mentioned fluyt *'s-Graveland*, coming from the fatherland, whose skipper told the governor-general how on the sixth of this month on the latitude of 13° 20′ and longitude 124° 51′ he saw floating several signs of a wrecked ship and among other things also the back piece of a boat with two oarlocks of which [it] was thought that the aforementioned unlucky vessel has to be the new ship the *Fortuijn* which left the Cape of Good Hope the 17th of January of this year and to date has not appeared.[8]

This report, including both latitude and longitude, provided coordinates which, after adjusting longitude for the Greenwich meridian, indicate a position approximately 200 nautical miles southeast of Christmas Island: 145 nautical miles south and 140 nautical miles east of that island. If the ship struck Christmas Island and wreckage drifted southeast at an average speed of 1 knot, it might have taken eight days to reach a location 200 miles southeast of the island. The distance from the reported floating wreckage location to landmasses other than Christmas Island is much greater: 700 nautical miles to the Cocos (Keeling) Islands and 800 nautical miles to Cartier Island off Western Australia. Longitude measurement at that time was still generally inaccurate, but de Vlamingh had been less than 25 nautical miles out in his measurement of the longitude of Rottnest Island off the coast of Western Australia.[9] Jan Diephout, the 's-*Graveland*'s skipper, had done the voyage to Batavia four times previously, so notwithstanding the general inaccuracy of the time, some credence can be placed on his calculation. He would have known roughly where he was when he saw the floating wreckage from the *Fortuyn*. The *Fortuyn* would have arrived from the Cape to that area in early March, when the currents were flowing from the north,[10] so the coordinates are consistent with the *Fortuyn* having struck the southwest side of Christmas Island and sunk, leaving flotsam to drift southward.

Other, less likely, causes for the *Fortuyn* to have been wrecked include cyclones and submarine mountains known as seamounts. The area south of Christmas Island has a low cyclone risk, but there is still the potential for major wind impact on a vessel.[11] The *Times Atlas of the World*[12] shows the Maria Augustina Bank, which lies south of Christmas Island, rising to 9 metres depth, close to the coordinates given by Diephout for the floating wreckage of the *Fortuyn*. However, depth charts from satellite data now show deep water in that location and nothing to indicate a shallow seamount in the near vicinity.[13] Another bank, the Muirfield Seamount, was discovered accidentally in 1973 when the 82,000 gross tonnage cargo ship MV *Muirfield* suddenly struck an unknown reef, resulting in keel damage.[14] This bank is located 77 nautical miles southwest of the Cocos (Keeling) Islands, rising to 16–18 metres below the surface of the ocean.

Consideration must also be given to a passage in French hydrographer Jean-Baptiste d'Apres de Mannevillette's 1745 atlas *Neptune Oriental*, which reads: '77 [old French] miles south of the west point of the island Java, at 10° 30' latitude lies the island that is called Christmas by the English and Moni by the Dutch. Some years ago a ship from this country [meaning the Netherlands?] touched there at night and was wrecked'.[15] The question arises as to whether Mannevillette's wreck at Christmas Island is the *Fortuyn*, the *Aagtekerke*, another Dutch vessel or a French vessel. The passage might also refer to an East Indiaman lost while bound from Indonesia to Europe.

The evidence points to the *Fortuyn* having struck Christmas Island and sunk nearby. It is not likely that it struck the island and bounced off, to float away from the island for some hours as a semi-intact derelict. In such circumstances, it can be expected that boats would have been launched and survivors would have reached Batavia, 300 nautical miles to the north. Such evidence would be consistent with the rapid-sinking experience of the crew on the *Vice Admiraal Rijk*.

For the *Fortuyn* to be wrecked against Christmas Island indicates that it would have been travelling the shorter October–March monsoon period route. This route, coming from the southwest, makes Smithson Bight, on the southwest side of the island, the most likely location. The lack of any survivors suggests a sudden catastrophe at night, such as the vessel colliding against a sheer cliff and rapidly sinking. The VOC ship *Zeewijk*, of the same length as the *Fortuyn* and built in 1725, had a draft of 6 metres. So the *Fortuyn* may be expected to have struck directly against, or close, to the cliffs in around 6 metres of water, and to have then drifted away from the cliffs before sinking, or rolled down the sloping seabed into the deep after sinking.

Christmas Island is the peak of a basalt volcanic seamount, which rose steeply 5,000 metres from the ocean floor about 60 million years ago. Charles Andrews observed that 'the present fringing reef forms a narrow shelf around the island, being only interrupted where deep water occurs close to the foot of the sea cliff'.[16] The Australian Hydrographic Service chart Aus. 00608 of Christmas Island has soundings varying from 10 metres depth to 50 metres depth just 200 metres offshore. At 1.6 kilometres offshore in Smithson Bight, the water depth is 1,000 metres.

Aagtekerke

The 850-ton, 145-foot *Aagtekerke* was built for the Zeeland chamber of the VOC in 1724 and armed with 36 cannon and swivel guns. On 27 May 1725, it sailed from Rammekens on its first voyage to Batavia under the command of Jan Witboom, with a crew of

212 men, a cargo of merchandise and a consignment of bullion and specie amounting to about 200,000 guilders. When on 3 January 1726 it anchored off Cape Town, 16 men had died during the voyage, and another 45 of the sick were put ashore. Fresh provisions and crew replacements were taken on board and the *Aagtekerke* sailed eastward on 23 January 1726. The cargo included 214 elephant tusks.[17] The *Aagtekerke* never reached Batavia.

The journals of the *Zeewijk* contained reports that survivors saw wreckage ashore on the Houtman Abrolhos, including a ship's frame-timber bearing the sculpted figure of a woman. Subsequently, VOC officials based in Batavia during the late 1720s also thought that the *Aagtekerke* might have been wrecked there.[18] However, it appears that most if not all of this wreck material, and other VOC wreckage reported by later visitors to the southern Abrolhos, is from the *Zeewijk* wreck.

Some of the wreckage reported by *Zeewijk* survivors may have been flotsam from the 1629 wreck of the *Batavia*, 50 kilometres to the north, notwithstanding the efforts of Commandeur Francisco Pelsaert (previously of the *Batavia*) to collect such material. The 1712 wreck of the *Zuytdorp*, 192 kilometres to the north, may also have contributed wreckage. Until the late 1970s there was little awareness of the Leeuwin Current, running south at 1–2 knots past the west coast before turning east along the south coast. In 1979 Abrolhos rock-lobster fisherman Maurie Glazier told members of a Western Australian Museum expedition based at the south end of Pelsaert Island that he was well aware of the current and that a few years before he had seen wreckage from a fishing boat that had been lost on the Zuytdorp Cliffs but transported southward to the lagoon at the southern end of Pelsaert Island by the Leeuwin Current.[19] A well and a pair of corroded sailmaker's scissors found on Middle Island by *Zeewijk* wreck survivors might have been left there by *Vergulde Draeck* survivors, sailing a boat northward for help after the wreck of their ship in 1656. The *Zeewijk* skipper who suggested that the *Aagtekerke* had been lost on the Abrolhos was convicted of falsifying journals. Perhaps he thought that if he could convince his accusers that the treacherous Houtman Abrolhos reefs had trapped many an unsuspecting skipper, then they would look upon him with an element of forgiveness.

During the 1960s a wreck found close to the coast of the Perth suburb of South Cottesloe was thought by some, because of the size and number of the cannon on the site, to be Dutch – the *Aagtekerke* or the *Fortuyn*.[20] However, subsequent contemporary investigations by Graeme Henderson from Wreck Check showed that the wreck contained a ship's chronometer and that the cannon were broken post–Napoleonic War pieces carried as ballast. It represents the regional trading barque *Elizabeth*, wrecked in 1839.[21] More recently it has been suggested, based on the number of cannon and anchors reported on the *Zeewijk* wreck site, and the presence of several elephant tusks found on the *Zeewijk* wreck site, that the *Aagtekerke* wreck lies beneath or beside the *Zeewijk* wreck.[22] However, others have concluded that the number of cannon reported (a total of 39) and the presence of the tusks are consistent with the *Zeewijk* wreck. A minimum of 84 cannon would be expected if the remains of both the *Zeewijk* and the *Aagtekerke* lie on the same site.[23] Three aerial magnetometer searches over the water adjacent to the *Zeewijk*, most recently during 2016, and in-water investigations by Western Australian Museum staff in 2019, did not locate any convincing evidence of another Dutch wreck.

Researchers Megan Coghlan and Michael Bunce, of the Trace and Environmental DNA Laboratory in Western Australia's Curtin University, applied DNA analysis to three of the tusks found on the *Zeewijk* site. DNA analysis has the potential to answer such historical questions as to whether the two Dutch ships *Zeewijk* and *Aagtekerke* lie on the same site on the Houtman Abrolhos and, perhaps, whether the tusk found on the Cocos (Keeling) Islands is from the *Aagtekerke* or the English brig *Sir Francis Nicholas Burton*.

DNA analysis shows what part of the world elephants lived in before their tusks were shipped for the Indies. If the tusks found on the *Zeewijk* site came from savanna elephants, the type that lives in East Africa, it would increase the likelihood that they are from the

Aagtekerke, because, during the 1720s, the Dutch officially shipped ivory from Mozambique in East Africa to the Cape of Good Hope for export to the Indies. Shipments to the Cape from other parts of Africa were not officially registered by the VOC and so were considered by the Dutch to be illegal.[24] The DNA analysis indicates that the tusks found on the *Zeewijk* site came from forest elephants of Central Africa, rather than from Mozambique, indicating in turn that they represent unofficial and illegal trade: that is, cargo from the *Zeewijk* wreck, not from the *Aagtekerke*, which had ivory as official cargo.[25]

If the *Aagtekerke* wreck is not on the Abrolhos, where is it most likely to be? As previously mentioned, the VOC sailing route in 1726 required outward-bound vessels, departing the Cape of Good Hope in January, to turn to the northeast after passing St Paul and Amsterdam islands, to travel up to 30° south and then to sail north-northeast, to bring themselves west of Sunda Strait. So, notwithstanding the Australian Abrolhos location of the *Zeewijk* wreck, whose skipper disobeyed instructions and continued eastward from the Cape of Good Hope to the Southland, the eighteenth-century VOC ships generally turned to the northeast after passing Amsterdam Island. Hence it is more likely that the *Aagtekerke* would have struck the Cocos or Christmas Island than the Abrolhos.

After a cyclone in 1981, Ed Dekker, at that time a schoolteacher on the Cocos (Keeling) Islands, was beachcombing on the south side of West Island, near Burton Point. During the cyclone, waves had broken onto the airport runway, depositing coral debris. Among the debris, approximately five feet above the sea level, he found an elephant tusk, encrusted with marine algae. Cyclones have the power to shift wreckage – both ship structure and cargo such as ivory – a substantial distance. After a cyclone on West Island in 1909, the governor wrote:

> The cyclone was accompanied by great waves ... and these waves left hardly anything standing. The whole of the villages as well as the working sheds were levelled to the ground, or wasted and

carried away by the sea. I could scarcely credit my eyes when daylight came; the wreckage was so thorough and complete that the islands were unrecognizable. Of my plantations of coconuts, I am sure that not more than one tree in a hundred stood it; in consequence, I have lost 800,000 trees more or less. As for lighters and boats, more than 40 per cent are lost, broken or damaged. Only five buildings stood upright and these without roofs upon them. The whole of that night we were practically underwater, wet and miserably bedraggled ... the waves swept right across the islands and deposited sand upon a tower fifty feet high.[26]

In 1845 Charles Darwin had written of the Cocos atolls that the long strips of land:

... have been raised only to that height to which the surf can throw fragments of coral, and the wind heap up calcareous sand. The solid flat of coral rock on the outside, by its breadth, breaks the first violence of the waves, which otherwise, in a day, would sweep away these islets and all their productions.[27]

So, the tusk found by Dekker is evidence of a ship having been wrecked on the outside reef – the rim of the atoll, which lies approximately half a mile seaward from Burton Point.

Dekker wrote to the Queensland Museum reporting his find, and the letter (minus his Perth address) was sent on to the Western Australian Museum. In 2015 we Wreck Check members were keen to locate Ed Dekker, to examine the tusk he had found, and to establish whether the tusk had come from the wreck of the *Aagtekerke*. At that time we knew that he had been on Cocos in 1981, but we were not aware that he had been a teacher there. We understood him to have been a visitor or resident of the Cocos (Keeling) Islands in 1981.

Figure 68. Talking shipwrecks in the classroom on Home Island.

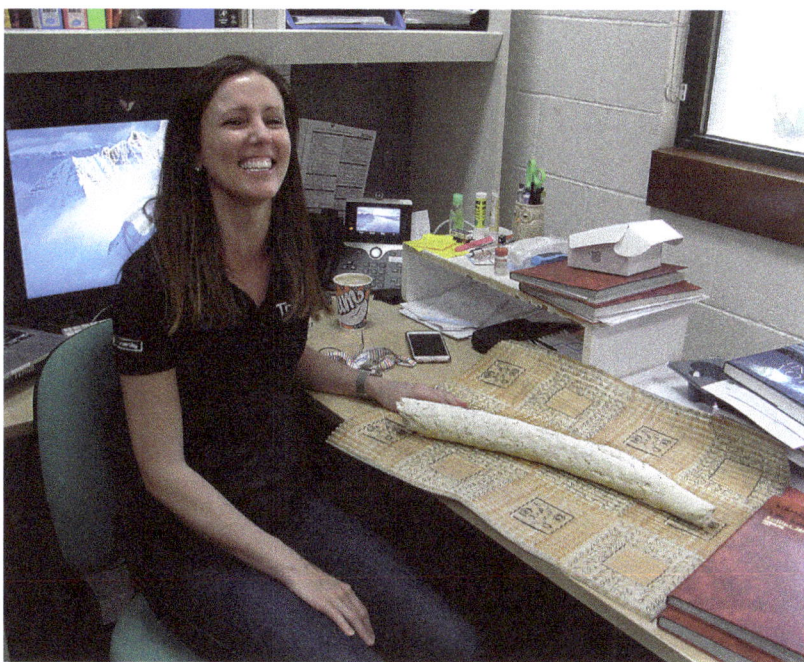

Figure 69. Megan Coghlan with the tusk at the Trace and Environmental DNA Laboratory at Curtin University.

Wreck Check's fieldwork programme on Christmas Island and the Cocos (Keeling) Islands

Wreck Check members James Parkinson, Alex Moss, Andy Viduka and Graeme Henderson conducted remote-sensing fieldwork on Christmas Island and the Cocos (Keeling) Islands in 2015 and 2016.[28] The 2016 team also included David Steinberg and Amer Khan (members of the Australian Institute for Maritime Archaeology), and Shinatria Adhityatama and Robert de Hoop (representing cultural heritage organisations in Indonesia and the Netherlands). The intention of the work was a general survey of the underwater cultural heritage of both territories, with a specific interest in whether the *Fortuyn* had been lost in the vicinity of Christmas Island or the Cocos (Keeling) Islands, and whether the then unsubstantiated report of the finding of an elephant tusk indicated that the *Aagtekerke* had been lost on the South Keeling atoll.

Considering community consultation as a high priority, we delivered slide lectures at the Cocos (Keeling) Islands school and leisure centre and the Christmas Island secondary school to let the communities know what we were doing and to seek their input about the shipwreck heritage. In response to the question of whether anyone knew of Ed Dekker, Home Island teacher Mak Laisa, now Nek Laisa (Susan Dixon), said that Ed had been a teacher there during the early 1980s and then had returned to Perth. Back in Perth, old phone books provided addresses, and Ed Dekker responded to a Wreck Check letter of inquiry and provided access to the tusk for analysis.

Methodology

For the 2015 Wreck Check fieldwork season, the Maritime Archaeology Association of Victoria (MAAV) loaned a proton magnetometer. Magnetic anomalies (local variations in the Earth's magnetic field from what is expected) were assessed and prioritised for further investigation and inspection in case they represented wreckage from shipwrecks.

Figure 70. Wreck Check members Alex Moss, James Parkinson and Andy Viduka set up the remote-sensing equipment.

Diving was constrained to 30 metres depth for work health and safety reasons. Shallow waters were searched because the drafts of the target vessels, including the *Fortuyn* and *Aagtekerke*, were estimated to be less than 7 metres. A coroner's report about the wreck of the asylum-seeker boat SIEV 221 was also considered as a model to follow. In 2010 the SIEV 221 had approached the cliffs at Rocky Point on the north side of Christmas Island and was caught in what the coroner called a 'washing machine effect'.[29] Observers of that disaster noticed that a deep ocean swell struck the low cliffs and washed repeatedly out to sea and back again, creating the washing-machine effect. One man from the SIEV 221 was able to scramble onto the jagged cliffs as the vessel came into contact, and some of the refugees were rescued by men on inflatable dinghies as the vessel broke up and sank in 10 metres of water, claiming 50 lives.

Wreck Check members explored two questions. Firstly, might the *Fortuyn* also have been caught in a washing-machine effect and broken up close to the Christmas Island cliffs, spilling its many cannon and anchors before the broken timbers floated out to sea? Secondly, might any of that material culture remain on the seabed and be detectable using the magnetometer? After the VOC ship *Zuytdorp* struck cliffs in a washing-machine environment on the Western Australian coast in 1712, some wreckage had remained trapped in gutters near the cliffs. Diving in the cliff-side location of the SIEV 221, Wreck Check members noticed small, scattered, metal fittings on the seabed, so it seemed possible that if the *Fortuyn* had struck cliffs on Christmas Island, then some wreck material would be detectable.

The volcanic nature of Christmas Island meant that magnetometer signals had to be assessed against a possible high magnetic background and submerged outcroppings of basalt. Nevertheless, the instrument revealed the known shipwrecks and anchors around the coast. The magnetometer runs were primarily focused on the southwest side of Christmas Island, and the main South Keeling atoll. Both island groups have rapidly shelving seabeds, so the width of the 0–30 metre depth mark was narrow. The magnetometer used in 2015 had a much lower detection rate than more-modern magnetometers, and that could lead to significant data gaps even at a fairly slow towing speed of 4 knots. So the primary instrument employed for the 2016 fieldwork season was a leased Geometrics G-882 caesium vapour marine magnetometer with greater sensitivity.

Results and interpretation after the fieldwork

The remote-sensing survey and the diver ground-truthing yielded no underwater evidence of the presence of the *Aagtekerke* at the Cocos (Keeling) Islands or of the *Fortuyn* at Christmas Island. In 2016, using the caesium vapour magnetometer with excellent sea conditions, an intensive search on the southwest point of Christmas

Figure 71. Andy Viduka about to start the towing of the magnetometer transducer.

Figure 72. Divers ground-truthed the remote-sensing information.

Island revealed no wreckage. A similar survey of the outside reef off Burton Point on the South Keeling Islands revealed no wreckage. With greater understanding of the environment came the realisation that these wrecks, if there, will be found to lie in water deeper than the search penetrated.

During and after the 2016 season, several new pieces of information brought a modification of the team's approach and understanding of the disposition of any Dutch eighteenth-century wrecks on the Cocos (Keeling) Islands or Christmas Island.

The *Vice Admiraal Rijk* as an example of the movement of wrecks on a sloping Christmas Island seabed

Dutch researcher Thomas Creemers provided information about the 1852 wreck of the Dutch 34-metre barque *Vice Admiraal Rijk* that struck and sank near the southwest point of Christmas Island.[30]

The account by survivor Roelof Bennet gave information about its location (see Chapter 6). We judged that if the *Vice Admiraal Rijk*, known to have sunk not far from the cliffs, could be found in a depth of less than 30 metres, then the wreck of the *Fortuyn* might also be found in such depth. Alternatively, if searching in such a depth failed to find the *Vice Admiraal Rijk*, it would indicate that both wrecks likely lie at a greater depth of water because they had similar site formation processes.

Illegal fishing vessels as examples of the movement of wrecks on a sloping seabed

Both Christmas Island and the Cocos (Keeling) Islands have very steep underwater drop-offs close to shore.[31] Wreck Check members initially used the SIEV 221, which struck and broke up in shallow water leaving metal fittings scattered on the seabed in the location of the wreck event, as a predictive model for the *Vice Admiraal Rijk*'s location. However, searching for the *Vice Admiraal Rijk* in the location indicated by Bennet has not resulted in its discovery, so another model is now considered more appropriate.

On Christmas Island, local dive operator Hama Hamanaka[32] told the team that, around 2001, an illegal fishing vessel was deliberately scuttled as a dive site in 25 metres of water in Flying Fish Cove. He observed the wreck remaining intact in situ for about a year, after which it disappeared into the abyss beyond scuba-diving depth limits. This postdeposition process contrasts with the coroner's observation regarding the wrecking event of the SIEV 221 and reflects a steeper underwater terrain.

The illegal fishing vessel was so impacted by the underwater current movement that it slid down the slope into water deeper than 30 metres. So too could shipwreck material from the *Vice Admiraal Rijk* and the *Fortuyn*. Perhaps large, heavily constructed VOC vessels such as the *Fortuyn* would not immediately break up on striking Christmas Island but would bounce off the cliff or steeply sloping reef, sink and slide into depths beyond the search limit.

It is unlikely that the steep drop-off of Christmas Island's southwest coast is so linear that no artefacts could settle in crevices. Wreck Check members are working on the hypothesis that during the wrecking process some cultural material from the *Vice Admiraal Rijk*, and potentially from the *Fortuyn*, would have accumulated on the slope at an unknown height above the deep seafloor. A deep-water survey is now required to map the bathymetry of the seamount walls in the target area and to overlay the flatter areas of potential interest with magnetometer data, to ascertain whether heavier metallic artefacts from the wreck settled in those likely locations. This envisages a different system of searching to that employed to date, perhaps utilising an autonomous underwater vehicle, a remotely operated vehicle or an airborne magnetometer. Of course, if the *Fortuyn* wreck lies in a depth more than 30 metres its condition may be expected to be superior to that of the four previously discovered Dutch shipwrecks in shallow, turbulent, highly oxygenated waters off Australia's west coast.

Figure 73. Local divers inspect the scuttled boat off Christmas Island. Image courtesy Hama Hamanaka.

A new interpretation of the wreckage reported on the Cocos (Keeling) Islands in 1825

The numerous archaeological surveys conducted in the Houtman Abrolhos have failed to locate the wreck of the *Aagtekerke*, and there are reasons to consider that it was wrecked some 1,375 nautical miles to the north-northwest of the Abrolhos, at the Cocos (Keeling) Islands.

The report about the Cocos made in 1825 by Captain Driscoll is evidence of a shipwreck located nearby – not the 90-ton brig *Mauritius* but a large East Indiaman. If the reported structural items represent a Dutch VOC shipwreck at the Cocos (Keeling) Islands, then the 850-ton VOC ship *Aagtekerke*, with a cargo that included ivory, is the most obvious candidate.

Analysis of the elephant tusk found on the Cocos (Keeling) Islands

Knowing that the *Aagtekerke* carried 214 ivory tusks before disappearing, Wreck Check members arranged for the tusk found by Dekker to be analysed by the DNA experts Coghlan and Bunce, who had previously analysed the ivory from the *Zeewijk* wreck. They, in turn, arranged further analysis by Rachel Wood of the radiocarbon dating facility at the Australian National University. It was hoped that analysis by these experts would provide information indicating whether the tusk came from the *Aagtekerke*, known to have been carrying tusks obtained from southeast Africa in 1726, or the brig *Sir Francis Nicholas Burton*, wrecked in 1826.[33]

A chart of the South Keeling atoll, dated to approximately 1830, shows a 'Burton Point' at the southwest extremity of West Island, and, nearby, the words 'wreck' and 'heavy surf'.[34] The *Sir Francis Nicholas Burton* was wrecked on the southwest corner of the atoll in December 1826.[35] A question raised is whether 'Burton Point' and 'wreck' both mark the *Sir Francis Nicholas Burton*, or whether they mark two separate wreck events near that point, the second being the wreckage reported by Driscoll in 1825, the *Aagtekerke* or another of the missing Dutch ships.

Live elephants have had a presence on the South Keeling atoll. For many years, animals destined for import to Australia have been landed on West Island for quarantine purposes, and circus elephants were among these. In 2006, eight Asian elephants destined for Melbourne Zoo and Sydney's Taronga Zoo were held there for three months.[36] However, the tusk found by Ed Dekker was marked with marine algae, having come from a marine environment, and there is no suggestion that any of the elephants destined for Australian zoos were disposed of at sea.

In 1821 the 1,100-ton Dutch ship *Arinus Marinus* left Batavia bound for the Netherlands with a shipment of natural-history objects for a Royal Cabinet of Rarities in The Hague (planned initially in 1808 by King Louis Bonaparte). Live exotic animals, including an elephant, were kept in cages on the upper deck.[37] The ship overturned during a storm about 60 miles south of Sunda Strait and the elephant was spilled into the sea. A passing ship found just

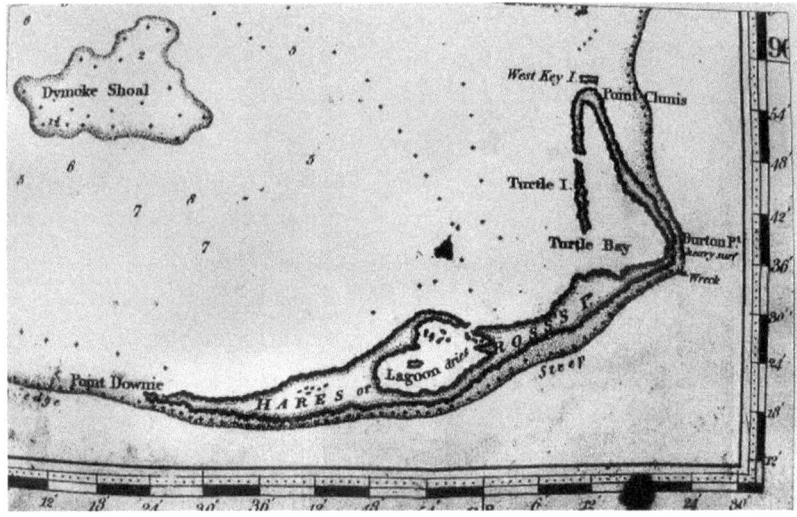

Figure 74. An early chart of the south end of West Island shows a 'wreck' near Burton Point at the far right on the chart.

four survivors, clinging to the floating elephant's cage. However, it is inconceivable that this elephant's remains could have floated to the Cocos (Keeling) Islands. In any case, the *Arinus Marinus* elephant was Asian, whereas the tusk found on the Cocos was from an African elephant.

In 1827 the British brig *Sir Francis Nicholas Burton* was listed in *Lloyds Shipping Register* as bound from London, under the command of W. Hare, to the Mexican port of Vera Cruz, a port of entry for African enslaved people during the eighteenth century, when the Atlantic 'triangular trade' involved shipping trinkets from Europe to Africa, enslaved people (and on Dutch ships, ivory) to the Americas, and sugar and ivory back to Europe.[38] Given its route, the *Sir Francis Nicholas Burton* was possibly involved in the trading, or more likely the transporting, of slaves. The Atlantic slave trade had been made illegal in 1807, so the owners of British slave-trading vessels disguised their activities and whereabouts, and owners of enslaved people could continue to transport them in ships.

However, things were becoming more difficult for slave owners throughout the Atlantic. The 1834 *Slavery Abolition Act* was soon to abolish slavery itself in most of the British Empire, including South Africa and Mauritius. The Lloyds Register reference to Vera Cruz was likely a subterfuge. Perhaps the *Sir Francis Nicholas Burton* was always intended to sail to one of the more remote Indian Ocean islands, delivering a cargo of enslaved people collected en route from Africa.

Financial pressures were also increasing on slave owners in the less remote parts of the Indian Ocean. Keen observer James Holman wrote:

> When I left the Mauritius [December 1829] it was considered to be in a very deplorable state, owing to the dissatisfaction of the French planters at the orders of the British Government, relative to the amelioration in the condition of slaves. These had fallen in value from 800 dollars per head to an exchange of 500 dollars each ... by considering the multitude of slaves that are smuggled

into Bourbon from Madagascar, and the east coast of Africa, it is not, therefore, the less a grievance to the planters, who one and all desire to dispose of their estates and return to France.[39]

Did Captain W. Hare collect ivory in Africa while en route in the *Sir Francis Nicholas Burton* to the Cocos (Keeling) Islands, perhaps from Alexander Hare's farm near Cape Town or, more likely, from Mozambique where the slave trade continued, albeit illegally? There is no obvious reason for the *Sir Francis Nicholas Burton* to have been carrying African ivory to the Cocos (Keeling) Islands, other than for the making, by Alexander Hare's 'manumitted' slaves, of small objects of decorative value for sale to crews of passing ships.[40] Holman, travelling in East Africa, noted that the small tusks were greatly prized by the natives of India for making rings for their arms and ankles.

Having analysed the tusk found on the Cocos (Keeling) Islands, Coghlan observed that it matched most closely with African savanna elephant reference sequences. Within the three mitochondrial DNA groups for savanna elephant, the tusk matches with elephants from a region encompassing southeast savanna countries including Mozambique, South Africa, Botswana, Zimbabwe, Zambia and Tanzania. Coghlan concluded:

> It is possible that the tusk originated from an elephant individual that was from one of these countries. The DNA sequences do not as closely match the other species of African elephant, the Forest elephant, or the Asian elephant.[41]

In the 1720s, ivory was being legally exported from Mozambique to Cape Town. The *Aagtekerke* loaded 214 legal tusks at Cape Town in 1726, so the DNA information is consistent with the idea that the tusk found on the Cocos (Keeling) Islands comes from the *Aagtekerke*. A West African, mainland Asian, or Sumatran elephant-tusk origin would have supported the idea that the Cocos (Keeling) Islands wreck is the *Sir Francis Nicholas Burton*. However, a southeast

African origin does not rule out the *Sir Francis Nicholas Burton* as the carrier. The DNA analysis indicates that the tusk came from southeast Africa. This fits with the *Aagtekerke*'s legal trade in 1726, but it would also fit with *Sir Francis Nicholas Burton* calling at one of the Mozambiquan ports to collect enslaved people and ivory.

The analytical approach utilised by Rachel Wood was radiocarbon dating, a method for determining the age of an object containing organic material by using the properties of radiocarbon, a radioactive isotope of carbon. A carbon date for the tusk leaning towards 1726 would be indicative of the *Aagtekerke* having been the carrier, whereas a carbon date leaning towards 1826 would be indicative of the *Sir Francis Nicholas Burton*. However, there are challenges in the use of the method in this case. The calibration curve of the rate of carbon radioactive decay between the years 1300 and 1900 is interrupted by a major fluctuation between 1726 and 1826, meaning that carbon dating may need to have a correction applied or may prove not to be reliable for shipwrecks of those two dates.[42] With the sample analysed it has not been possible to discriminate between the two wreck dates.

Chapter 8

Conclusions

The research conducted for this book has provided the opportunity to lift the veil and remove misconceptions about the pre-settlement history of the Cocos (Keeling) Islands and Christmas Island. The very isolation of the many islands scattered across the southern Indian Ocean increased their attraction for the myth-makers among explorers, travel writers, cartographers, hydrographers, naval officers, natural scientists and fiction writers. Given their trade routes across the Indian Ocean, some South-East Asian and Arab vessels possibly visited Christmas and Cocos pre-settlement, but if they did, they left no obvious footprints.

European and American travellers and writers who put their minds to the southern Indian Ocean include Marco Polo (history's most famous and influential traveller), Antonio Pigafetta

(Magellan's literary assistant during the first circumnavigation of the world), Cornelis de Houtman (commander of the first Dutch expedition to the East Indies), William Dampier (first Englishman to explore parts of what is today Australia, and the first person to circumnavigate the world three times), John Milton (poet and intellectual), Jonathan Swift (foremost prose satirist in the English language) with his island of Lilliput, Lewis Carroll (children's fiction writer), H. G. Wells (science fiction novelist), Edgar Alan Poe (American writer, poet, editor, and literary critic, with his Flying Dutchman), British explorer and Arabist Sir Richard Burton (translator of the literary fantasy *The Book of the Thousand Nights and a Night*) and James Holman (blind travel writer). Each of them increased international public interest and understanding about this area without ever setting foot on (or, in the case of Holman, ever sighting) either the Cocos (Keeling) Islands or Christmas Island.

Today, new versions of Milton's metaphorical gods and devils of the Indian Ocean are potentially 'live' and multiplying, as the world's superpowers establish and expand their military bases and geopolitical influence. In 2021 Iran's Revolutionary Guards fired long-range ballistic missiles into the Indian Ocean. In April 2022, Russia's President Putin announced his 'unstoppable' Sarmat nuclear-powered global cruise missile, dubbed by journalists as 'Satan-2', with 'practically unlimited' range. Satan-2 is said to be capable of striking a target 11,200 miles away, and powerful enough to wipe out territories the size of Britain in a single strike. *Business Insider* reported, in terms reminiscent of Milton's flying Satan, that Putin 'showed an animation of the device bobbing and weaving around the globe'.[1]

The presence of coconut palms on the Cocos (Keeling) islands does not represent conclusive evidence of human visitation before the period of European exploration because ocean currents could bring coconuts to the atoll. Marco Polo's late-thirteenth-century islands of Condur and Sondur, shown on maps as located south of Java, nevertheless belonged in the northern hemisphere. Also, it is generally thought that Chinese Admiral Zheng travelled the northern rim of the Indian Ocean, rather than straying into the southern hemisphere, during his fifteenth-century voyaging.

It would be interesting to know whether the Cocos (Keeling) Islands Museum, or one of the Darwin repository museums in England, has a 'well-rounded' piece of greenstone labelled number 3581 and preserved 'as a curiosity' in its collection. If either the boulder or the sample referred to by Darwin can be located and examined, it should be possible to determine its origin: Indonesia, the Gambia in West Africa, the Murchison Range in the Limpopo Province of South Africa, the Xikuangshan antimony mine in Hunan, China, or New Zealand. Two Darwin notebooks of the 1830s, that mysteriously disappeared from the Cambridge University Library in 2000, have recently been returned, so Darwin's greenstone may also turn up at some time.[2]

The three most likely explanations for the presence of greenstone on North Keeling are: it came as a floating piece of scoria (heavier, black pumice) from the 1815 eruption of Mount Tambora on Sumbawa Island in Indonesia; it came attached to a floating tree trunk from one of the Indonesian islands after an eruption; or it came with a ship. If, between the stranding and removal of the hull of the *Earl of Liverpool*, part of the heavier cargo was offloaded on the northwest point of North Keeling Island, marked as 'Wreck Pt' on Fitzroy's chart of 1836, there might still be some pieces of greenstone, olivine, antimony ore or scoria scattered among holes in the shallow reef. If so, samples could, on a low-swell, low-tide day, be located and examined to determine their nature and origin. These three options appear more likely than an Austronesian or Chinese origin, and of the three options, Darwin's floating tree trunk seems most plausible.

Thanks to the myth-makers of the region and the imaginations of the European cartographers, the charts of the southern Indian Ocean were adorned with giant birds, numerous imagined islands and intriguing stories to accompany them. There remain unanswered questions. Have previous folds or joins in the 1502 Cantino planisphere obscured toponym letters in a manner that

that could influence their interpretation? Could it be that on his 1522 map García de Toreno painted chestnut-bellied guans astride southern Indian Ocean islands after receiving a brief description about the chicken-sized, chicken-flavoured Buff-banded Rails of the Cocos (Keeling) Islands, information transmitted to Europe from Indigenous voyagers who had visited the Cocos before 1522? Or has García simply followed Cantino's 1502 map, in his placement of Java and Ceram too far to the west in the southern Indian Ocean, and (like Roelant Savery with his parrots in Figure 18) not been concerned that his glorious-bird images were not representative of any Indian Ocean islands?

Some of the islands marked on late-sixteenth-century charts in the locations of the Cocos (Keeling) Islands and Christmas Island are the result of the proliferation of phantom islands. Others are the result of inaccurate longitude readings. Cartographers misaligned islands such as the Diego Garcia atoll, known to Indigenous cowrie-collecting inhabitants of the Maldives and then seen by the Portuguese early in the sixteenth century.

Notwithstanding the above reference to Rails, the available evidence indicates that because the early European trade routes approached the islands of Indonesia from the northwest or the northeast, both the Cocos (Keeling) Islands and Christmas Island lay unseen by Europeans until the beginning of the seventeenth century. Then the Dutch developed new shipping routes, taking vessels ever further south to capture the most favourable winds. These new shipping routes led to the sighting and exploration of these islands by the Dutch and the English.

Jodocus Hondius' 1610 chart showing Polvero Island in 10° south, 95° east, close to the position of the Cocos (Keeling) Islands, is a strong indication of Dutch discovery in 1609 or before. Then the 1612 world map by Dutch cartographer Hessel Gerritsz represents the earliest clear evidence that the Cocos (Keeling) Islands had been found and recorded, by Dutch mariners. However, the Dutch had richer prospects further northeast in the Spice Islands. The successive names appearing on charts of the islands reflect the changing interests of European nations. The peripheral Dutch en route interest in edible birds, coconuts and water as sources of refreshment was finally replaced by an English interest in the formal acquisition of the islands, driven by ambitious British hydrographers, controllers of ex-slave communities and a confused naval officer.

During the second half of the eighteenth century, a new period of mythmaking commenced, as claims of discovery were used to support ambitions to form colonies. In 1787 Alexander Dalrymple first claimed a link between the words 'Killing' and 'Keeling' – fully 178 years after William Keeling's 1609 homeward voyage, and 141 years after Robert Dudley named North (Keeling) Island as 'Killing' Island. Then it was not until 1857 that Captain Stephen Fremantle, keen to justify his mistaken annexation of the islands, was the first to state that Keeling, 248 years previously, had passed 'to the Northward of the single Northern Isle'. With those words, he created a direct link between Captain Keeling and North Keeling Island. The British Government had ignored the 1829 petition by John Clunies-Ross seeking incorporation of the islands into the British Empire, and it was simply confusion over toponyms that led to the Cocos (Keeling) Islands, rather than Coco Island in the Bay of Bengal, being annexed as British territory by Captain Stephen Fremantle in 1857.

Journals of the expedition led by Dutch merchant Cornelis de Houtman, who returned home to Europe via the south coast of Java, do not indicate that men on his ships saw Christmas Island in 1597. However, the 'roaring forties' route established by Hendrick Brouwer of the Verenigde Oostindische Compagnie (VOC) in 1611 included an approach to Sunda Strait from the south. This made it inevitable that European vessels would encounter Christmas Island, and an English captain, John Milward of the East India Company (EIC), did so by accident in 1615.

Later, explorers from both Britain and the Netherlands called at Christmas Island – William Dampier in 1688 to collect boobies for eating and water for drinking, and Willem de Vlamingh in 1697, searching for shipwreck survivors and taking note of any potential resources. The first clearly documented Christmas Island settlers, albeit temporary and reluctant, were Dutchmen from the wreck of the *Vice Admiral Rijk* in 1852. The loss of this vessel did nothing to encourage further interest by the Dutch. So, it was not until the discovery of phosphate fertiliser in the 1880s that Britain formally annexed the island and George Clunies-Ross initiated a settlement at Flying Fish Cove.

Wreck Check's investigations into possible Dutch shipwrecks at Christmas Island and the Cocos (Keeling) Islands are incomplete. There remain mysteries to be solved. The historical VOC documents indicate that the *Fortuyn* was wrecked on or near the south coast of Christmas Island. However, indications are that the wreck lies in water deeper than 30 metres. Wreck Check members are exploring the feasibility of acquiring access to an autonomous underwater vehicle for a deeper search at the southwest point of the island to locate the wreck of the *Vice Admiraal Rijk* as a pointer to the likely depth location of the *Fortuyn* wreck, should it lie along the western or southern sides of the island.

Numerous searches have failed to find the wreck of the *Aagtekerke* on the Abrolhos Islands off Western Australia. The modifications to the Dutch trade route across the Indian Ocean by the eighteenth century, and Captain Driscoll's 1825 report of substantial wreckage on Horsburgh Island in the South Keeling atoll, suggests the presence somewhere on the atoll of the *Aagtekerke* or another Dutch wreck. It is unlikely that the *Fortuyn* was wrecked on the Cocos. In June 1724, just five months after the *Fortuyn* had departed from Cape Town, the VOC's search vessel *Windhond* searched the South Cocos atoll unsuccessfully. If the wreck had occurred on the Cocos, then flotsam would have been abundant and obvious at that time.

There are just two apparent reasons for the presence of the tusk found near the shore of West Island, in the Cocos (Keeling) Islands, by Ed Dekker. Either it was part of the cargo of the *Sir Francis Nicholas Burton* or it was part of the cargo of the *Aagtekerke*. The proximity of the tusk find to 'Burton Point' makes the wreck of the *Sir Francis Nicholas Burton* the most likely source. In 1826 the captain of this vessel would likely have found Mozambique to be the most convenient source for both a cheap labour supply for the Cocos settlement and for a supply of savanna elephant ivory for indentured Cocos labourers to craft into saleable products.[3]

It is currently not possible to date the tusk. However, another option is further intensive in-water searching around Burton Point, using an autonomous underwater vehicle in the deeper water, combined with metal detector and visual survey work in the unexplored shallows immediately shoreward of the South Keeling atoll rim to check for structural and cargo items.

The known Dutch shipwrecks on the Western Australian coast might now, arguably, have been fully investigated, at least for the present, and aerial remote-sensing searches in the Pelsaert Group of the Abrolhos have not located evidence of the *Aagtekerke* or *Fortuyn*. The archival evidence makes it more likely that these ships were lost in the waters of Australia's Cocos (Keeling) Islands and Christmas Island.

Advances in oceanography and increased interest in the deep seabed of the southeastern Indian Ocean are reasons for optimism that the deeper shipwrecks around Cocos and Christmas islands will be found during the United Nations Decade of Ocean Science 2021–2030, with its focus on charting the oceans. The Nippon Foundation's General Bathymetric Chart of the Oceans (GEBCO) Seabed 2030 Project, for example, aims to bring together bathymetric data to produce the definitive chart of the world ocean floor by 2030 and make it available to all. The Woods Hole Oceanographic Institution would have the capacity to do a deep-water search, as does the Minderoo-UWA Deep-Sea Research Centre (with state-of-the-art equipment housed at the Indian Ocean Marine Research Centre in Perth) and Australia's Marine National Facility research vessel *Investigator*.[4] Combining the historical data with the increasing oceanographic data and activity should eventually lead to discovery of the wrecks.

Acknowledgements

Supporting organisations
Generous financial and in-kind support by several organisations made possible the Christmas and Cocos (Keeling) Islands fieldwork and the preparation of this book. The principal supporters were the Embassy of the Kingdom of the Netherlands in Canberra; the International Programme for Maritime Heritage of the Cultural Heritage Agency of the Netherlands (part of the Ministry of Education, Culture and Science); Parks Australia; the Silentworld Foundation; the Australian Government Department of the Environment and Energy; and the University of Western Australia's Oceans Institute; and UWA Publishing.

Supporting individuals
Many individuals made the research and writing possible. Peter Veth, as Director of the UWA Oceans Institute, arranged for artefact analysis, and provided the opportunity for the work to be published as the first in an intended series of monographs on islands; Julian Partridge and Christophe Gaudin, as successive Oceans Institute directors, facilitated that part of the publication process; Erika Techera provided valuable comments on a late draft; Martijn Manders, head of the International Programme for Maritime Heritage in the Netherlands, brought international collaboration to the project and arranged the input of Pablo Boorsma to locate archival sources about early Indian Ocean voyagers; Thomas Creemers drew our attention to and translated the Bennet account; Ed Dekker opened up tantalising new directions of research and joined in the process of seeking the analytical expertise regarding the elephant tusk from the Cocos (Keeling) Islands; Megan Coghlan and Michael Bunce of Curtin University's Trace and Environmental DNA Laboratory provided valuable DNA information

ACKNOWLEDGEMENTS

on the Cocos (Keeling) Islands elephant tusk; Rachel Wood of the Australian National University gave expert advice on carbon dating; Jan Tent of the Australian National University provided linguistic information; Brendan Whyte, curator of maps at the National Library of Australia, gave comments on an early draft; Femke Withag, senior policy officer cultural affairs and public diplomacy at the Embassy of the Kingdom of the Netherlands, provided encouragement throughout the project; Rosalia Di Nisio translated Italian phrases from Treviso; Heather McGinty solved the French translation issues; Filipe Castro, the Frederick Mayer II professor of nautical archaeology and director of the Richard Steffy Ship Reconstruction Laboratory, Texas A&M University, with his associates, translated crucial Portuguese text; Patrick Armstrong shared most generously his extensive knowledge about Charles Darwin's visit to the Cocos (Keeling) Islands; Patrick Baker applied his masterful touch to the images in the book; and Kate Pickard, publishing manager, UWA Publishing, steered us through the publishing process.

On the islands, many people gave us help, in particular Parks Australia staff Robert Muller, Ismail MacRae, Trish Flores and Michael Misso. We also received support from local dive operators Dieter Gerhard and Hama Hamanaka, and information about island history from John Clunies-Ross and Meiko Scholes.

Fellow Wreck Check members Alex Moss and James Parkinson, who joined us in the field, helped throughout the project. Shinatria Adhityatama, the maritime archaeologist at the National Research Center for Archaeology (Pusat Arkeologi Nasional) in Indonesia, joined the team for the 2016 fieldwork season.

Our thanks to the following for their help in various ways during the project: Atholl Anderson, Douglas Bateman, Jaco Boshoff, Bobbie Bruce, Pauline Bunce, Heather Campbell, Alec Coles (CEO, WA Museum), Ian Crawford, Tim Eastwood, Joshua Esler, Antonietta De Felice, George Finch, Ross Fletcher, Peter Gesner, Kathleen Granger (principal, Cocos Islands District High School), Jeremy Green (previous head of maritime archaeology, WA Museum), Sue Grey-Smith, Yasmin Haskell, Alan Henderson, Ali McGovern,

ACKNOWLEDGEMENTS

Andrea Mangoni, Steven Marcuson (of Trowbridge), Sally May, Zoe Richards, Pat Sedgwick, Andrea Selvey (chief executive, Shire of Cocos Islands), Elly Spillekom, Alasdair Wardle, Andrew White, Anne Worden and Tina Zhang.

Kandy Henderson provided inspiration throughout the fieldwork and writing phases.

Illustration sources and credits

Figure 1. The Cocos (Keeling) Islands and Christmas Island lie in the tropical eastern waters of the Indian Ocean. Map reproduced with the permission of CartoGIS Services, Scholarly Information Services, The Australian National University.

Figure 2. Relief panel of the Borobudur ship. Image G. Henderson.

Figure 3. Section of the Fra Mauro 1450 map of the world showing Sumatra, the Laccadive-Maldive-Chagos Ridge and Madagascar. Image Piero Falchetta, viewed 12 August 2020, <https://commons.wikimedia.org/wiki/File:FraMauroDetailedMap.jpg>.

Figure 4. The Cantino planisphere, completed by an unknown Portuguese cartographer in 1502, is now kept in the Biblioteca Universitaria Estense, Modena, Italy, viewed 14 November 2021, <https://commons.wikimedia.org/wiki/File:Cantino_planisphere_(1502).jpg>.

Figure 5. Detail from the 1502 Cantino planisphere showing a blue island and a red island. Source Biblioteca Estense Universitaria, Modena, Italy, viewed 18 July 2020, <https://commons.wikimedia.org/wiki/File:Cantino_planisphere_(1502).jpg>. A fold in the map to the east of the red island rendered three of the toponyms incomplete. For the detail used, photographer Patrick Baker has connected the sight lines to show (in white) where the letters appear to be missing.

Figure 6. The modern 1-cedi coin of Ghana bears the cowrie image, recalling the shell money. Image Bill Maurer, Institute for Money, Technology and Financial Inclusion, on Flickr, viewed 24 August 2020, <https://commons.wikimedia.org/wiki/File:Ein-Cedi-M%C3%BCnze.jpg>.

Figure 7. Cowries from Diego Garcia. The flesh-coloured *Nymphae Nymphae* cowrie of Diego Garcia is now very rare. Image Cowries World, viewed 2 June 2020, <http://www.cowries-world.com/crbst_153.html>.

Figure 8. Magellan's *Victoria*. Detail from a 1590 Ortelius map, viewed 25 August 2019, <https://commons.wikimedia.org/w/index.php?curid=1593812>.

ILLUSTRATION SOURCES AND CREDITS

Figure 9. Parrot-hunting on Mauritius in 1598, by Johann Theodor de Bry. The long-legged birds are thought to be erroneous depictions of dodos, viewed 4 November 2021, <http://julianhume.co.uk/wp-content/uploads/2010/07/History-of-the-dodo-Hume.pdf>.

Figure 10. Section of Gerard de Jode's 1593 chart Hemispheriv Ab Aeqvinoctiali. Note the islands of Augama and Sondur below Java Major and Taprobana (Sumatra). Viewed 12 August 2019, <https://commons.wikimedia.org/wiki/File:Gerard_de_Jode_1593_Map_Southern_hemisphere.jpg>.

Figure 11. Detail of Emanuel Bowen's 1729 chart showing Marco Polo's Sondur and Condur, and an island named 'Palvoreira' further west. Source *Carte du Voyages tres-curieux et fort remarquables, Achevees par toute L'Asie, Tartarie, Mangi, Japan, les Indes Orientales, Iles, Adjacentes Et L'Afrique. Commences l'An 1252 Par Marc Paul, Venitien*. National Palace Museum, Taipei.

Figure 12. Marco Polo in Tartar costume. Source *Scanné de Coureurs des mers, Poivre d'Arvor, 18th century*. Author Grevembrock Viewed 2 February 2020, <https://upload.wikimedia.org/wikipedia/commons/3/3d/Marco_Polo_-_costume_tartare.jpg>.

Figure 13. Detail of 'The probable view of Marco Polo's own geography', drawn by Henry Yule, 1871. From 'Marco Polo, 1254–1323', 'Sir Henry Yule, 1820–1889', *The book of Ser Marco Polo, the Venetian: concerning the kingdoms and marvels of the East*, John Murray, London, 1871, p. 143, viewed 12 August 2019, <https://archive.org/details/bookofsermarcopo01polo/page/n143/mode/2up>.

Figure 14. Henry Yule showed the Islands of the Ruc as lying eastward of Madagascar. From Yule, vol. 2, bk 3, part VII.

Figure 15. A Charles Maurice Detmold (1883–1908) impression of the Roc, which fed its young on elephants. Plate from 'The Arabian Nights', *The Second Voyage of Sinbad the Sailor*, Hodder & Stoughton, 1924, viewed 3 February 2020, <https://commons.wikimedia.org/wiki/File:Edward_Julius_Detmold49.jpg>.

Figure 16. Detail from the Nuño García de Toreno map of 1522. Fragment preserved at the Biblioteca Reale di Torino, Italy. By permission del © MiBACT – Royal Musems, Royal Library of Turin, viewed 28 September 2019, <https://www.museireali.beniculturali.it/opere/carta-nautica-2/>.

Figure 17. The chestnut-bellied guan of Brazil, now on the International Union for Conservation of Nature's Red List of Threatened Species. Transpantaneira, Poconé, Mato Grosso, BRAZIL Image Bernard Dupont, France, viewed 30 July 2020, <https://commons.wikimedia.org/wiki/File:Chestnut-bellied_Guan_(Penelope_ochrogaster)_(30850197103).jpg>.

ILLUSTRATION SOURCES AND CREDITS

Figure 18. A dodo as painted by Roelant Savery, late 1620s. The bird at the lower right may be the extinct Red Rail, and the two parrots may be the extinct Lesser Antillean Macaw (left) and Martinique Macaw (right). Natural History Museum, London. Presented to the British Museum by George Edwards in 1759, having previously been in the collection of Sir Hans Sloane, viewed 1 March 2021, <https://www.stuff.co.nz/science/103723368/newlydiscovered-pigeon-species-related-to-the-dodo-lived-in-nz-millions-of-years-ago>.

Figure 19. An 1865 artist's impression of the Chrocho egg. Author Gustave Dore, 'An episode from the 5th voyage of Sinbad the Sailor' in the *One Thousand and One Nights*. Illustration from 'Les Mille et une nuits', par Galland, Paris, 1865, viewed 20 August 2020, <https://upload.wikimedia.org/wikipedia/commons/b/b0/Sinbad_the_Sailor_%285th_Voyage%29.jpg>.

Figure 20. The Cocos (Keeling) Islands. North Keeling is at top of the image. Image: NASA's Earth Observatory, viewed 25 August 2019, <https://eoimages.gsfc.nasa.gov/images/imagerecords/76000/76791/cocoskeeling_ali_2009202_lrg.jpg>.

Figure 21. Wreckage of a refugee boat washed ashore near the West Island airstrip. Image Wreck Check.

Figure 22. Detail from the 1550 Desceliers map of the world showing Diego Garcia. Add MS 24065, British Library, viewed 7 August 2020, <https://commons.wikimedia.org/wiki/File:Map_of_the_world_-_Pierre_Desceliers,_1550_-_BL_Add_MS_24065.jpg>.

Figure 23. NASA image of Diego Garcia atoll (British Indian Ocean Territory) in the Indian Ocean. The profile is similar to a sock or boot, viewed 16 July 2020, <https://commons.wikimedia.org/wiki/File:Nasa_diego_garcia.jpg>.

Figure 24. Detail from Jodocus Hondius' Asia Nova chart of 1610 showing I de Polvero in the location of the Cocos (Keeling) Islands, viewed 2 March 2020, <https://commons.wikimedia.org/wiki/File:CEM-19-Asiae-nova-description-1610-Jodocus-Hondius-2538.jpg>.

Figure 25. Detail from Henricus Hondius II's, 1630 chart, 'New Geographic and Hydrographic Map of the Whole World', taking 'I da Polvera' back westward to resume its place as an extension of the Laccadive-Maldive-Chagos Ridge, viewed 2 March 2020, <https://upload.wikimedia.org/wikipedia/commons/b/b5/Nova_totius_Terrarum_Orbis_geographica_ac_hydrographica_tabula_%28Hendrik_Hondius%29_balanced.jpg>.

ILLUSTRATION SOURCES AND CREDITS

Figure 26. Detail of the Hessel Gerritsz world map of 1612, viewed 13 September 2019, <https://en.wikipedia.org/wiki/Hessel_Gerritsz#/media/File:Hessel_Gerritsz_-_Worldmap_of_1612_including_the_discovery_of_La_Austrialia_del_Espiritu_Santo_by_Pedro_Fernandes_de_Queirós.png>.

Figure 27. The Hessel Gerritsz 1612 world map, including the discovery of La Austrialia del Espiritu Santo by Pedro Fernandes de Queirós.

Figure 28. A Polverara chicken. Image courtesy Andrea Mangoni 2019.

Figure 29. A red-footed booby. Image Gregg Yan 2001, viewed 28 December 2019, <https://commons.wikimedia.org/wiki/File:Sula_sula_by_Gregg_Yan_01.jpg>.

Figure 30. Alice's dodo. *Liddell & Boyd (Alice in the looking glass works)* by Karl Beutel, 2011, following earlier depictions. Perceived and imagined resemblances between dodos, chickens and boobies appear to have influenced the mythology of the southern Indian Ocean, viewed 1 August 2019, <https://commons.wikimedia.org/wiki/File:Liddell_%26_Boyd_(Alice_in_the_looking_glass_works)_by_Karl_Beutel_2011.jpg>.

Figure 31. Woodcut of the *Dragon*, or *Red Dragon*, as it was sometimes referred to, Captain Lancaster, in the Strait of Malacca, 1602. Artist unknown. From the Dutch collection of East India voyages, 1645–6, viewed 12 August 2019, <https://en.wikipedia.org/wiki/Red_Dragon_(1595)#/media/File:Reddragonship.jpg>.

Figure 32. Cabinet miniature of Sir Robert Dudley (1574–1649), English explorer, styled Earl of Warwick and Duke of Northumberland. Artist Nicholas Hilliard, viewed 1 August 2019, <https://commons.wikimedia.org/wiki/File:Nicholas_Hilliard_Sir_Robert_Dudley,_styled_Duke_of_Northumberland.jpg>.

Figure 33. Dudley's Cocos (Keeling) Islands. Source Asia Carta III.

Figure 34. Dudley's Coco Islands in the Bay of Bengal. Source Asia Carta V.

Figure 35. Detail showing Cocos Eylanden off the south coast of Sumatra in 2°S, 100°E, from van Keulen, J., 1753, Sea chart of Sumatra, the Malacca Straits, the islands of Singapore, Banca, Sunda and surrounding islands. In the sixth volume of *Lichtende Zee-Fakkel*, the great sea atlas begun by his grandfather (Johannes). MAP RM 4186, National Library of Australia, viewed 2 June 2019, <http://nla.gov.au/nla.obj-232434475>. Modern charts show some similarity in disposition.

ILLUSTRATION SOURCES AND CREDITS

Figure 36. Detail from the bottom left corner of Hessel Gerritsz's 1627 'Caert van't Landt van d'Eendracht (Chart of the Land of Eendracht)'. This map possibly influenced Dudley in his representation of the Cocos (Keeling) Islands, viewed 12 August 2019, <https://en.wikipedia.org/wiki/Tryal_Rocks#/media/File:Caert_van%27t_Landt_van_d%27Eendracht_(detail_showing_Tryal_Rocks).jpg>.

Figure 37. Aerial view of North Keeling Island in 1976, showing a white sand channel to the ocean. Image courtesy Trish Flores, Acting Chief Ranger Pulo Keeling National Park, Parks Australia.

Figure 38. North Keeling Island in 2012, showing the channel permanently blocked and overgrown. Image PalawanOz, licensed under CC BY-SA 3.0 via Wikimedia Commons, viewed 12 August 2019, <https://commons.wikimedia.org/wiki/File:North_Keeling_Island_01.JPG>.

Figure 39. Illustration 2 to Milton's *Paradise Lost*: Satan, Sin, and Death: Satan Comes to the Gates of Hell, Maker, William Blake, 1807, Object number: 000.2, The Huntington Library, Art Museum, and Botanical Gardens, viewed 13 April 2012, <https://emuseum.huntington.org/objects/69/illustration-2-to-miltons-paradise-lost-satan-sin-and>. © Courtesy of the Huntington Art Museum, San Marino, California.

Figure 40. Frontispiece to the Dutch version of Dampier's book.

Figure 41. Left: It appears that Swift has reinterpreted Sir Robert Dudley's 1661 map 'Il Mare Del Indie Orientales' portraying North Keeling (Riling Island) and South Keeling Islands, rather than envisaging Christmas Island as Gulliver's Lilliput. See also Malaysian Island as Gulliver's Lilliput, viewed 24 April 2020, <https://christmasislandarchives.com/malaysian-island-as-gullivers-lilliput/>. Right: Gulliver's Lilliput, shown on his woodcut map as southwest of Sunda Strait, in the general location of the Cocos (Keeling) Islands. Source J. Swift, *Gulliver's Travels*, in *Gulliver's Travels and Other Writings*, The Riverside Press 1960 edn, Cambridge, Mass., 1726.

Figure 42. Godlob Silo's 'Compass chart of the Kokos Islands', circa 1724. Title in the Leupe catalogue: 'Platte paskaart van de Cocus-Eylanden, diens Zuydelijks liggende op de Z.Br. van 12 gr. 15 min., en 't Noordl. op de Z.Br. van 11 gr. 38 à 40 min., Lengte 118 gr', 1724?, Nationaal Archief, viewed 12 August 2019, <www.atlasofmutualheritage.nl/en/Compass-chart-Kokos-islands.5134>.

ILLUSTRATION SOURCES AND CREDITS

Figure 43. Johannes van Keulen's 1753 map of the Cocos Islands. Source Pas caart van de Cocos-Eylanden. MAP RM 3771, National Library of Australia, viewed 12 August 2019, <https://catalogue.nla.gov.au/Record/3081704>.

Figure 44. Alexander Dalrymple, 'Plan of the Keeling and Cocos Islands… from John van Keulen', Map 160, Dalrymple's charts, 1771–1806, vol. 5, Library of New South Wales, 1787. The form and extent of the Northern Island are from a Swedish MS by C. G. Egeberg 1749, viewed 2 July 2019, <http://library.sl.nsw.gov.au/record=b4113886~S2>.

Figure 45. Fiction writer James Otis, in 1902, even provided a directions map for the Aymara Inca treasure on the Cocos (Keeling) Islands rather than the Costa Rican islands. *The treasure of Cocos Island: a story of the Indian Ocean*. A. Burt, New York, p. 63, viewed 12 August 2019, <https://babel.hathitrust.org/cgi/pt?id=hvd.hn1lti;view=1up;seq=8>.

Figure 46. 'Eckeberg's Island of 1749', with Dalrymple's modification and Guppy's 1889 alteration and comments. From H. Guppy, 'The Cocos-Keeling Islands', p. 16. Reprinted from the *Scottish Geographical Magazine*, June 1889, viewed 2 July 2019, <access.bl.uk/item/pdf/lsidyv3756a1b1>.

Figure 47. James Holman, the blind travel writer. Painting by George Chinnery, 1830, viewed 24 December 2019, <https://commons.wikimedia.org/wiki/File:James.Holman.by.George.Chinnery.1830.jpg>.

Figure 48. A chart of the Cocos Keeling Islands in the southern Indian Ocean, 1840. Source Holman, *A Voyage Round the World*, viewed 15 August 2019, <https://upload.wikimedia.org/wikipedia/commons/3/3b/Chart_of_Cocos_Keeling_Islands.png>.

Figure 49. Cornelis de Houtman. From G. Rouffaer, and J. IJzerman, *De Errste Schipvaart der Nederlanders Naar Oost-Indie onder Cornelis de Houtman 1595–1597*, Martinus Nijhoff, 's-Gravenhage, 1915.

Figure 50. Cornelis de Houtman's fleet, seventeenth-century artist. Source W. Hanna, *Bali Chronicles*, viewed 12 August 2019, <https://en.wikipedia.org/wiki/First_Dutch_Expedition_to_Nusantara#/media/File:Fleet_of_Cornelis_de_Houtman.jpg>.

Figure 51. Detail of Sebastian Munster's Tabula Orientalis, 1580, published in *Geographia universalis vetus et nova*, an updated edition of Ptolemy's *Geographia*, viewed 20 March 2020, courtesy Steven Marcuson, Trowbridge Claremont, <https://trowbridgegallery.com.au/product/1580-munster-sebastian-asia/>.

ILLUSTRATION SOURCES AND CREDITS

Figure 52. Portrait of Hendrik Brouwer (1581–1643), explorer and Governor-General of the Dutch East Indies. Artist anonymous. Rijksmuseum Amsterdam, viewed 1 August 2019, <https://commons.wikimedia.org/wiki/File:Hendrik_Brouwer.jpg>.

Figure 53. English explorer, buccaneer, navigator and naturalist William Dampier. Artist Thomas Murray (1663–1734), National Portrait Gallery UK, viewed 13 September 2019, <https://en.wikipedia.org/wiki/William_Dampier#/media/File:Dampier-portrait.jpg>.

Figure 54. 'A map of the world shewing the course of Mr Dampier's voyage round it. From 1679 to 1691'. Author H. Moll. From William Dampier, *A New Voyage Round the World*, viewed 15 August 2019, <http://gutenberg.net.au/ebooks05/0500461h.html>.

Figure 55. The outflow of a stream into the ocean on the northwest coast of Christmas Island. Image: Wreck Check.

Figure 56. Dolly Beach on the southeast coast of Christmas Island is now covered with coconut palms. Image: Wreck Check.

Figure 57. In 1718 Captain Daniel Beekman sketched the island from the sea. From D. Beeckman, *A voyage to and from the island of Borneo, in the East-Indies. With a description of the said island: giving an account of the inhabitants*. T. Warner, London, 1718.

Figure 58. Christmas Island robber crabs and red crabs. Image: Wreck Check.

Figure 59. The Dutch barque *Vice Admiraal Rijk*. 'Technische tekening van barkschip *Vice Admiraal van Rijk*'. Source Maritiem Museum Rotterdam, viewed 12 August 2019, <https://www.maritiemdigitaal.nl/index.cfm?event=search.getdetail&id=100022255>.

Figure 60. Swell conditions on the southwest coast of Christmas Island. Image: Wreck Check.

Figure 61. Christmas Island showing water depths. Source: AUS 00608 Australian Hydrographic Service. Not to be used for navigation.

Figure 62. The *Amicitia* rescue ship. 'De barkschepen *Amicitia* en *Azia* in het zeegat van Texel'. Creator Jacob Spin, A.2583(02), Scheepvaart National Maritime Museum, viewed 15 August 2019, <https://www.maritiemdigitaal.nl/index.cfm?database=MaritimeDigitalObjects&museum=&allfields=&title=&keyword=&creator=&collection=&shipname=Amicitia&invno=&event=search.getadvancedsearch&saveToHistory=1>.

ILLUSTRATION SOURCES AND CREDITS

Figures 63a and 63b. Two views of a bottle identified as a 'Dutch gin' bottle, collected from near the number two Dale waterfall near the west coast of Christmas Island. Images courtesy Mieko Scholes.

Figure 64. The location of the bottle find. Map courtesy of Dion Maple, Christmas Island National Park, Parks Australia.

Figure 65. Medal awarded to boatswain Gerd Addicks of the *Amicitia* for saving the lives of the three crew members from the *Vice Admiraal Rijk*. 1853 / Z.H.M.R.S. Beloningsmedaille aan Gerd Addicks. Posted 20 May 2014, <http://scheepvaartpenningen.nl/?p=5233>.

Figure 66. George Clunies-Ross. From F. Wood-Jones, Corals and Atolls, Lovell Reeve and Co. Ltd, London, 1912, viewed 2 June 2019, <https://archive.org/stream/coralatollshisto00jone#page/n7/mode/2up>.

Figure 67. Climatological Database of the World's Oceans (CLIWOC) ships position plots 1750–1850, showing evidence from logs of the shipping route between Christmas and Cocos, a great distance from Australia. Source CLIWOC, viewed 27 August 2019, <http://projects.knmi.nl/cliwoc/cliwocmeta.htm>.

Figure 68. Talking shipwrecks in the Home Island classroom. Image: Wreck Check.

Figure 69. Megan Coghlan with the tusk at the Trace and Environmental DNA Laboratory at Curtin University. Image: Wreck Check.

Figure 70. Alex Moss, James Parkinson and Andrew Viduka set up the remote-sensing equipment. Image: Wreck Check.

Figure 71. Andrew Viduka about to start the towing of the magnetometer transducer. Image: Wreck Check.

Figure 72. Divers ground-truthed the remote-sensing information. Image: Wreck Check.

Figure 73. Local divers inspect the scuttled fishing boat in 24 m off Christmas Island. Image courtesy Hama Hamanaka. The seabed profile of the Cocos (Keeling) Islands is, like that of Christmas Island, very steep.

Figure 74. An early chart of the south end of West Island shows a 'wreck' near Burton Point. Source: Early Charts of Australia and the Pacific, Essex Institute Library, folio 592, PMB 213, State Library of Western Australia.

References and notes

Chapter 1. Islands of Misadventure
1. C. Van Duzer, 'Hic sunt dracones': the geography and cartography of monsters, in A. Mittman & P. Dendle, *The Ashgate research companion to monsters and the monstrous*, Routledge, 2017.
2. See wreckcheckinc.org. See also <https://www.facebook.com/FortuynProject>.
3. Gilder Lehrman Institute of American History, *The doctrine of discovery*, 2012, viewed 2 September 2019, <https://www.gilderlehrman.org/sites/default/files/inline-pdfs/04093_FPS.pdf>.
4. F. Wood-Jones, *Coral and atolls: a history and description of the Cocos-Keeling Islands with an account of their flora and fauna, and a discussion of the method and development of transformation of coral structures in general*, Lovell Reeve and Co. Ltd, London, 1912, p. 1, viewed 2 June 2019, <https://archive.org/details/coralatollshisto00jone>.

Chapter 2. Marco Polo's Islands and the Cantino planisphere
1. B. Fagan, *Beyond the blue horizon*, Bloomsbury Press, New York, 2012, p. 21. Michael Pearson refers to boat use on the Red Sea coast at least 125,000 years ago in *The Indian Ocean*, Oxford, Routledge, 2003, p. 47.
2. B. Chatwin, *The songlines*, Franklin Press, UK, 1987.
3. R. Norris, et al., *Emu Dreaming: an introduction to Australian Aboriginal astronomy*, Emu Dreaming, 2009.
4. P. Manguin, 'Austronesian shipping in the Indian Ocean', in Gwyn Campbell (ed.), *Early exchange between Africa and the wider Indian Ocean world*, Palgrave Series in Indian Ocean World Studies, 2016.
5. N. Burningham, 'The Borobudur Ship: recreating the first trans-ocean voyaging', *MHA Journal*, viewed 4 September 2020, <https://www.wuestenschiff.de/Phoenicia/Boro_Exped.pdf>.
6. S. Fitzpatrick and R. Callaghan, Figure 3, in 'Seafaring simulations and the origin of prehistoric settlers to Madagascar', in G. Clark, F. Leach and S. O'Connor (eds), *Islands of inquiry: colonisation, seafaring and the archaeology of maritime landscapes*, Terra Australis 29, pp. 47–58, ANU E Press, 2008, viewed 6 July 2020, <https://web.archive.org/web/20110310063635/http://epress.anu.edu.au/terra_australis/ta29/pdf/ch03.pdf>. See the Roger Blench 2009 map 'Austronesia with hypothetical greatest expansion extent' in his 'Remapping the Austronesian', in B. Evans, *Discovering history through language: papers in honour of Malcolm Ross*, Pacific Linguistics, viewed 6 July 2020, <https://upload.wikimedia.org/wikipedia/commons/f/f0/Austronesia_with_hypothetical_greatest_expansion_extent_%28Blench%2C_2009%29_01.png>. See also P. Manguin,

'Austronesian shipping in the Indian Ocean: From outrigger boats to trading ships', in G. Campbell, *Early exchange between Africa and the wider Indian Ocean world* ch. 3. See also I. Goodwin, S. Browning and A. Anderson, 'Climate windows for Polynesian voyaging to New Zealand and Easter Island', in *Proceedings of the National Academy of Sciences of the United States of America*, published online, 2014, viewed 2 February 2020, <https://www.ncbi.nlm.nih.gov/pmc/articles/PMC4205595/>. See also R. Blench, 'Almost everything you believed about the Austronesians isn't true', in M. Tajoa-Bonatz et al. (eds), *Crossing borders: Selected papers from the 13th International Conference of the European Association of Southeast Asian Archaeologists*, vol. 1, ch. 12, NUS Press, 2012, viewed 13 November 2020, <http://www.rogerblench.info/Archaeology/SE%20Asia/Berlin%202010/Blench%20Austronesians%202012%20offprint.pdf>.

7. S. Gerke and H. Evers, 'Looking east, looking west: Penang as a knowledge hub', in *Proceedings of the PIO Conference 2011*, George Town, Malaysia, 2012, p. 143, viewed 2 June 2018, <https://www.academia.edu/2830987/Looking_East_looking_West_Penang_as_a_knowledge_hub>.

8. J. van Braam and F. Valentyn, *Nieuwe kaart van het Eyland Sumatra*, 1726? Library of Congress, viewed 2 July 2019, <https://www.loc.gov/item/2014585053/>.

9. H. Yule and H. Cordier (eds), *The Travels of Marco Polo, by Marco Polo and Rustichello of Pisa*, vol. 2, bk III, ch. VII, The Project Gutenberg eBook, 2004, viewed 2 June 2019, <http://www.gutenberg.org/cache/epub/12410/pg12410-images.html>.

10. R. Skelton, *Explorers' Maps*, Hamlyn Publishing Group edn, 1970, p. 9. Regarding the value of place names see W. A. R. Richardson, 'An Indian Ocean Pilgrimage in Search of an Island', *The great circle: Journal of the Australian Association of Maritime History*, vol. 11, no. 2, 1989. See also J. Tent and D. Blair, Motivations for Naming, a toponymic typology. *ANPS technical paper no. 2, Australian National Placenames Survey*, 2009, viewed 15 October 2020, <https://www.anps.org.au/upload/ANPSTechPaper2.pdf>.

11. N. Germanus (after Ptolomey's *Geographica*, 1st/2nd century CE), *Cosmographia Claudii Ptolomaei Alexandrini*, source National Library of Poland, viewed 29 July 2020, <https://commons.wikimedia.org/wiki/File:Ptolemy_Cosmographia_1467_-_world_map.jpg>. See also L. Holle, 'World Map from Ptolemy', *Cosmographiia*, Ulm, 1482, James Ford Bell Library, University of Minnesota, viewed 7 August 2020, <https://apps.lib.umn.edu/bell/map/PTO/TOUR/1482ulg.html>.

12. Cantino planisphere 1502, viewed 1 January 2020, <https://upload.wikimedia.org/wikipedia/commons/9/9c/Cantino_planisphere_%281502%29.jpg>. See also M. Ferrar, The Cantino Planisphere; 1502AD Portuguese Expertise, Is It Copied? + Caverio; 1505AD Planisphere Is Not A Copy, viewed 7 August 2020. <https://www.cartographyunchained.com/chcan1/>. Some cartographers sprinkled spice names in areas where they were not grown. See C. Burdick, 'Patagonian cinnamon and pepper: blurring geography in Alonso de Ovalle's Tabula

Geographica Regni Chile (1646)', *Imago Mundi*, 66.2 (2014): 196-212, <https://www.academia.edu/6733276/_Patagonian_Cinnamon_and_Pepper...>

13. See J. Gaspar, 'Blunders, errors and entanglements: scrutinising the Cantino planisphere with a cartographic eye', *Imago Mundi, the International Journal for the History of Cartography*, vol. 64, issue no. 2, 2012, note 15, viewed 10 July 2020, <https://www.tandfonline.com/doi/full/10.1080/03085694.2012.673762>. Unfortunately, Gaspar omitted the Indian Ocean from his analysis. He notes that all inscriptions are transcribed and translated into English in Cortesao and Teixeira da Mota, *Portugaliae Monumenta Cartographica* (see note 3), vol. 1, pp. 11–13. His note 3 reads, 'For more detailed descriptions, see Armando Cortesão and Avelino Teixeira da Mota, *Portugaliae Monumenta Cartographica*, 6 vols (Lisboa, Comissão para a Comemoração do V Centenário da Morte do infante D. Henrique, 1960; Imprensa Nacional-Casa da Moeda, Lisboa, 1987 [facsimiled edition]), vol. 1, p. 9; Duarte Leite, 'O mais antigo mapa do Brasil', in *História da Colonização Portuguesa do Brasil*, Litografia Nacional, Porto, vol. 2, 1923, pp. 227–32.

14. Information provided by Filipe Castro (Frederick Mayer II Professor of Nautical Archaeology Director at the J. Richard Steffy Ship Reconstruction Laboratory, Texas A&M University) and Antonio Canas from Cortesão (1975, pp. 52–3).

15. H. Thomas, *The Slave Trade*, Phoenix, London, 2006, p. 323.

16. J. Hogendom and M. Johnson, *The shell money and the slave trade*, African Studies Series, Cambridge University Press, 2003. See also Pearson, p. 151, and R. Raben, 'European periphery at the heart of the Indian Ocean: the Maldives, 17th–18th centuries', in *International Conference on Shipping, Factories and Colonisation* (Brussels, 24–26 November, 1994), Brunela, Konenklijke Academie van Belgie, 1996.

17. E. Yiridoe, 'Economic and sociocultural aspects of cowrie currency of the Dagaaba of Northwestern Ghana', *Nordic Journal of African Studies* vol. 4, no. 2, 1995, pp. 17–32, viewed 30 August 2020, <http://www.njas.helsinki.fi/pdf-files/vol4num2/yiridoe.pdf>. During the nineteenth century, captured Africans were taken south from this area and exported to the Americas from the port of Whydah. See the references to the enslaved person referred to as Daaga (perhaps because of his origins) in G. Henderson, *Redemption of a slave ship: the James Matthews*, Western Australian Museum, Welshpool, 2009.

18. The letters 'Cal...am' are clear on the map, but a join makes it difficult to see whether 'Caleirciram' is the complete word. Waldseemuller the mapmaker interpreted the word on the map to indicate the head dress worn by Roman women – the *caliendorium*. The word 'ciram' can be translated as meaning 'a long time' in Sanskrit (<https://www.wisdomlib.org/definition/ciram>). 'Cal...uam' could feasibly have come from 'calendarum' (the first day of the Roman month), 'calenture' (a Portuguese word for a feverish delirium formerly thought of as afflicting sailors in the tropics, in which the sea is mistaken for green fields), or sunstroke. The letter c was sometimes interchangeable with g in Latin, raising the possibility of a reference to poultry (gallus). So 'Cal...uam' might refer to 'gallinarium' (from the Latin 'gallingha' meaning 'little hen'). However, the word

interpreted by Cortesão as 'clauo', referring to clove, is compelling and their conclusions make sense. See also Pearson, pp. 82–3.

19. Gan (Addu Atoll), viewed 7 October 2014, <https://en.wikipedia.org/wiki/Gan_(Addu_Atoll)>.
20. A. A. Fauvel, 'Unpublished documents on the history of the Seychelles Islands anterior to 1810', Government Printing Office, Mahé, Seychelles, viewed 4 November 2012 <https://catalogue.nla.gov.au/Record/1614203>. Fauvel's footnotes read as follows: '(2) …a lot of benzoin (fragrant gum resin used in medicine and perfume), (3) …a lot of clove, (4) …a lot of gold and silver and silk and sulfur and more amber'. See Ferrar, op. cit. See also <https://en.wikipedia.org/wiki/4th_Portuguese_India_Armada_(Ga…>.
21. The interpretation of damaged toponyms is a minefield. 'Ganga' is Portuguese for waterfowl; 'ganso' is Portuguese for gander or male goose.
22. M. Waldseemuller, 'Universalis cosmographia secundum Ptholomaei traditionem et Americi Vespucii alioru[m]que lustrationes', 1507, Library of Congress, viewed 13 July 2020, <https://www.loc.gov/resource/g3200.ct000725>. See also, viewed 2 October 2021, <Introduction_to_the_Carta_Marina (2).pdf>. Iona is shown east of Madagascar on Sheet 11 of the *Carta marina*, p. 136, in C. Van Duzer, 'Martin Waldseemuller's *"Carta marina" of 1516: study of the long legends*', viewed 19 November 2021, <https://doi.org/10.1007/978-3-030-22703-6>. Regarding cowries, Van Duzer, p. 138, notes that Waldseemuller's legend on his 1507 map reads, 'Iona In ista insula reperiuntur panni de serico texti et porcellana vel bombex (Java. In this island are found silk cloth and porcelain or shells)'.
23. A. Pigafetta, *Magellan's voyage around the world*, original text of the Ambrosian ms. translated by James Robertson, The Arthur H. Clark Company, Cleveland, vol. 2, 1906 edn, note 581, p. 226, viewed 8 April, 2021 <https://archive.org/details/magellansvoyagea02piga>. Pigafetta refers to the disease of St Jop, while the editor in note 581 refers to Job. See also Machado–Joseph disease, <https://en.wikipedia.org/wiki/Machado%E2%80%93Joseph_disease>.
24. Pigafetta, p. 181.
25. Pigafetta, pp. 169–71. The ancient Sri Lankan chronicle *Mahawamsa* refers to an island called 'Mahiladiva', possibly meaning 'Island of Women'. See 'Maldives', viewed 7 August 2020, <https://en.wikipedia.org/wiki/Maldives>.
26. 'Log-Book of Francisco Alvo or Alvaro', in A. Pigaferra (trans. Lord Stanley of Alderley), viewed 4 November 2021, <https://en.wikisource.org/wiki/The_First_Voyage_Round_the_World/Log…>
27. Pigafetta, note 637.
28. J. Miguel Alonso Rojo, 'Nuño García de Toreno: The first cartographer of the Casa de la Contratacion', 2020 Magazine of Columbian Studies, viewed 2 October 2021, <https://www.academia.edu/49081971/Nuño_García_de_Toreno_El_primer…>. See 'Nuño García de Toreno Map of the Moluccas', 1522. Fragment preserved at the Biblioteca Reale in Turin. Copy in 'Why does the map drawn right after the first world circumnavigation show two fantastic

giant birds?', 2019, viewed 28 August 2019, <historyandmaps.wordpress.com>. See also left edge, <map-pacific-munster-1540.jpg (3078×2496) (princeton.edu)>, in <https://library.princeton.edu/visual_materials/maps/websites/pacific/pacific-ocean/pacific-ocean-maps.html>. See also reference to Griffins? In the southern Indian Ocean, in Typus Orbis Universalis 1550 by Münster – CartaHistorica <https://www.cartahistorica.com/our-catalogue/world-polars-oceans/typus-orbis-universalis-1550/>.

29. See N. Peters, 'Eredia Map 1602', *Cartography*, December 2003. See also M. Cowan, *Reptiles of Dirk Hartog Island*, Department of Biodiversity, Conservation and Attractions, Government of Western Australia, 2018, viewed 20 October 2020, <https://www.cartahistorica.com/our-catalogue/world-polars-oceans/typus-orbis-universalis-1550/>.

30. E. Heawood, *A history of geographical discovery in the seventeenth and eighteenth centuries*, Cambridge University Press, Cambridge, 1912, viewed 2 July 2019, <http://gutenberg.net.au/ebooks13/1305581h.html#ch-03>.

31. A. Burnell, *The voyage of John Huyghen van Linschoten to the East Indies*, vol. 1, Hakluyt Society, London, 1876, viewed 2 July 2019, <https://archive.org/details/voyagejohnhuygh00tielgoog>.

32. B. Langhenez, 'The description of a voyage made by certaine ships of Holland into the East Indies, with their aduentures and successe; together with the description of the countries, townes, and inhabitantes of the same: who set forth on the second of Aprill, 1595, and returned on the 14 of August, 1597', translated out of Dutch into English by W. P., London, 1598. *Principal navigations, voyages, traffiques and discoveries of the English nation, by Richard Hakluyt*, E. Goldsmid (ed.), vol. X (Asia), part III, E. & G. Goldsmid, Edinburgh, 1889, p. 262, viewed 19 March 2020, <https://archive.org/details/cihm_33126/page/n235/mode/2up/search/Holland>.

33. Mercator_1569_world_map_sheet_12.PNG (980×1142) (wikimedia.org), viewed 11 April 2022, <https://commons.wikimedia.org/wiki/File:Mercator_1569_world_map_sheet_12.PNG>.

34. G. de Jode, 'The Southern Hemisphere', map published in the atlas *Speculum Orbis Terrae*, C. de Jode, 1593, viewed 2 July 2019, <https://commons.wikimedia.org/wiki/File:Gerard_de_Jode_1593_Map_Southern_hemisphere.jpg>.

35. J. Tent, 'The ghosts of Christmas (Island) past: an examination of its early charting and naming', *Terrae Incognitae: The Journal of the Society for the History of Discoveries*, 2016, pp. 1–23, viewed 2 July 2019, <https://www.researchgate.net/publication/305646738_The_Ghosts_of_Christmas_Island_Past_An_Examination_of_its_Early_Charting_and_Naming>.

36. 'Cologne Digital Sanskrit Dictionaries: Monier-Williams Sanskrit–English Dictionary', viewed 3 March 2020, <https://www.wisdomlib.org/definition/agama>. Oxford Dictionary has the words 'agamia' and 'agami' referring to the chestnut-bellied heron of Central America, and the presence of herons on the

Indonesian islands may be the reason for the toponym 'Augama' to have been used.

37. E. Bowen, 'Carte du Voyages tres-curieux et fort remarquables, Achevees par toute L, Asie, Tartarie, Mangi, Japan, les Indes Orientales, Iles, Adjacentes Et L'Afrique. Commences l'An 1252 Par Marc Paul, Venitien', 1729.
38. Yule, vol. 2, bk III, ch. VII, note 2. They appear as on Waldseemuller's, 1507 Universalis Cosmographia as Candur and Sandur.

Chapter 3. Discovery of the Cocos (Keeling) Islands.

1. See legend on sheet 17, 'Mercator 1569 world map', viewed 26 March 2020, <https://en.wikipedia.org/wiki/Mercator_1569_world_map#legend9>. See also W. A. R. Richardson, 'An Indian Ocean Pilgrimage in Search of an Island', *The great circle*, vol. 11, no. 2, 1989, pp. 32–51.
2. Yule, vol. 2, bk 3, part VII.
3. Yule, vol. 2, bk 3, ch. XXXIII, Concerning the island of Madeigascar.
4. Anonymous, transcriptions of notes and legends on Fra Mauro's map of 1459, viewed 6 January 2020, <www.myoldmaps.com/late-medieval-maps-1300/249-fra-mauros-mappamundi/>.
5. C. Swan, 'Exotica on the move: Birds of Paradise in early modern Holland', p. 623, viewed 9 November 2021, <https://www.academia.edu/15118766/Exotica_on_the_Move_Birds_of_Paradise_in_Early_Modern_Holland>. See also A. Pigafetta, *Magellan's voyage around the world*, vol. 2, 1906 edn, p. 105, viewed 27 August 2019. <https://archive.org/details/magellansvoyagea02piga/page/180>.
6. T. Juniper, *Spix's macaw: the race to save the world's rarest bird*, Fourth Estate, London, 2002, pp. 40, 42>
7. L. Macias, 'Why does the map drawn right after the first world circumnavigation show two fantastic giant birds?', posted on 14 January 2019 in *History of cartography, navigation and discoveries*, viewed 23 December 2019, <https://historyandmaps.wordpress.com/2019/01/14/why-does-the-map-drawn-right-after-the-first-world-circumnavigation-show-two-fantastic-giant-birds/>.
8. See The journal of Syms Covington, <https://www.asap.unimelb.edu.au/bsparcs/covingto/chap_7.htm> See also J. Reid, 'Survey of the Buff-banded Rail (Rallus philippensis andrewsi)', in *Pulu Keeling National Park, Cocos Islands, Indian Ocean*, consultancy report to Parks Australia North, RM87, the author, Canberra, 2000. Mauritius had a Red Rail, now extinct. See also 'Chinese Pond Heron', viewed 30 July 2021, <https://en.wikipedia.org/wiki/Chinese_Pond_Heron>. See also https://en.wikipedia.org/wiki/Cocos_buff-banded_rail.
9. U. Marzolph, 'Arabian Nights', in K. Fleet, G. Kramer, D. Matringe, J. Nawas and E. Rowson (eds), *Encyclopaedia of Islam*, 3rd ed., 2007.
10. See W. A. R. Richardson, 'Cartographical clues to three sixteenth-century shipwrecks in the Indian Ocean', *The great circle*, vol. 14, no. 1, 1992, pp. 1–20.

11. From a poem in a journal published in H. Soeteboom (ed.), W. van West-Zanen, *Derdevoomaemste na de Oost-Indien*, Amsterdam, 1648, and translated in E. Fuller, *Dodo from extinction to icon*, Collins, London, 2002, p. 56.
12. J. Forshaw, *Parrots of the world*, Landsdowne Editions, Willoughby, NSW, 1989, p. 307. See also M. Cotti, 'Pappagalli Estinta', viewed 3 March 2020, <https://es-la.facebook.com/notes/marco-cotti/pappagalli-estinti/2360163854010510/>.
13. J. Long, P. Vickers-Rich, K. Hirsch, E. Bray and C. Tuniz, 'The Cervantes egg: an early Malagasy tourist to Australia', *Records of the Western Australian Museum*, vol. 19, 1998, pp. 39–46, viewed 23 December 2019, <museum.wa.gov.au/sites/default/files/THE%20CERVANTES%20EGG%20AN%20EARLY%20MALAGSY%20TOURIST%20TO%20AUSTRALIA.pdf>.
14. 'Anonymous, ZSL names world's largest ever bird – *Vorombe titan*', ZSL Institute of Zoology, 26 September 2018, viewed 23 December 2019, <https://www.zsl.org/science/news/zsl-names-world's-largest-ever-bird-–-vorombe-titan>.
15. H. G. Wells, *Aepyornis Island*, viewed 9 October 2021, <www.online-literature.com/wellshg/1>. Wells was welcomed in Perth by the WA Fellowship of Writers in 1938 as 'the seer with a vision of the shape of things to come'. See Norman Bartlett, 'Science, Sex and Mr Wells', *Westerly*, June 1978.
16. C. Allibert, cited in B. Gunn, L. Baudouin and K. Olsen, *Independent origins of cultivated coconut (Cocos nucifera L.) in the old-world tropics*, 2011, viewed 2 July 2019, <https://doi.org/10.1371/journal.pone.0021143>.
17. K. Olsen, in *Independent origins*. See also D. Lutz, 'Deep history of coconuts decoded', *The Source*, Washington University in St Louis, 2011, viewed 2 July 2019, <https://source.wustl.edu/2011/06/deep-history-of-coconuts-decoded/>. Clunies-Ross exported coconut oil in 1829, which indicates that the established palms were not of the Pacific variety.
18. Anonymous, 'The seed salting experiments of Charles Darwin', *Awkward Botany*, 2 May 2018, viewed 9 November 2020, <https://awkwardbotany.com/2018/05/02/the-seed-salting-experiments-of-charles-darwin/>. See also J. Costa, *Darwin's backyard. How small experiments led to a big theory*, W. W. Norton & Company, New York, 2017.
19. Darwin, quoted in A. Keith, *Darwin revalued*, Watts & Co. London, p. 115. See C. Darwin, *Journal of researches into the natural history and geology of the countries visited during the voyage of H.M.S. Beagle round the world, under the Command of Capt. Fitz Roy, R.N.*, 2nd edn, John Murray, London, 1845, p. 454, viewed 2 July 2019, <http://darwin-online.org.uk/content/frameset?itemID=F14&viewtype=text&pageseq=1>.
20. P. Armstrong, *Under the blue vault of heaven: a study of Darwin's sojourn in the Cocos (Keeling) Islands*, Indian Ocean Centre for Peace Studies, Nedlands, 1991, p. 37, viewed 24 November 2020, <http://darwin-online.org.uk/content/frameset?itemID=A588&viewtype=text&pageseq=1>.
21. J. Dana, *Corals and coral islands*, 3rd edn, Dodd Mead, New York, 1890, p. 327.

22. H. Guppy, 'The dispersal of plants as illustrated by the flora of the Keeling or Cocos Islands', Victoria Institute lecture, 1890, p. 5, viewed 2 July 2019, <https://babel.hathitrust.org/cgi/pt?id=hvd.32044106359169;view=1up;seq=1>.
23. Darwin, in his *Voyage of the Beagle*, quotes Holman's *A voyage round the world*, vol. 4, p. 378. Balci is not in the *Indonesia Gazetteer*. See <<https://indonesia.places-in-the-world.com/>.
24. Darwin regarded Liesk as 'very intelligent', and 'intimately acquainted with every part of this reef, and likewise with that of North Keeling atoll'. Guppy wrote of Darwin 'Deriving his information [on North Keeling] from Mr Liesk in 1836', in his 'The Cocos-Keeling Islands'. Reprinted from the *Scottish Geographical Magazine*, June 1889, p. 14, viewed 15 September 2022, <https://access.bl.uk/item/viewer/ark:/81055/vdc_0000000151F2#?c=0&m=0&s=0&cv=17&xywh=95%2C470%2C1913%2C1500>.
25. C. Darwin, 'Notes on the geology and corals of Keeling Islands', 4.1836, CUL-DAR41. 40–57, transcribed and edited by Alistair Sponsel, viewed 1 December 2020, <http://darwin-online.org.uk/content/frameset?viewtype=side&itemID=CUL-DAR41.40-57&pageseq=1>, p. 14 verso. It might have been expected that the greenstone sample would have been placed in the Sedgwick Museum of Earth Sciences collection in Cambridge, but Collections Manager Dan Pemberton advises that it is not shown on their records. Darwin advised mineral collectors to: 'Put a number on every specimen, and every fragment of a specimen; and during the very same minute let it be entered in the catalogue, so that if hereafter its locality be doubted, the collector may say in good truth, "Every specimen of mine was ticketed on the spot". Any thing which is folded up in paper, or put into a separate box, ought to have a number on the outside (with the exception perhaps of geological specimens), but more especially a duplicate number on the inside attached to the specimen itself'. Cited by D. Bressan, 'How Charles Darwin classified his mineral collection', viewed 13 November 2020, <https://www.forbes.com/sites/davidbressan/2016/04/20/how-charles-darwin-classified-his-mineral-collection/?sh=1bf9b4ff381c>. Darwin's notebook words regarding plural rocks on the Cocos are puzzling, but they were simply his field notes – thoughts he had as he went about his tasks for the day, rather than his considered opinion. He mentions greenstone rocks in the same sentence as his reference to earthquakes, implying that he saw an association between earthquakes and greenstone. Then he appears to say that one of these rocks (which he never saw) was found in the sand-breccia on an island. He has added, in a pencilled circle, the words 'NB. Greenstone Rock. brought by roots of trees', as an apparent afterthought. The impression given is that, after reflection about how plant varieties might migrate to distant islands, he has concluded that floating trees had the potential to carry stones, entangled in their roots, to these islands. However, the later reference, in his *Journal of researches*, to the 'one block of greenstone' appears to contradict his notebook entry about a number of greenstone rocks on the 'Northern Islands'

(North Keeling and Horsburgh?) of Cocos. The notes provide an insight to his hypothesis generation process.
26. C. Lyell, *Principles of geology*, Appleton and Co., New York, 1854. Patrick Armstrong's Figure 11 shows coral rock with 'petrified' corals on the outer beach of West Island, another example of coral breccia. Darwin noted that Clunies-Ross had found the greenstone embedded in the conglomerate. In Clunies-Ross' absence from the island, Liesk would have told Darwin of this. The words could mean 'to lay in a bed of mixed ingredients', or conversely 'to be cemented into a coral conglomerate'. If it took decades for that boulder to become 'embedded', it would rule out the *Earl of Liverpool* as the source. In some environments, concretions grow quite rapidly. Henderson has seen a modern-design 1990s? toy car, part diecast metal and part plastic, thickly embedded in a matrix of rock-hard cement. The item had been lying buried under an exposed section of ocean shoreline at Leighton Beach, just north of Fremantle.
27. D. Bressan, 'How Charles Darwin classified his mineral collection', forbes.com.
28. W. Norton, 'A classification of breccias', *The Journal of Geology*, University of Chicago Press, vol. 25, no. 2, Feb. – Mar. 1917, pp. 160–94, 1917, viewed 8 December 2020, <https://www.jstor.org/stable/30060966?seq=1>.
29. C. Darwin, *Journal of researches into the natural history and geology of the countries visited during the voyage of HMS Beagle round the world, under the command of Capt. Fitzroy, R.N.*, 2nd edn, John Murray, London, 1845, p. 461.
30. Darwin, *Journal of researches*, p. 465.
31. Darwin, *Journal of researches*, p. 493.
32. Guppy, *The Cocos-Keeling Islands*, pp. 5–9, viewed 2 July 2019, <access.bl.uk/item/pdf/lsidyv3756a1b1>.
33. Footnote by Darwin, in G. Bettany (ed.), *Charles Darwin's coral reefs, volcanic islands and South American Geology, The Minerva Library of Famous Books*, Ward, Lock and Co, London 1890, p. 89.
34. Patrick Armstrong, pers. comm. See C. Darwin, *On the origin of species by means of natural selection, or the preservation of favoured races in the struggle for life*. John Murray, London, 1859, chs 11 and 12, viewed 13 November 2020, <http://darwin-online.org.uk/converted/pdf/1861_OriginNY_F382.pdf>. See also R. Winkworth, 'Darwin and dispersal', *Biology International*, vol. 47, pp. 139–44, viewed 13 November 2020, <https://www.researchgate.net/publication/258120865_Darwin_and_Dispersal>
35. 'Greenstone', viewed 13 November 2020, <https://en.wikipedia.org/wiki/Greenstone_(archaeology)>. See also W. Whitecar, *Four years aboard the whaleship: embracing cruises in the Pacific, Atlantic, Indian, and Antarctic Oceans*, Lippincott & Co., Philadelphia, 1860, p. 114. <https://archive.org/details/fouryearsaboardw00whitrich>.
36. R. Hall, in *Empires of the monsoon*, Harper Collins, 1998, p. 81, states that part of Zheng's fourth expedition fleet was detached near Sumatra and sailed straight across the Indian Ocean to East Africa on 'the route taken centuries before by the

Waqwaqs'. An account, possibly fictitious, by *Ajayeb al-Hind* refers to an invasion in Tanganyika and Mozambique by people called Wakwak or Waqwaq, perhaps the Malay people of Srivijaya or Javanese people of Medang kingdom, in 945–946 CE, viewed 18 November 2021, <https://en.wikipedia.org/wiki/Al-Wakwak>

37. See G. Henderson, *Unfinished voyages: Western Australian shipwrecks 1622–1850*, 2nd edn, University of Western Australia Press, Nedlands, 2007, pp. 184–7.
38. Holman, p. 382. See also Henderson, *Unfinished voyages*, 2nd edn, p. 184.
39. Henderson, *Unfinished voyages*, pp. 184–86.
40. T. Pearton and M. Viljoen, 'Antimony mineralisation in the Murchison Greenstone Belt', *Mineral deposits of Southern Africa*, 1986, pp. 293–320, viewed 27 December 2020, <https://www.researchgate.net/publication/309236862>.
41. Visiting naturalist Henry Forbes wrote that 'Mr Leisk, who was in charge, showed Mr Darwin over the place and gave him a great deal of information, but though given in good faith, much of it was not quite accurate'. *A naturalist's wanderings in the eastern archipelago*, London, 1885, p. 15, viewed 4 December 2020, <https://archive.org/details/naturalistquots00Forb>.
42. The Mineral and Gemstone Kingdom, 'The mineral antimony', viewed 12 November 2020, <https://www.minerals.net/mineral/antimony.aspx>.
43. Maps of the Dieppe School have received criticism from some historians because they also include the landmass titled 'Jave la Grande', suggesting Portuguese exploration of Australia in the sixteenth century, well before the Dutch explorations. E. Scott (*Australian discovery by sea*, London, Dent, 1929, vol. 1, pp. xi–xii) and R. King (*Mapping our world: discovery day*, National Library of Australia, 10 November 2013, 'JAVE LA GRANDE, A PART OF TERRA AUSTRALIS?' viewed 2 August 2020, <https://www.anzmaps.org/wp-content/uploads/other_publications/JaveLaGrande-King.pdf>) have criticised the makers of the Dieppe maps for their portrayal of Java Major, but those particular criticisms do not invalidate the Dieppe School presentation of other Indian Ocean islands.
44. P. Desceliers, 'Map of the world, 1546', viewed 12 April 2022, <https://johannes.library.manchester.ac.uk/luna/servlet/detail/maps002~1~1~1968~118509?qvq=q:desceliers&mi=11&trs=32>.
45. 'The Harleian Mappemonde', British Library, Add. MS 5413, copy held by the National Library of Australia. See also, 'Theory of the Portuguese discovery of Australia', viewed 10 March 2016, <https://en.wikipedia.org/wiki/Theory_of_the_Portuguese_discovery_of_Australia#/media/File:Harleian.jpg>. It may be stretching it to read desponoada as 'despenhadeiro', meaning a precipice – the edge of the world.
46. P. Desceliers, 'Map of the world, 1550', Add. MS 24065, British Library, viewed 7 August 2020, <https://commons.wikimedia.org/wiki/File:Map_of_the_world_-_Pierre_Desceliers,_1550_-_BL_Add_MS_24065.jpg>. Another possibility, which matches reasonably the image on the Desceliers map, is 'pouldron', from the Spanish 'espandaron' meaning a shoulder plate of one piece,

introduced in the reign of England's and France's Henry VI (between 1422 and 1471).

47. The island is reincorporated with the Chagos-Laccadive Ridge as 'Poueada' in Abraham Ortelius' 1570 world map. Library of Congress, viewed 23 March 2020, <https://upload.wikimedia.org/wikipedia/commons/e/e2/OrteliusWorldMap1570.jpg>. De Jode's 1578 map depicts three islands southwest of Java marked Condur and Proban. Plancius' 1594 map, similar to the Mercator map, shows an island named Poulada west of Sunda Strait. See G. Mercator, 'New and more complete representation of the terrestrial globe properly adapted for use in navigation', 1569, viewed 23 March 2020, <https://upload.wikimedia.org/wikipedia/commons/2/22/Mercator_1569_world_map_sheet_11.PNG>. See also G. Masselman, *The cradle of colonialism*, Yale University Press, Newhaven, 1963, p. 67, viewed 23 March 2020, <https://archive.org/details/cradleofcolonial0000mass/mode/1up>. See also <http://www.atlascoelestis.com/desu%20Plancius.htm>, regarding Plancius' use of Gallus, the rooster, in navigating south of the Tropic of Capricorn. The term 'pollarde', meaning young fattened hen, was used in 1562; see <https://www.cnrtl.fr/lexicographie/poularde>.

48. G. Rouffaer and J. Ijzerman (eds), *De eerste schipvaart der Nederlanders naar Oost-Indië onder Cornelis de Houtman, 1595–1597*, vol. 3, p. 366, viewed 23 March 2020, <https://archive.org/details/deeersteschipvaa03rouf/page/n16/mode/2up>.

49. J. Linschoten, *Iohn Huighen van Linschoten his Discours of voyages into ye Easte & West Indies: deuided into foure books*, John Wolfe, London, 1598, viewed 8 January 2020, <https://www.loc.gov/resource/rbc0001.2007kis1964006000001/?sp=36>.

50. J. Hondius, 'A new description of Asia', from the special collection China in Maps, of the Hong Kong University of Science and Technology Library, Hong Kong 2003, viewed 19 March 2020, <https://commons.wikimedia.org/wiki/File:CEM-19-Asiae-nova-description-1610-Jodocus-Hondius-2538.jpg>. Hondius may have been referring to Cornelis Ceullen's 1596, Houtman voyage, noting of Polvera/Poluara.

51. J. Bruijn, F. Gaastra and I. Schoffer (eds), *Dutch-Asiatic shipping in the 17th and 18th centuries*, vols 1–3. Martinus Nijhoff, The Hague, 1987, p. 72, viewed 2 July 2019, <http://resources.huygens.knaw.nl/retroboeken/das/#page=90&accessor=toc&source=1>.

52. Schilder, p. 20.

53. J. Heeres in his *The part borne by the Dutch in the discovery of Australia 1606–1765*, London, 1899, p. 9, cautioned that 'at times in subsequent issues of certain charts the dates given in the first issue were retained, while numerous corrections were made in the chart itself'. However, such criticism does not appear to have been levelled at Gerritsz's 1612 world map.

54. National Library of Australia, *Mapping our world: Terra Incognita to Australia*, National Library, Canberra, 2013, p. 119.

55. H. Gerritsz, 'Chart of the Indian Ocean 't Amsterdam, 1622', State Library of New South Wales, M M1 990/1622/1, viewed 2 July 2019, <http://digital.

sl.nsw.gov.au/delivery/DeliveryManagerServlet?embedded=true&toolbar=false&dps_pid=IE3775991>.

56. See Schilder, p. 301. Gerritsz's introduction of the term 'Cocos' to the 1622 map is important for an unfortunate reason: many other islands were similarly named and this led to confusion among cartographers. For example, a Dutch chart by Braam (1726) shows 'de Cocos Eylanden' as six islands forming a semicircle with 'I Moni' (Christmas Island) close by and, south of Sunda Strait, 'I Zelam' and 'I Christina' both representing Christmas Island. This chart also shows a 'Cocos I' north of the Andaman Islands, 'Cocos' west of Sumatra, and 'Cocus Hooft' on the south side of Java.

57. Rosalia Di Nisio, pers. comm.

58. See Poule de Polverara, viewed 2 April 2020, <https://www.wikizero.com/fr/Poule_de_Polverara>, citing:

i). Bernardino Scardeone, *Bernardini Scardeonii, canonici Patavini, De antiqvitate vrbis Patavii, and claris ciuibus Patauinis, libri tres, in quindecim classes distincti. Eivsdem appendix De sepvlchris insignibvs exterorvm Patavii iacentivm ... Baseleae, apvd Nicolaum Episcopium iuniorem*, 1560, p.17, *Hujus territorium frumento et lino is exuberantissimum, and gallinarum mirae magnitudinis copia supramomomomoitatum: praesertim in pulverario pagosi oppido propinquo.*

ii). Alessandro Tassoni, *La secchia: poema eroicomico by Androvinci Melisone. Con gli argomenti del can. Alber. Baris. Aggiuntoui in ultimo il primo canto de l'oceano del medesimo autore Paris*, 1622, 1830 edn, p.136... *Polverara, dov'è il regno de' galli e la sementa famosa in ogni parte.*

59. Director of National Parks, *Pulu Keeling National Park Management Plan 2015–2025*, Commonwealth of Australia, 2015, p. 37, viewed 2 May 2020, <https://www.environment.gov.au/system/files/resources/83e459f1-dc59-4fcc-9255-2bbb9cc23951/files/pknp-management-plan-web-v1.2.pdf>.

60. Fondation Bertarelli, 'Marine science research continues in the Indian Ocean', 10 July 2019, viewed 29 June 2020, <https://www.fondation-bertarelli.org/marine-science-research-continues-in-the-indian-ocean/>. See also Ramsar Wetlands Information Sheet, viewed 10 June 2019, <http://www.ukotcf.org/pdf/Ramsar/61BIOT.pdf>.

61. S. Bown, *A most damnable invention*, Penguin Books, Camberwell, Victoria, 2007, p. 2.

62. W. Dampier, 'His voyage from Achin in Sumatra to Tonquin and other places in the East Indies', in *A collection of voyages*, vol. 11.1, James Knapton, London, 1729 (2), p. 11, viewed 10 December 2019, <www.canadiana.ca/view/oocihm.29536/208?r=0&s=4>.

63. W. Dampier, 'Mr Dampier's voyages to the Bay of Campeachy', in *A collection of voyages*, vol. 11.11, James Knapton, London, 1729 (3).

64. P. Mortier, 'Carte des Costes de L'Asie sur L'Ocean Contenant les Bancs Isles et Costes etc: levee sur les memoires les plus nouveau; Partie Orientale de L'Asie sur L'Ocean', 1700?, MAP RM 3465, National Library of Australia.

65. F. Danvers, in Letters received by the East India Company, vol. 1: 1602–1613, London, 1896, viewed 2 July 2019, <https://archive.org/stream/lettersreceivedb01east#page/n4/mode/1up>. See also H. Gray, *Spice at any price, the life and times of Frederick de Houtman 1571–1627*, Westralian Books, Geraldton, 2019, for an account of the voyage.
66. S. Purchas, Purchas His Pilgrimes, vol. 1, printed by William Stansby for Henrie Fetherstone, London, 1625, p. 188, viewed 2 July 2019, <https://books.google.com.au/books?id=0jSN5RNaVNkC&printsec=frontcover&source=gbs_ge_summary_r&cad=0#v=onepage&q&f=false>.
67. R. Kerr (ed.), 'Third voyage of the English East India Company, in 1607, by Captain William Keeling', in *Early voyages of the English to India, after the establishment of the East India Company*, vol. VIII, ch. X, sect. IV, 1824, viewed 2 July 2019, <http://www.columbia.edu/itc/mealac/pritchett/00generallinks/kerr/vol08chap10sect04.html>.
68. A. & V. Palmer, *Who's who in Shakespeare's England*, St. Martin's Press, New York, 1981, p. 138.
69. B. Kliman, 'At sea about Hamlet at sea: a detective story', *Shakespeare Quarterly*, vol. 62, no. 2, 2011, pp. 180–204, 2011, viewed 2 July 2019, <http://muse.jhu.edu/article/446527/pdf>.
70. Purchas, 1625, bk 6, p. 203.
71. T. Mutch, 'The first discovery of Australia, with an account of the voyage of the *Duyfken* and the career of Captain Willem Jansz', reprinted from *Journal of the Royal Australian Historical Society*, vol. 28, no. 5, 1942, p. 20, viewed 2 June 2019, <http://gutenberg.net.au/ebooks06/0600631h.html>.
72. Purchas, 1625, p. 204.
73. S. Dunn, *A new directory for the East Indies*, 5th edn, London, 1780, p. 380.
74. A. Dalrymple, 'A collection of plans of ports in the East Indies', [microform], published by A. Dalrymple in 1774 and 1775, vol. 5, chart 160, Library of New South Wales, viewed 2 July 2019, <http://digital.sl.nsw.gov.au/delivery/DeliveryManagerServlet?embedded=true&toolbar=false&dps_pid=IE3800936>.
75. J. van Keulen, 'Sea chart of Sumatra, the Malacca Straits, the islands of Singapore, Banca, Sunda and surrounding islands', in the sixth volume of *Lichtende Zee-Fakkel*, the great sea atlas begun by his grandfather Johannes, 1753 (1), viewed 2 June 2019, <http://nla.gov.au/nla.obj-232434475>.
76. P. van der Aa, *Der hollanderen eerste scheepstogt na Oost-Indien onder den Hr. Cornelis Houtman gedaan in't Iaar 1595 = Le premier voyage par Mer des Hollandois aux Indes Orientales, fait en l'an 1595, sous le commandement de Corneille Houtman, avec les routes marquées, suivant la description qu'il en a donnée, conferée avec les cartes les plus correctes, qui en ont été faites sur les lieux, de nouveau mis au jour / par Pierre vander Aa, à Leide, avec privilege*, 1714?, viewed 2 July 2019, <https://nla.gov.au/nla.obj-232523439/view>.
77. W. Dampier, *A voyage to New Holland, etc. in the year 1699*, 3rd edn, James and John Knapton, London, 1729 (1), viewed 3 July 2019, <http://gutenberg.net.au/ebooks/

e00046.html>. See also J. Thornton, *A new map of the world, 1700*, Library of Congress, viewed 2 July 2019, <https://www.loc.gov/resource/g3201pm.gct00234/?sp=8&r=0.752,0.477,0.103,0.043,0>.

78. R. Dudley, *Dell' Arcano del Mare* (The Secret of the Sea), self-published, 1646, viewed 2 July 2019, <https://en.wikipedia.org/wiki/Dell%27Arcano_del_Mare>.
79. Rosalia Di Nisio, pers. comm.
80. It is less likely that Dudley's islands were based on islands at the north end of the Andaman Islands, named the Coco Islands by the Portuguese in the sixteenth century. Those islands, also marked 'I; di Cocos' on Dudley's *Asia Carta V*, are of a similar longitude to the Cocos (Keeling) Islands but lie in the northern hemisphere. If Dudley's engraver had to rely on loose sheets of information assembled by Dudley, it is conceivable that the relevant hemisphere was not provided to the engraver. Van Keulen's 1753 chart of Cocos Eylanden (Figure 35), lying beside Siberut Island off the south coast of Sumatra, is geographically the closest like-named group to the Cocos (Keeling) Islands. It is in a similar longitude, and bears some cartographic resemblance, but was probably engraved well after Dudley's charts.
81. Gerritsz was not the first to mark this phantom island. With a variation in the spelling (Poulada) Petrus Plancius shows such an island in c 12° south on his 1594 'Orbis Plancius' map, viewed 2 June 2019, <https://commons.wikimedia.org/wiki/File:1594_Orbis_Plancius_2,12_MB.jpg>. Waldseemuller, in 1516, labelled as Iona a similar shaped island close to Poueada.
82. Dudley was also perhaps antagonistic towards the Dutch because of his father's unpopularity as Lord Regent of the Netherlands after William of Orange's assassination, leading him to attribute discoveries to the English rather than the Dutch.
83. See J. Henderson, *Phantoms of the Tryall*, St George Books, Perth, 1993. See also J. Green, 'Australia's oldest wreck: the loss of the *Trial 1622*', *BAR Supplementary Series 27*, Oxford, 1977, p. 8.
84. In Gerritsz's 1627 chart, the upright sock above a group of rocks can be seen, in a roughly similar alignment to that later depicted by Dudley. Later mapmakers continued the idea. See the 1747 map by Emmanuel Bowen, titled 'A new and accurate map of all the known world', plate 90, in William Innys et al., *A complete system of geography*, London, viewed 15 September 2021, <https://searchworks.stanford.edu/view/10448789>. This map shows the toponym 'Cocos' beside a group of three or more islands in approximately 20° south, off the northwest coast of Australia in the location of Trial Rocks, which were discovered by the English. Bowen had conflated the Cocos (Keeling) Islands with Trial Rocks, as Dudley may also have done previously.
85. C. Darwin, *Journal of researches*, p. 462, viewed 2 July 2019, <http://darwin-online.org.uk/content/frameset?itemID=F14&viewtype=text&pageseq=1>. See also A. Wulf, *The invention of nature. The adventures of Alexander von Humboldt*, John Murray, London, p. 223.

86. C. Darwin, *The structure and distribution of coral reefs. Being the first part of the geology of the voyage of the Beagle, under the command of Capt. Fitzroy, R.N. during the years 1832 to 1836,* Smith Elder & Co., London, 1842, viewed 16 September 2019, <darwin-online.org.uk/content/frameset?pageseq=1&itemID=F271&viewtype=side>.
87. Darwin, 1845, pp. 476–7.
88. J. Veron, 'Re-examination of the reef corals of Cocos (Keeling) Atoll', in *Records of the Western Australian Museum*, vol. 14, no 4, 1990, pp. 553–81.
89. Trish Flores, acting chief ranger Pulu Keeling National Park, pers. comm., 26 September 2019. Earthquakes and tsunamis have produced distinctive igneous rock formations that might also be termed 'rills' on the Coco Islands in the Bay of Bengal. (See P. Chakrabarti et al., 'Earthquake and tsumani effects, Andaman Islands, India', in *Geomatrics in tsunami*, S. Ramasamy, et al. (eds), Department of Science and Technology, New Delhi, 2006, p. 43). If Dudley transposed the Coco Islands to the location of the Cocos (Keeling) Islands, he was not alone in such confusion. Wood-Jones (1912, p. 4) wrote that 'the Cocos of treasure fame, the Cocos in the Andaman group, the Cocos off the west coast of Sumatra, and other smaller islands so named from their bearing coconut palms are apt to be confounded with this atoll'.
90. Darwin, 1845, p. 459.
91. It is also possible that he was referring to a small rivulet on Christmas Island. Some maps produced in the 1630s and 1660s show 'Cocos Eyland' in the location of Christmas Island, making it difficult to know which of the two island groups was being referred to. See Schilder, 1976, p. 329.
92. The Cocos (Keeling) Islands were uninhabited until the nineteenth century and there is no obvious indication in the records that the Coco Islands were violent places. Polo has been cited (C. Van Duzer, 'Hic sunt dracones: the geography and cartography of monsters', in A. S. Mittman and P. J. Dendle (eds), *The Ashgate research companion to monsters and the monstrous*) as saying that the inhabitants were cannibals, but Dampier understood that two friars sent to convert the natives reported that they were 'very honest, civil, harmless people; that they were not addicted to quarrelling, theft, or murder'. In 1522 a pilot told Pigafetta that the women, on an island 'below Java' named Ocoloro, habitually killed all males born or visiting there. Writers have conjectured disparately that Ocoloro represents the small island of Enggano, or part of the continent of Terra Australis (Yule: book ii, p. 340). However, it is unlikely that Ocoloro was seen by Dudley as another manifestation of the phantom island 'Polverara', the upright-sock-shaped island that he apparently placed above his triangle of islands representing South Keeling Islands.
93. The Dordtse Kil in South Holland was a small tidal creek until the nineteenth century. There is a Bronx Kill between the Bronx and Randalls Island in an area of Dutch influence in the Hudson and Delaware Valleys in the United States. See <https://en.wikipedia.org/wiki/Kill_(body_of_water)>, viewed 12 April 2022.
94. Atholl Anderson, pers. comm.

95. C. Edmondson, 'Viability of coconut seeds after floating in sea', *Bernice P. Bishop Museum Occasional Papers*. vol. 16, 1941, pp. 293–304. See <https://en.wikipedia.org/wiki/File:Chronological_dispersal_of_Austronesian_people_across_the_Pacific_(per_Benton_et_al,_2012,_adapted_from_Bellwood,_2011).png>, viewed 12 April 2022.

Chapter 4. Exploration of the Cocos (Keeling) Islands

1. Thornton, 'A new map of the world'.
2. Paradise Lost (1667)/Book II – Wikisource, the free online library, lines 630–653. See <https://emuseum.org/objects/80/Illustration 2 to Milton's "Paradise Lost": Satan, Sin, and Death: Satan Comes to the Gates of Hell>. See also The Flying Dutchman (Wagner), <https://www.musicwithease.com/flying-dutchman-source.html>. For one present day Christian interpretation of some of the themes see 'The lord of the monsoon: as the tide of world attention shifts to the Indian Ocean so must the mission of the church (michaelmilton.org)', viewed 20 April 2022 <https://michaelmilton.org/2012/04/20/the-lord-of-the-monsoon-as-the-tide-of-world-attention-shifts-to-the-indian-ocean-so-must-the-mission-of-the-church/>.
3. D. and M. Preston, *A pirate of exquisite mind. the life of William Dampier*, Corgi Books, London, 2004, p. 454.
4. J. Bach, Dampier, William (1651–1715), *Australian dictionary of biography*, National Centre of Biography, Australian National University, 1966, viewed 2 July 2019, <http://adb.anu.edu.au/biography/dampier-william-1951/text2345>. See also J. Swift, 'Gulliver's travels', in *Gulliver's travels and other writings*, The Riverside Press 1960 edn, Cambridge, Mass., 1726, viewed 2 June 2019, <http://www.gutenberg.org/cache/epub/17157/pg17157-images.epub?session_id=e3ebf4b88205e68f553c721d301e788e7e6822d3>.
5. 'Where the "little people" of Ireland came from', *Irish Central*, viewed 28 December 2020, <https://www.irishcentral.com/roots/where-the-little-people-of-ireland-came-from-96552649-237700421>. Samuel Dunn's Plate 4 shows Houyhnhnms Land not far from Lewins Land at the southwest corner of the State, and Edels Land which runs north of Fremantle to include the Abrolhos.
6. E. A. Poe, 'Ms found in a bottle', *Baltimore Saturday Visiter,* 19 October 1833.
7. Poe, 'Ms Found in a Bottle'.
8. S. Saenz-Lopez Perez, *Marginalia in cartography*, Exhibition at the Chazen Museum of Art, Madison, February 28–May 18, 2014, p. 24, viewed 21 November 2021, <https://www.academia.edu/6249602/Marginalia_in_cARTography>. See H. Moll, 'Map of Lilliput and Blefuscu', 1726, British Library, viewed 7 July 2019, <https://www.bl.uk/collection-items/map-of-lilliput-and-blefuscu>. See also F. Bracher, 'The maps in "Gulliver's Travels"', Huntington Library Quarterly, vol. 8, pp. 59–74, 1944. Moll has written 'Discovered A.D. 1699' beside his islands so it may be that he also had in mind Dampier's visit to Shark Bay in August 1699.
9. Pigafetta, vol. 2, p. 161. See also B. Douglas, 'Terra Australis to Oceania', *The Journal of Pacific History*, vol. 45, no. 2, 2010, p. 187, viewed 3 December 2021,

<http://dx.doi.org/10.1080/00223344.2010.501696>. C. Braga notes that Greek historian Strabo referred to a Ptolemaic myth of 'men with ears like beds', in her 'Marvelous India in medieval European representations', viewed 3 December 2021, <https://rupkatha.com/marvelous-india-medieval-european-representations/>.

10. T. Sutikna, 'Revised stratigraphy and chronology for Homo floresiensis at Liang Bua in Indonesia', *Nature*, vol. 532, pp. 366–9, 30 March 2016.
11. J. Harley, 'Deconstructing the map', *Cartographica*, vol. 26, no. 2, 1989, pp.1–20.
12. G. Silo, 'Compass chart of the Kokos Islands'.
13. Gerhard de Kok, Facebook Fortuyn Project page, 28 January 1015.
14. Open Archives, Godlob Silo on 3 October 1752 in the Service of the Dutch East India Company, Nationaal Archief (Netherlands), Dutch East India Company, archive 1.04.02, inventory number 62860, folio 3, viewed 2 June 2019, <https://www.openarch.nl/ghn:258f1502-eaf5-49bf-9946-f158e4647e11/en>.
15. Open Archives, Jan de Marre on May 10, 1728, in the service of the Dutch East India Company, viewed 2 June 2019, <https://www.openarch.nl/ghn:f93396c8-de03-4847-86f1-2552d8e32fe8/en>.
16. I. Schoffer, P. Emmer and D. Kolff, *Editorial Committee Intercontinenta Series*, Centre for the History of European Expansion, Leiden, undated, p. 108, viewed 15 September 2022, <https://scholarlypublications.universiteitleiden.nl/access/item:31401...>. See also Bruijn et al., vol. II, p. 541 and vol. III, p. 415.
17. Open Archives, Silo.
18. The *Gleanings in Science* editor, clearly influenced by John Clunies-Ross, wrote that 'Mr Hare was attended by a number of followers, including women and children, originally, it appears, enslaved people, but manumitted in consequence of our abolition laws'. John Clunies-Ross, 'Some account of the Cocos or Keeling Islands; and of their recent settlement', *Gleanings in Science*, Baptist Mission Press, Calcutta, pp. 293–301, October 1830, viewed 1 January 2021, <https://archive.org/details/gleaningsscienc2>. Manumission was the formal freeing of enslaved people before the end of the slave system. Darwin commented that, 'The Malay slaves [belonging to Mr Hare] ran away from the Isd on which Mr Hare was settled and joined Capt. Ross's party ... The Malays are now nominally in a state of freedom, and certainly so as far as respects their personal treatment; but in most other points they are considered as slaves.' R. Keynes (ed.), *Charles Darwin's Beagle diary*, Cambridge University Press, Cambridge, p. 414. Captain Fitzroy commented that 'they are still slaves, and only less ill-used than they were by the man who purchased them'. See Armstrong, p. 54.
19. Eckeberg cited on Dalrymple chart 160. Accepting Eckeberg's 1' to mean 1 nautical mile, his description of North Keeling Island is of an island 5–6 miles by 3–4 miles, whereas the Management Plan records the island today as 2 kilometres long and 1.3 kilometres wide. In other respects (latitude and disposition of the two groups) the description fits that of the Cocos (Keeling) Islands.
20. J. van Keulen, Map of the Cocos Islands showing rhumb lines. From De Nieuwe Groote Lichtende Zee-Fakkel / by een gebragt en opgestelt door Jan de Marre,

... in 't Licht gebragt door Joannes van Keulen, 1753 National Library of Australia Digital Collection, viewed 2 June 2019, <https://catalogue.nla.gov.au/Record/3081704>.

21. B. Flon, van Keulen family history, 2018, viewed 2 July 2019, <http://lushergallery.com/van-keulen-family-history>. Several men with that name were employed by the VOC (Open Archives, Jan de Marre). Woodroffe (p. 1) attributes the map to the navigator Jan de Marre in 1729, following Guppy who stated that: 'Mr. G. D. Bom, a member of the firm that has succeeded the ancient house of the van Keulens of Amsterdam, informs me that it was made in 1729–30 by Jan de Marre, the noted Dutch navigator and poet, when in command of the *Heesburg*. I have, however, not yet obtained the necessary reference'. Guppy, 1889, p. 16.

22. See Dunn, 1780, p. 380. In the 1770s Dunn was appointed as a mathematics examiner for the EIC. Describing himself as a teacher of mathematics and master of longitude, he published works under the company's auspices including *The navigators guide to the Oriental or Indian Seas, or the description and use of a Variation Chart of the Magnetic Needle* (1775).

23. Anonymous, 'Dalrymple, Alexander, (1737–1808)', *Australian dictionary of biography*, vol. 1, MUP, 1966, viewed 2 July 2019, <http://adb.anu.edu.au/biography/dalrymple-alexander-1949?>.

24. C. Simpson, 'The East Indies', *The National Library of Australia Magazine*, September 2014, pp. 24–6.

25. Dalrymple's full text reads 'View of the Keeling, or Cocos, Islands; by c.g Ekeberg, 19th Jan.y 1749. a. Red Rock with a Reef stretching to the SE ab.t1'. b. The Northmost Shoar overgrown wth Coconut Trees. c. Some Rocks above-water. d. Here supposed to be shoal water, being discoloured. e. An higher Island about 4 lea. s dis.t. f. The smallest 5 or 6 leagues'.

26. S. Dunn, *A general map of the world*, 1794, viewed 2 July 2019, <https://nla.gov.au/nla.obj-232160746/view>.

27. R. Fitzroy, *Narrative of the surveying voyages of His Majesty's Ships* Adventure *and* Beagle *between the years 1826 and 1836, describing their examination of the southern shores of South America, and the Beagle's circumnavigation of the globe. Proceedings of the second expedition, 1831–36, under the command of Captain Robert Fitzroy, R.N.*, Henry Colburn, London, 1839, pp. 630–2, viewed 2 July 2019, <https://archive.org/details/narrativeofsurve02king/page/632>.

28. 'circumstantial evidence', *The Free Dictionary*, viewed 2 July 2019, <https://legaldictionary.thefreedictionary.com/circumstantial+evidence>.

29. S. Fremantle, 'HMS Juno, Account of the Origins and Progress, 1857', Australian Joint Copying Project, Reel 2712, Adm 125/135. Fremantle's reference to Dutch shipwreck survivors living on the islands then going to Padang is probably derived from his reading of James Holman's travel book, *A voyage round the world*, vol. 4, London, 1834. Holman told the story of Arthur Keating, who lived on the Cocos (Keeling) Islands with the crew of the brig *Mauritius* (wrecked in 1825) and got away by vessel, going to Padang in November 1829. In referring

to the buccaneers of South America having named the Cocos (Keeling) Islands, Captain Fremantle was conflating a story about the pirate Captain William Thompson, who in 1820 was thought to have buried the 'treasure of Lima' on Cocos (Costa Rica) Island, a site credited by some as the inspiration for Robert Louis Stevenson's *Treasure Island*. In 1855 the governor of New South Wales sent Stephen Fremantle to Pitcairn Island to see whether the inhabitants wanted to move to Norfolk Island. The people voted in favor of the idea and were landed at Kingston in 1856 (KAVHA Heritage Mgt Plan, p. 29).

30. P. Richards to senior officer of HM's Ships, Sydney, 6 October 1856, Adm 125/135, No. 172, AJCP 2712.
31. S. Fremantle to R. Asbarne, 12 June 1857, AJCP 2712, Adm 125/135.
32. H. Guppy, 'The Cocos-Keeling Islands', reprinted from the *Scottish Geographical Magazine*, June 1889, p. 14, viewed 2 July 2019, <access.bl.uk/item/pdf/lsidyv3756a1b1>.
33. It may also be that, like other cartographers, Dudley confused the Cocos (Keeling) Islands with Christmas Island, reputedly discovered by the Englishman John Milward in 1615.
34. Wood-Jones, p. 3.
35. Guppy, *The Cocos-Keeling Islands*, part III., p. 16.
36. C. Gibson-Hill, 'Documents relating to John Clunies-Ross, Alexander Hare and the early history of the settlement on the Cocos-Keeling Islands', *Journal of the Malaysian Branch of the Royal Asiatic Society*, vol. 25, no. 4, 1952, p. 61, viewed 18 November 2021, <https://www.jstor.org/stable/i40073616>.
37. Gibson-Hill, p. 145.
38. B. Tan, *Carl Alexander Gibson-Hill*, National Library Board Singapore, 2008, viewed July 2019, <https://web.archive.org/web/20090509105328/http://infopedia.nl.sg/articles/SIP_1348_2008-12-01.html>.
39. A. Keating cited in J. Holman, *A voyage round the world, including travels in Africa, Asia, Australasia, America, etc. etc. from MDCCCXXVII to MDCCCXXXII*, Smith Elder and Co, London, 1834, p. 374.
40. Gibson-Hill, p. 87.
41. Gibson-Hill, p. 88.
42. J. Horsburgh, *The India Directory, or directions for sailing to and from the East Indies*, Allen & Co., London, 1843, p. 132, viewed 2 July 2019, <https://archive.org/stream/indiadirectoryor02hors#page/130/mode/2up/search/Keeling>.
43. Reference HA42, Mauritius Archives. Information from Yann von Arnim.
44. Holman, p. 374.
45. Holman, p. 382. See also G. Henderson, *Unfinished voyages. Western Australian shipwrecks 1622–1850*, 2nd edn, University of Western Australia Press, Nedlands, 2007, p. 184.
46. Director of National Parks, p. 13.
47. L. Reilly, 'The blind traveler: how James Holman felt his way around the world to become history's most prolific explorer', 2017, viewed 6 June 2019,

<https://www.mentalfloss.com/article/502774/blind-traveler-how-james-holman-felt-his-way-around-world-become-historys-most>.
48. Holman, vol. 1, p. 4.
49. Gibson-Hill, p. 209. During the 1870s an enterprising American planted his flag on the guano-rich Lacepede Islands to claim possession. See Henderson, *Unfinished voyages*, p. 213.
50. J. Slocum, *Sailing alone around the world*, London, 1949 edn, p. 201.
51. Gibson-Hill citing J. Clunies-Ross, p. 61.
52. Gibson-Hill, p. 145.
53. Koninklijk Instituut, *Bujdragen tot de Taal-Land-en Volkenkunde van Nederlandsch Indie*, Frederik Muller, Amsterdam, 1860, p. 16, viewed 2 July 2019, <https://books.google.com.au/books?id=caHQiqLUknAC&dq=molukko&pg=PA16&redir_esc=y#v=onepage&q=molukko&f=false>.
54. A. Smith, Borneo's first 'White Rajah': new light on Alexander Hare, his family and associates', *Borneo Research Bulletin*, vol. 44, 2013, pp. 93–131.
55. H. van der Jagt cited in Gibson-Hill, p. 148.
56. Holman, p. 379.
57. Gibson-Hill, p. 227.
58. Gibson-Hill, p. 135.
59. J. Clunies-Ross, cited in Gibson-Hill, p. 144.
60. H. Twiss, 1 July 1830, cited in Gibson-Hill, p. 148.
61. H. van der Jagt cited in Gibson-Hill, p. 149. See Gibson-Hill for more on the Dutch involvement in these discussions. See *Gleanings in Science,* October 1830, viewed 7 January 2021, <https://archive.org/details/gleaningsscienc2>. For the Clunies-Ross perspective. For the Hare perspective, see David Oates, 'Alexander Hare in the East Indies: a reappraisal', *The Great Circle*, vol. 21, no. 1, 1999, pp. 1–15.
62. Gibson-Hill, p. 79.

Chapter 5. Discovery of Christmas Island

1. W. Phillip, *The description of a voyage made by certain ships of Holland into the East Indies: With their adventures and success, together with the description of the countries, towns, and inhabitants of the same, who set forth on the second of April 1595, and returned on the fourteenth of August 1597*, London, 1598, p. 403, viewed 2 April 2020, <https://archive.org/details/descriptionofvoy00hout/page/n13/mode/2up>.
2. Burnell, vol. 1, p. 130.
3. Phillip, p. 403. See also S. Lee (ed.), 'Phillip, William', *Dictionary of national biography*, vol. 45, Smith, Elder & Co. London, 1896.
4. Phillip, p. 404. A 1581 chart, 'Die Eigentliche und Warhafftige Gestalt der Erden Und des Meers', by Heinrich Bunting depicts Taprobana midway between the southern tip of India and 'India Meridionalis', a continent with a likeness to Australia, viewed 2 April 2020, <https://trowbridgegallery.com.au/blog/rare-maps-of-australia/>.

5. G. Rouffaer and J. Ijzerman, *De eerste schipvaart der Nederlanders naar Oost-Indië onder Cornelis de Houtman, 1595–1597; journalen, documenten en andere bescheiden, uitg. en toegelicht door*, vol. 3, 'S-Gravenhage M Nijhoff, 1915, viewed 4 April 2020, <https://archive.org/stream/deeersteschipvaa03rouf/#page/n3/mode/2up>.
6. L. Biesman, cited in F. Swart, 'Lambert Biesman (1573–1601) of the Company of Trader Adventurers, the Dutch Route to the East Indies, and Olivier van Noort's circumnavigation of the globe', *The Journal of the Hakluyt Society*, December 2007, viewed 2 June 2019, <https://www.hakluyt.com/journal_articles/2007/Lambert%20Biesman.pdf>.
7. Heawood, ch. 2.
8. E. Satow (ed.), *The voyage of Captain John Saris to Japan, 1613*, The Hakluyt Society, London, 1900, p. 223, viewed 3 May 2020, <https://archive.org/details/voyageofcaptainj00saririch/page/222/mode/2up/search/diamond>.
9. J. Milward, 'Memorials of a voyage, wherein were employed three ships, the *Samaritan*, *Thomas* and *Thomasine*, 1614, written by John Milward, Merchant who went in the *Thomas*', in Samuel Purchas, 1905, *Hakluytus Posthumus*, vol. 4, part 14, p. 283, viewed 12 April 2022, <https://archive.org/stream/hakluytusposthum04purcuoft#page/n7/mode/1up>.
10. W. Foster (ed.), *Letters received by the East India Company from its servants in the East*, vol. 6, Sampson, Low, Marston and Company, London, 1896, p. 307, viewed 2 July 2019, <http://www.archive.org/stream/lettersreceivedb06east/lettersreceivedb06eas>.
11. J. Bruijn et al.
12. See Schilder, p. 305.
13. Tent, pp. 1–23.
14. W. Foster, 'The discovery of Christmas Island', *The Geographical Journal*, vol. 37, no. 3, 1911, pp. 281–2.
15. Cited in Foster, p. 281.
16. N. Comerford, Comerford family blog, 2007, viewed 2 July 2019, <http://comerfordfamily.blogspot.com.au/2007/12/comerford-profiles-6-nicholas.html>.
17. S. Thornton, A new and correct mapp of the world, 1711, viewed 2 July 2019, <https://nla.gov.au/nla.obj-232475651/view>.

Chapter 6. Exploration of Christmas Island

1. W. Dampier, *A new voyage round the world*, 1937 edn, Adam and Charles Black, London, 1697, ch. 16, viewed 2 July 2019, <http://gutenberg.net.au/ebooks05/0500461h.html>.
2. Dampier, 1697, ch. 10. See also W. Hill, 'The original home and mode of dispersal of the coconut', *Nature*, vol. 124, 1929, pp. 133–34.
3. F. Swart, 'The circumnavigation of the globe by Pieter Esaiasz de Lint 1598–1603', *The Journal of the Hakluyt Society,* January 2007, viewed 15 September 2022, <https://www.hakluyt.com/downloadable_files/Journal/pieter_de_lint.pdf>, citing Ohio State University Extension online, 'Chow line: coconuts helpful on

desert islands', viewed 2 January 2020, <http://extension.osu.edu/~news/story.php?id=2289>. See also Z. Prinzo, 'Scurvy and its prevention and control in major emergencies', WHO/NHD, 1999, viewed 2 January 2020, <https://www.unhcr.org/4cbef0599.pdf>. See Alan Everett, Too much has been made of the contributions by Lind and Cook to the cure of scurvy at sea, *The Great Circle*, 44.1, pp. 51–75.
4. Dampier 1697. Dampier's reference to a 'fine small brook near the southwest point of the island' appears odd because the coast is more approachable on the northwest side, where streams can be observed emptying into the ocean from the low cliffs. He makes no mention of *Cocos Nucifera*, the coconut palm, being present on Christmas Island. It seems that coconuts were not yet established on Christmas Island. Nor are they mentioned by Charles Andrews in his *A monograph of Christmas Island*. Printed by order of the Trustees, London, 1900, viewed 11 November 2021, <http://www.archive.org/details/monographofchris00andruoft>.
5. W. de Vlamingh, cited in Schilder, 1985, p. 142.
6. G. Henderson, 'The American China Trader *Rapid* (1811): an early Western Australian shipwreck site identified', *The Great Circle*, vol. 3, no. 1, 1981, pp. 125–36.
7. *Bataviasche Koloniale Courant*, 8 March 1811.
8. Image at https://en.wikipedia.org/wiki/Bulldog_rat
9. Dampier, 1697.
10. Stichting Maritiem Historische Databank, Vice Admiraal Rijk – ID 13822, viewed 30 December 2019, <https://www.marhisdata.nl/schip?id=13822>.
11. Warshipresearch, viewed 30 December 2019, <https://warshipsresearch.blogspot.com/2011/09/survivors-rescued-of-wrecked-dutch-bark.html>.
12. Anonymous, Verslag van het beheer en den staat der Oost-Indische bezittingen over 1853, pp. 26, National Archives, Studbook Marine: Stamboeken officieren, 1814–1868, archive 2.12.14, inventory number 10, folio 83, viewed 12 January 2020, <http://lampje.leidenuniv.nl/KITLV-docs/open/Metamorfoze/Kol.%20Verslag/MMKITLV01_PDF_TS4159_1853-1.pdf>.
13. R. Bennet, 'The shipwreck of the three-master merchant ship *Vice Admiraal Rijk* on Christmas Island. Dutch museum: historical and literary curiosities…', part 18, from *Weekblad van Den Helder en het Nieuwediep*, 17 January 1853.
14. See Geneanet, 'Arnold Roelof Herman Tollius Benneth', viewed 12 January 2020, <https://gw.geneanet.org/gluesi60?n=tollius+benneth&oc=&p=arnold+roelof+herman>, Open Archives, 'Registration Arnold Bennet', viewed 12 January 2020, <https://www.openarch.nl/gae:89f3ef3d-caf0-fdd9-d2e8-5f86cf252294/nl>, Open Archives, 'Registration Arnold Bennet', viewed 12 January 2020, <https://www.openarch.nl/ghn:6386fd86-1c56-102e-8011-0050569c51dd>.
15. Bennet. Translation by Thomas Creemers from article in *Nederlandsch Museum*, part XVIII, 1855, printed by N. de Zwaan, Utrecht, viewed 12 January 2020,

<https://www.delpher.nl/nl/boeken1/gview?query=christmas-+of+kerstijds eiland&coll=boeken1&identifier=czFTAAAAcAAJ>.
16. J. Carpenter, Western Australian Museum, pers. comm.
17. J. MacLear, 'Report on Christmas Island', *Proceedings of the Zoological Society of London*, London, 1887, p. 510, viewed 2 June 2019, <http://www.archive.org/stream/proceedingsofgen87zool#page/n898/mode/1up>.
18. Robide van der Aa, 1866, cited in Tent, p. 5.
19. Elsewhere, Murray propounded a new theory of coral reefs, arguing that Darwin's view that they were formed by subsidence was not tenable. Murray was supported in this argument by Guppy, according to J. Judd. See G. Bettany, p. 8.
20. J. MacLear, 'Report on Christmas Island'.
21. Andrews, p. 19. An article in *Current Biology*, 9 March 2022, 'Probing the genomic limits of de-extinction in the Christmas Island rat', probes the genomic limits of de-extinction in another Christmas Island rat, Rattus macleari, prompting newspaper articles such as 'The "lab" rat to test the Jurassic theory' in the *West Australian*, 12 March 2022, p. 35
22. R. Richards, 'The cruise of the *Kingston* and the *Elligood* in 1800 and the wreck found on King Island in 1802', *The Great Circle*, vol. 13, no. 1, 1991, p. 45.
23. Whitecar, p. 114, viewed 20 November 2012, <https://archive.org/details/fouryearsaboardw00whitrich>.
24. W. Wharton, 'Account of Christmas Island, Indian Ocean', *Proceedings of the Royal Geographical Society and Monthly Record of Geography*, vol. 10, no. 10, 1888, pp. 613–24.
25. Andrews, p. 19.

Chapter 7. VOC disasters along the spice-trade route
1. Centre for International Heritage Activities, 'Inventory and analyses of archival sources in the Netherlands in order to contribute to possible locations and identification of VOC shipwrecks off the Western Australian coast', unpublished report commissioned by Western Australian Museum Foundation Welshpool, Western Australia, 2014. Alan Villiers, in his *The Indian Ocean*, p. 22, refers to a reported touching by the ship *Le Lys* (*de Lys*?) on the Le Lys rock, in the Mergui Archipelago (Andaman Sea), in a similar longitude to the Cocos (Keeling) Islands. See also P. Boorsma, 'Concerning the locations of the missing Dutch East Indiamen *Fortuin* (1724) and *Aagtekerke* (1726)', unpublished report for the Cultural Heritage Agency of the Netherlands, Leiden University, Netherlands, 2014, viewed 17 January 2020, <https://www.academia.edu/21691991/Concerning_the_locations_of_the_missing_Dutch_East_Indiamen_Fortuin_1724_and_Aagtekerke_1726>.
2. Bruijn et al., p. 71.
3. M. Gibbs and E. McPhee, 'The Raine Island entrance: wreck traps and the search for a safe route through the Great Barrier Reef', *The Great Circle*, vol. 26, no. 2, 2004, pp. 24–54.

4. A. van der Kraan, 'Disaster in the Indian Ocean: the lost company fleet of 1662', *The Great Circle,* vol. 35, no. 1, 2013, pp. 29–74.
5. See Appendix 16, 'Extract from a letter from Nicolaes Witsen to Dr Martin Lister, 3 October 1698', in G. Schilder (ed.), *Voyage to the Great South Land: Willem de Vlamingh 1696–1969*, trans. C. de Heer, Royal Australian Historical Society, Sydney, 1985, pp. 221–2.
6. Cited in Centre for International Heritage Activities, p. 12.
7. C. Halls, 'The loss of the Dutch East Indiaman *Aagtekerke*', *Annual Dog Watch*, 1966, vol. 23, pp. 101–27.
8. J. Diephout, 'Report of the '*s-Graveland*. Kopie-dagregisters, gehouden in het kasteel Batavia', National Archief, VOC: 7613, 1724. See also Boorsma, p. 5.
9. See Schilder, 1986, p. 59.
10. See M. Tomczak and S. Godfrey, *Regional oceanography: an introduction*, Daya Publishing House, Delhi, 2003, p.180.
11. Bureau of Meteorology, 'Tropical cyclones affecting Cocos Islands and Christmas Island', viewed 2 July 2019, <http://www.bom.gov.au/cyclone/history/wa/cocos.shtml>.
12. *Times atlas of the world*, Times Books, London, 1974, p. 81.
13. Tim O'Hara, Museum of Victoria, pers. comm., 27 July 2018.
14. 'Muirfield Seamount', viewed 6 June 2019, <https://en.wikipedia.org/wiki/Muirfield_Seamount>.
15. J. D'Apres de Mannevillette, *Le Neptune Oriental, ou routier general des cotes des Indes Orientales et de la Chine; enrichi de cartes hydrographiques tant generals que particulieres, pour server d'instruction a la navigation de ces differentes mers*, J. Robustel, Paris, 1745.
16. Andrews, p. 5.
17. Generaal Journaal 1725–1726, NA 1.04.18.02 (Boekhouder Generaal Batavia) 10764, cited in Inventory and analyses of archival sources, Centre for International Heritage Activities, p. 76.
18. Centre for International Heritage Activities.
19. Patrick Baker, pers. comm. 2021. Adriaen Van Der Graeff's *Zeewijk* Journal, translation by C. de Heer, 28 January 1728 entry. See G. Henderson, 'The mysterious fate of the Dutch East Indiaman *Aagtekerke*. A review of the eighteenth and nineteenth century sources', *Westerly*, University of Western Australia, vol. 23, no. 2, June 1978, pp. 71–8. See also J. Green, *The mystery of the missing VOC shipwreck in the Houtman Abrolhos Islands, Western Australia*, Department of Maritime Archaeology, Western Australian Museum, report 20, 2018, viewed 6 May 2020, <http://museum.wa.gov.au/maritime-archaeology-db/maritime-reports/mystery-missing-voc-shipwreck-houtman-abrolhos-islands-western-australia-0>.
20. The presence of olive jars (of a type superficially similar to jars seen on Roman period wrecks in the Mediterranean), and cannon without trunnions, presented a confusing picture. See H. Edwards, 'Local wreck the richest?', *Daily News*, 2 February 1965, p. 6.

21. G. Henderson, 'The wreck of the *Elizabeth*', *Studies in Historical Archaeology*, no. 1, Australian Society for Historical Archaeology, Sydney, 1973.
22. H. Edwards, 'Where is the *Aagtekerke*?', unpublished report, Swanbourne, 2012.
23. J. Green, 'The wreck of the VOC retourschip *Zeewijk*: an archaeological and historical puzzle', *Bulletin of the Australasian Institute for Maritime Archaeology*, 2015, vol. 39, pp. 9–26. See J. Green and A. Paterson (eds), *Shipwrecks of the roaring forties: researching some of Australia's earliest shipwrecks*, UWA Publishing, Crawley, 2020, p. 42. See also Centre for International Heritage Activities 2014.
24. Centre for International Heritage Activities, p. 33.
25. M. Coghlan and J. Green, 'Helping to identify historic shipwrecks: the DNA analysis of ivory', in J. Rodrigues and A. Traviglia (eds), 2020, *Shared heritage: proceedings from the Sixth International Congress for Underwater Archaeology*, 28 November–2 December 2016, Western Australian Maritime Museum, Fremantle, Western Australia, Archaeopress, Oxford, UK. See also J. Green and A. Paterson (eds), p. 106.
26. Cited in Wood-Jones, pp. xxii–xxiii.
27. C. Darwin, *Journal of researches into the natural history and geology of the countries visited during the voyage of HMS Beagle round the world, under the command of Capt. Fitzroy, R.N.*, 2nd edn, John Murray, London, 1845, p. 457, viewed 2 July 2019, <http://darwin-online.org.uk/content/frameset?itemID=F14&viewtype=text&pageseq=1>.
28. G. Henderson, A. Viduka, J. Parkinson and A. Moss, 'Closing in on the *Fortuyn*: a progress report', *Bulletin of the Australasian Institute for Maritime Archaeology*, vol. 39, 2015, pp. 27–43. See also A. Viduka, G. Henderson, A. Moss and J. Parkinson, 'Closing in on the *Fortuyn*: report on fieldwork conducted in February–March 2016 at Christmas Island and the Cocos (Keeling) Islands', report for the Embassy of the Kingdom of the Netherlands in Australia, the Maritime Programme in the Netherlands Ministry of Culture and the Silentworld Foundation, 2016, viewed 10 October 2019, <https://www.academia.edu/27051924/Closing_in_on_the_Fortuyn_Report_on_fieldwork_conducted_in_2016_at_Christmas_and_the_Cocos_Keeling_Islands &gt>.
29. A. Hope, 'Inquest into the deaths of SIEV 221, Christmas Island', 2012, viewed 2 July 2019, <https://www.coronerscourt.wa.gov.au/_files/Christmas_Island_Findings.pdf>.
30. See Bennet.
31. Henderson et al., 2015, pp. 27–43.
32. Hama Hamanaka, pers. comm., February 2016.
33. VOC 1893, O.B. 1725, 1 fol.15vs, 389–90, 391, vs-303, 410–14, Algemeen Rijksarchief. See also H. van der Jagt, cited in Gibson-Hill, 1952, p. 151.
34. Essex Institute Library, undated, 'Early charts of Australia and the Pacific', fol. 592, PMB 213. State Library of Western Australia.
35. G. Henderson, *Unfinished Voyages*, p. 124.

36. Anonymous, 'Animals quarantined on Cocos Islands', *Sydney Morning Herald*, 1 August 2006, viewed 2 July 2019, <https://www.smh.com.au/national/elephants-quarantined-on-cocos-islands-20060801-gdo30c.html>.
37. T. van Heiningen, 'The correspondence of Caspar Georg Reinwardt (1773–1819)', part 1, The Hague, 2011, viewed 2 July 2019, <http://www.dwc.knaw.nl/wpcontent/bestanden/reinwardt.pdf>.
38. Lloyd's Register of Shipping 1827 Shipowners: Lloyd's Register Foundation, Heritage & Education Centre: Free Download, Borrow, and Streaming: Internet Archive, viewed 15 April 2022, <https://archive.org/details/HECROSS1827/page/n549/mode/7up>.
39. Holman, vol. 3, p. 162.
40. Holman, vol. 3. p. 46.
41. Megan Coghlan, Curtin University, pers. comm., 13 February 2017.
42. Michael Bunce, Curtin University, pers. comm., 8 March 2017.

Chapter 8. Conclusions

1. Nation states with bases in the Indian Ocean include the US and UK (at Diego Garcia), China (at Djibouti), Japan and France (at Djibouti). See P. Shukla, 'The Indian Ocean–the new power struggle', viewed 20 April 2022, <https://praneetshukla.substack.com/p/the-indian-ocean-the-new-power-struggle?s=r>. See 'Cocos (Keeling) Islands (globalsecurity.org)'. <https://www.globalsecurity.org/military/world/australia/cocos-islands.htm>. See <https://www.businessinsider.com/how-satan-2-icbm-nuclear-weapon-works-2018-3> and <https://www.jpost.com/international/iran-fires-long-range-missiles-into-indian-ocean-in-military-drill-media-655646> and <https://newstodaynet.com/2022/04/25/putin-says-satan-ii-missile-will-be-deployed-by-autumn>.
2. *The West Australian* 7 April 2022, p. 9.
3. Jack Boshoff, pers comm., 2017.
4. Nippon Foundation GEBCO Seabed 2030 Project, viewed 2 July 2019, <https://www.fugro.com/media-centre/seabed-2030>. See 'First new seafloor map of the decade collected on New Year's expedition in Australian waters', viewed 12 April 2022, <digital.ecomagazine.com/publication/frame.php?i=707374&p=&pn=&ver=html…>. See also *Oceans Institute News*, December 2021, viewed 21 December 2021.

Select bibliography

Alvo or Alvaro, F., 'Log-book of Francisco Alvo or Alvaro', viewed 12 April 2022, in A. Pigafetta, <https://en.wikisource.org/wiki/The_First_Voyage_Round_the_World/Log-Book_of_Francisco_Alvo_or_Alvaro>.

Andrews, C., *A monograph of Christmas Island*, printed by order of the Trustees, London, 1900, viewed 11 November 2021, <http://www.archive.org/details/monographofchris00andruoft>.

Armstrong, P., *Under the blue vault of heaven: a study of Darwin's sojourn in the Cocos (Keeling) Islands*, Indian Ocean Centre for Peace Studies, Nedlands, 1991, p. 37, viewed 24 November 2020, <http://darwin-online.org.uk/content/frameset?itemID=A588&viewtype=text&pageseq=1>.

Bach, J., 'Dampier, William (1651–1715)', *Australian dictionary of biography*, National Centre of Biography, Australian National University, 1966, viewed 2 July 2019, <http://adb.anu.edu.au/biography/dampier-william-1951/text2345>.

Bruijn, J., Gaastra, F. and Schoffer, I. (eds), *Dutch-Asiatic shipping in the 17th and 18th centuries*, vols 1–3, Martinus Nijhoff, The Hague, 1987, viewed 2 July 2019, <http://resources.huygens.knaw.nl/retroboeken/das/#page=90&accessor=toc&source=1>.

Campbell, G. (ed) *Early exchange between Africa and the wider Indian ocean world*, Palgrave Series in Indian Ocean World Studies, 2016, viewed 4 September 2020, <https://books.google.com.ph/books?id=XsvDDQAAQBAJ&lpg=PP1&pg=PA50#v=onepage&q&f=false>.

Centre for International Heritage Activities, 'Inventory and analyses of archival sources in the Netherlands in order to contribute to possible locations and identification of VOC shipwrecks off the Western Australian coast', unpublished report commissioned by Western Australian Museum Foundation Welshpool, Western Australia, 2014, viewed 17 January 2020, <https://www.academia.edu/21691991/Concerning_the_locations_of_the_missing_Dutch_East_Indiamen_Fortuin_1724_and_Aagtekerke_1726>.

Clunies-Ross, J., 'Some account of the Cocos or Keeling Islands; and of their recent settlement', *Gleanings in science*, Baptist Mission Press, Calcutta, October 1830, viewed 1 January 2021, <https://archive.org/details/gleaningsscienc2>.

Dampier, W., 1699, *A voyage to New Holland*, 3rd edn, James and John Knapton, London, 1729. viewed 3 July 2019, <http://gutenberg.net.au/ebooks/e00046.html>.

Dampier, W., *A collection of voyages*, vol. 11, no. 1, James Knapton, London, 1729, p. 11, viewed 10 December 2019, <www.canadiana.ca/view/oocihm.29536/208?r=0&s=4>.

Dampier, W., *A new voyage round the world*, 1937 edn, Adam and Charles Black, London, 1697, viewed 2 July 2019, <http://gutenberg.net.au/ebooks05/0500461h.html>.

Dana, J., *Corals and coral islands*, 3rd edn, Dodd Mead, New York, 1890.

Danvers, F., in *Letters received by the East India Company*, vol. 1: 1602–1613, London, 1896, viewed 2 July 2019, <https://archive.org/stream/lettersreceivedb01east#page/n4/mode/1up>.

D'Apres de Mannevillette, J., *Le Neptune oriental, ou routier general des cotes des Indes Orientales et de la Chine; enrichi de cartes hydrographiques tant generals que particulieres, pour server d'instruction a la navigation de ces differentes mers*, J. Robustel, Paris, 1745.

Darwin, C., *Journal of researches into the natural history and geology of the countries visited during the voyage of HMS Beagle round the world, under the command of Capt. Fitzroy, R.N.*, 2nd edn, John Murray, London, 1845, viewed 2 July 2019, <http://darwin-online.org.uk/content/frameset?itemID=F14&viewtype=text&pageseq=1>.

Darwin, C., *On the origin of species by means of natural selection*, John Murray, London, 1859, chs 11 and 12, viewed 13 November 2020, <On the origin of species by means of natural selection, or, the preservation of favoured races in the struggle for life (nla.gov.au)>.

Davies, S., 'The wondrous east in the renaissance geographical imagination: Marco Polo, Fra Mauro and Giovanni Battista Ramusio', viewed 23 April 2022, <https://www.tandfonline.com/doi/abs/10.1080/02757206.2012.675803>. – Academia.edu.

Dudley, R., *Dell' Arcano del Mare* (The Secret of the Sea), self-published, 1646, viewed 2 July 2019, <http://www.doria.fi/handle/10024/59106>.

Fitzroy, R., *Narrative of the surveying voyages of His Majesty's ships adventure and Beagle between the years 1826 and 1836, describing their examination of the southern shores of South America, and the Beagle's circumnavigation of the globe. Proceedings of the second expedition, 1831–36, under the command of Captain Robert Fitzroy, R.N.*, Henry Colburn, London, 1839, viewed 2 July 2019, <https://archive.org/details/narrativeofsurve02king/page/632>.

Foster, W. (ed.), *Letters received by the East India Company from its servants in the East*, vol. 6, Sampson, Low, Marston and Company, London,

1896, p. 307, viewed 2 July 2019, <http://www.archive.org/stream/lettersreceivedb06east/lettersreceivedb06eas>.

Gibson-Hill, C., 'Documents relating to John Clunies-Ross, Alexander Hare and the early history of the settlement on the Cocos-Keeling Islands', *Journal of the Malaysian Branch of the Royal Asiatic Society*, vol. 25.4, 1952, viewed 18 November 2021, <https://www.jstor.org/stable/i40073616>.

Gray, H., *Spice at any price: the life and times of Frederick de Houtman 1571–1627*, Westralian Books, Geraldton, 2019.

Green J., and Paterson A. (eds), *Shipwrecks of the roaring forties: researching some of Australia's earliest shipwrecks*, UWA Publishing, Crawley, 2020.

Gunn, B. Baudouin, L. and Olsen, K., *Independent origins of cultivated coconut (Cocos nucifera L.) in the Old World tropics*, 2011, viewed 2 July 2019, <https://doi.org/10.1371/journal.pone.0021143>.

Guppy, H., 'The dispersal of plants as illustrated by the flora of the Keeling or Cocos Islands', Victoria Institute lecture, 1890, p. 5, viewed 2 July 2019, <https://babel.hathitrust.org/cgi/pt?id=hvd.32044106359169;view=1up;seq=1>.

Hall, R., *Emperors of the monsoon: a history of the Indian Ocean*, Harper Collins, 1996.

Heeres, J., *The part borne by the Dutch in the discovery of Australia 1606–1765*, London, 1899.

Henderson, G., 'The mysterious fate of the Dutch East Indiaman *Aagtekerke*: A review of the eighteenth and nineteenth century sources'. *Westerly*, University of Western Australia, vol. 23, no. 2, June 1978, pp. 71–8.

Henderson, G., Viduka, A., Parkinson J. and Moss, A., 'Closing in on the *Fortuyn*: a progress report', *Bulletin of the Australasian Institute for Maritime Archaeology*, 2015, vol. 39, pp. 27–43.

Holman, J., *A voyage round the world, including travels in Africa, Asia, Australasia, America, etc. etc. from MDCCCXXVII to MDCCCXXXII*. Smith Elder and Co, London, 1834, p. 374.

Kerr, R. (ed.), 'Third voyage of the English East India Company, in 1607, by Captain William Keeling', in *Early voyages of the English to India, after the establishment of the East India Company*, vol. VIII, ch. X, sect. IV, 1824, viewed 2 July 2019, <http://www.columbia.edu/itc/mealac/pritchett/00generallinks/kerr/vol08chap10sect04.html>.

Langhenez, B., 'The description of a voyage made by certaine ships of Holland into the East Indies, with their aduentures and successe; together with the description of the countries, townes, and inhabitantes of the same: who set forth on the second of Aprill, 1595, and returned on the 14 of August, 1597', translated out of Dutch into English by W. P., London, 1598.

Principal navigations, voyages, traffiques and discoveries of the English nation, by

Richard Hakluyt. E. Goldsmid (ed.), vol. X (Asia), part III, Edinburgh 1889, viewed 19 March 2020, <https://archive.org/details/cihm_33126/page/n235/mode/2up/search/Holland>.

Linschoten, J., *Iohn Huighen van Linschoten his Discours of voyages into ye Easte & West Indies: deuided into foure books*, J. Wolfe, London, [1598], viewed 8 January 2020, <https://www.loc.gov/resource/rbc0001.2007kis1964006000001/?sp=36>.

Lyell, C., *Principles of geology*, Appleton and Co., New York, 1854.

Masselman, G., *The cradle of colonialism*, Yale University Press, New Haven, 1963, viewed 23 March 2020, <https://archive.org/details/cradleofcolonial0000mass/mode/1up>.

Mattietto, L., 'Environmental catastrophies law and literature: Maurice Blanchot's The Writing of the Disaster', *Public Policy Law*, vol. 2, no. 1, Jan 2020. Recovered from <http://www.seer.unirio.br/rdpp/article/view/10400>.

Miguel Alonso Rojo, J., 'Nuno Garcia de Toreno: the first cartographer of the Casa de la Contratacion', *Magazine of Columbian Studies*, 2020, viewed 2 October 2021, <https://uva-es.academia.edu/JoséMiguelAlonso>

Milward, J., 'Memorials of a voyage, wherein were employed three ships, the *Samaritan*, *Thomas* and *Thomasine*, 1614, written by John Milward, Merchant who went in the *Thomas*', in S. Purchas, *Hakluytus Posthumus*, 1905, vol. 4, part 14, viewed 2 June 2019, <https://archive.org/stream/hakluytusposthum04purcuoft#page/n7/mode/1up>.

Moorthy, S. & Jamal, A. (eds), *Indian Ocean studies, cultural, social and political perspectives*, Routledge, 2010.

Mutch, T., 'The first discovery of Australia, with an account of the voyage of the *Duyfken* and the career of Captain Willem Jansz, Sydney. Reprinted from *Journal of the Royal Australian Historical Society*, vol. 28, no. 5, 1942 viewed 2 June 2019, <http://gutenberg.net.au/ebooks06/0600631h.html>.

Pearson, M., *The Indian Ocean*, Routledge, 2003.

Phillip, W., *The description of a voyage made by certain ships of Holland into the East Indies: with their adventures and success, together with the description of the countries, towns, and inhabitants of the same, who set forth on the second of April 1595, and returned on the fourteenth of August 1597*, London, 1598, viewed 2 April 2020, <https://archive.org/details/descriptionofvoy00hout/page/n13/mode/2up>.

Pigafetta, A., 'Magellan's voyage around the world by Antonio Pigafetta', translated by James Robertson, The Arthur H. Clark Company, Cleveland, 1906 edn, vols 1–3, viewed 27 August 2019, <https://archive.org/details/magellansvoyagea02piga/page/180>.

Prazmari, V., Floating islands: the floating and wandering island in Medieval and Renaissance culture and isolarii, viewed 23 April 2022, <https://docgo.net/floating-islands-the-floating-and-wandering-island...>, Academia.edu.

Preston, D. and M., *A pirate of exquisite mind: the life of William Dampier*, Corgi Books, London, 2004.

Purchas, S., *Purchas His Pilgrimes*, vol. 1, printed by William Stansby for Henrie Fetherstone, London, 1625, viewed 2 July 2019, <https://books.google.com.au/books?id=0jSN5RNaVNkC&printsec=frontcover&source=gbs_ge_summary_r&cad=0#v=onepage&q&f=false>.

Richardson, W. A. R., 'Cartographical clues to three sixteenth-century shipwrecks in the Indian Ocean', *The Great Circle*, vol. 14, no. 1, 1992, pp. 1–20.

Rouffaer, G. and Ijzerman, J. (eds), *De eerste schipvaart der Nederlanders naar Oost-Indië onder Cornelis de Houtman, 1595–1597*, vol. 3, viewed 23 March 2020, <https://archive.org/details/deeersteschipvaa03rouf/page/n16/mode/2up>.

Saenz-Lopez Perez, S., *Marginalia in Cartography*, exhibition at the Chazen Museum of Art, Madison, February 28–May 18, 2014.

Satow, E. (ed.) *The Voyage of Captain John Saris to Japan, 1613*, The Hakluyt Society, London, 1900, viewed 3 May 2020, <https://archive.org/details/voyageofcaptainj00saririch/page/222/mode/2up/search/diamond>.

Schilder, G. and van Egmond, M., 'Maritime cartography in the Low Countries during the Renaissance' ', in David Woodward (ed.), *The history of cartography, volume three: cartography in the European Renaissance*, University of Chicago Press, 2007, pp. 1384–432, viewed 4 December 2021, <https://www.academia.edu/4673297/Maritime_Cartography_in_the_Low_Countries_during_the_Renaissance_G%C3%BCnter_Schilder_and_Marco_van_Egmond?email_work_card=view-paper>.

Sheriff, A. and Enseng, H., *The Indian Ocean: oceanic connections and the creation of new societies*, Hurst and Co., London, 2014.

Skelton, R., *Explorers' maps*, Hamlyn Publishing Group edn, 1970.

Slocum, J., *Sailing alone around the world*, London, 1949 edn, p. 201.

Smith, A., 'Borneo's first "White Rajah": new light on Alexander Hare, his family and associates', *Borneo Research Bulletin*, vol. 44, 2013.

Swift, J., *Gulliver's Travels*, in *Gulliver's travels and other writings*, 1726, Riverside Press edn, Cambridge, Mass. 1960.

Tent, J., 'The ghosts of Christmas (Island) past: an examination of its early charting and naming', *Terrae Incognitae: The Journal of the Society for the History of Discoveries*, 2016, pp. 1–23, viewed 2 July 2019, <https://www.researchgate.net/publication/305646738_The_Ghosts_of_Christmas_Island_Past_An_Examination_of_its_Early_Charting_and_Naming>.

Thomas, H., *The slave trade*, Phoenix, London, 2006.

Van der Kraan, A., 'Disaster in the Indian Ocean: the lost company fleet of 1662', *The Great Circle*, vol. 35, no. 1, 2013, pp. 29–74.

Van Duzer, C., 'Martin Waldseemuller's "Carta marina" of 1516', 2000, viewed 19 November 2021.

Viduka, A., Henderson, G., Moss A. and Parkinson, J., 'Closing in on the *Fortuyn*: Report on fieldwork conducted in February–March 2016 at Christmas Island and the Cocos (Keeling) Islands', report for the Embassy of the Kingdom of the Netherlands in Australia, the Maritime Programme in the Netherlands Ministry of Culture and the Silentworld Foundation, 2016, viewed 10 October 2019, <https://www.academia.edu/27051924/Closing_in_on_the_Fortuyn_Report_on_fieldwork_conducted_in_2016_at_Christmas_and_the_Cocos_Keeling_Islands&gt>.

Vigano, M., (99+) Prayers and Cornerstones. Wedges of gold, Prows of old. Ancient and medieval Ethiopia as an African Empire based on sea trade | Marco Vigano, ማርኮ ቪጋኖ - Academia.edu.

Wharton, W., 'Account of Christmas Island, Indian Ocean', *Proceedings of the Royal Geographical Society and Monthly Record of Geography,* vol. 10, no. 10, 1888, pp. 613–24.

Wood-Jones, F., *Corals and atolls: a history and description of the Cocos-Keeling Islands with an account of their flora and fauna, and a discussion of the method and development of transformation of coral structures in general*, Lovell Reeve and Co. Ltd, London, 1912.

Yule, H. and Cordier, H. (eds), *The travels of Marco Polo, by Marco Polo and Rustichello of Pisa*, vol. 2, bk III, ch. VII, The Project Gutenberg eBook, 2004, viewed 2 June 2019, <http://www.gutenberg.org/cache/epub/12410/pg12410-images.html>.

Author biographies

Graeme John Henderson AM, CitWA

Themes of special interest
Maritime archaeology, maritime history, maritime museums and protection of underwater cultural heritage

Professional biography
Graeme Henderson chairs Wreck Check, an Australian not-for-profit group formed to research maritime cultural heritage. He  has played a crucial role in developing maritime archaeology and maritime museums in Australia. His gifting in 1963, before the introduction of protective cultural heritage legislation, of *Vergulde Draeck* shipwreck finder's rights to the Western Australian Museum initiated that museum's involvement with underwater cultural heritage. His recommendation that the derelict Fremantle Commissariat building be transformed into a shipwrecks museum – now the WA Shipwrecks Museum – was adopted. He was the first director of the Western Australian Maritime Museum, from 1992 to 2005, and project director for the development of the WA Maritime Museum exhibition facility on Victoria Quay. In the 1990s he extended his activities to the international forum, establishing the International Council on Monuments and Sites (ICOMOS) International Committee on Underwater Cultural Heritage Inc. That committee played a lead role in developing the UNESCO *Convention for the Protection of the Underwater Cultural Heritage*. He was recognised as Western Australian Citizen of the Year (Arts, Culture and Entertainment Category) in 2002, and awarded the Centenary Medal in 2003, and the Order of Australia in 2012.

Andrew John Viduka FSA M.ICOMOS–ICUCH, PhD

Themes of special interest
Underwater cultural heritage management, public archaeology, maritime archaeology and conservation

Professional biography
Andy Viduka (ORCID 0000-0002-0348-4544) is a maritime archaeologist and conservator employed by the Australian Government as the assistant director, Underwater Cultural Heritage. In this role, Andy administers Australia's legislation that protects underwater cultural heritage and coordinates the Australian Underwater Cultural Heritage Program. Andy co-led the drafting of the *Underwater Cultural Heritage Act 2018* and led Australia's consideration of ratification of the UNESCO 2001 *Convention on the Protection of the Underwater Cultural Heritage*. Andy is actively involved in maritime archaeological projects with the not-for-profit research group Wreck Check Inc., continuing his research interest in linking community outcomes with the discovery and protection of underwater cultural heritage. Andy's PhD was on 'A public good conservation approach for underwater cultural heritage management through citizen science' and in 2018 he founded the citizen science project Gathering Information via Recreational and Technical Scientific Divers (GIRT). Andy is a fellow of the Society of Antiquaries, and member of ICOMOS – ICUCH, ICOMOS – ICAHM, the Australasian Institute for Maritime Archaeology (AIMA), and the Australian Citizen Science Association (ACSA). Andy is an honorary associate of the University of New England and a foundation member of the research group Wreck Check Inc.

Robert William de Hoop RCE

Themes of special interest
3D recording and documentation of cultural heritage, battlefield archaeology, difficult heritage, in situ preservation, maritime archaeology, shared cultural heritage and underwater cultural heritage management

Professional biography
Robert de Hoop is a maritime and underwater archaeologist working with the International Programme for Maritime Heritage at the Cultural Heritage Agency of the Netherlands (RCE), part of the Ministry of Education, Culture and Science, since October 2017. The projects within this programme deal with Dutch maritime heritage overseas and shared cultural heritage. Robert completed a bachelor in archaeology with honours at Saxion University of Applied Sciences in the Netherlands. His undergraduate thesis about predicting underwater cultural heritage was linked to an internship at the Maritime Programme of the Cultural Heritage Agency. He completed his masters at the Maritime Archaeology Programme at the University of Southern Denmark. During his masters, he obtained his commercial scuba diver ticket as well as his commercial SSE ticket. His thesis on the different values and the significance of WWII shipwrecks was nominated for the W.A. van Es prize. As a maritime heritage expert, Robert has travelled all over the world to cooperate with countries managing cultural heritage underwater. Robert participated in several national and international projects, including the excavation of the East Indiaman (VOC) ship the *Rooswijk* and writing the process and best practice guidelines for the EU-project SASMAP.

Index

f is figure; n is note

Aagtekerke ix, 4, 89, 93, 153, 155–157, 159–164, 166–168, 173–174, 176–177, 184–185
Africa 1, 4, 7, 14–15, 18–19, 52, 65, 79, 94, 162–163, 173, 176–177
   Gambia 52–53, 109, 181
   Mozambique 53, 109, 163, 176–177, 185, 207n26
   South Africa 2, 112–113, 175, 181
   see also Cape of Good Hope; Cape Town; Madagascar; Mauritius
Age of Exploration 1, 4–5
Age of Imperialism 92
Albo, Francisco 23
Aldrich, Pelham 151
Allibert, Claude 44
Amethyst 128, 149
Amicitia 139, 146–147, 149
Amsterdam 118–119f, 121
Amsterdam Island 25, 35, 59, 94, 155, 157, 163
Anderson, Atholl 79
Andreae, Ambassador Willem 3
Andrews, Charles 42, 151, 160
antimony 52–53, 109, 181
Apianus, Petrus 8
Arab seafarers 1, 12, 15, 18, 21, 35, 39, 80, 179
Arinus Marinus 149, 154, 174–175
Ascension Island 50
Australia 1–3, 9, 25, 44–46, 66, 73, 84, 100, 106–107, 157, 160, 163, 174, 180

   see also Houtman Abrolhos; Western Australia
Australian Institute for Maritime Archaeology 166, 232
Australian National University 173, 188
Austronesians 7, 9–11, 29, 44, 48, 52, 79–80, 108, 181

Bachstrom, Johann 131
Bali 47, 151
Batavia 155, 161
Beagle ix, 48, 99
Beekman, Daniel 127, 136f
Belgium 27
Bennet, Roelof 137, 139–150, 171
Biesman, Lambert 121
birds 33, 182, 203n36
   edible x, 8, 11–12, 25, 37, 39, 40f, 56–57, 62, 63f, 127, 133, 139, 143, 145, 154, 182–183
   giant 2, 33–37, 38f, 39–44, 40f, 43f, 56–57, 62–63f, 95, 181–182
   parrots 25, 26f, 37, 41, 42f, 182
   see also Cocos Buff-banded Rail; dodo; guano
Blaeu, Willem 56, 125
Blake, William 87f
Bligh, William 62
Borneo 124
Borneo 111, 115
Borobudur ship 9–11, 30, 52
Bounty 62
Bowen, Emanuel 29f, 82, 212n84

British Government x, 98, 115–116, 149, 175, 183
  see also slave trade
Bruin-Vis 41
Brookes, John 73
Brouwer, Hendrik x, 123f
  Route ix, 34, 59, 122, 155, 183
Bunce, Michael 162, 173, 187
Burningham, Nick 11
Burton, Richard 18, 180

Cabral, Pedro 15, 37
Cantino, Alberto 8–9, 15–22, 16f, 17f, 25, 37, 54, 181–182, 201n18
Cape of Good Hope 5, 8, 14–15, 23–25, 34, 39, 41, 52, 57, 66, 68, 93–94, 118, 124–125, 153, 156–158, 163
Cape Town 112, 161, 176
Caroline du Sud 151
Carroll, Lewis 41, 180
cartography 12, 54, 58, 92–93, 98, 105, 179, 181–182
  see also maps
Cavendish, Thomas 26
Central America 64, 88, 101, 203n36
Ceram 18–19, 54, 182, 201n18
Ceullen, Cornelis 8, 56, 209n50
Ceylon 9, 14, 22, 202n25
Challenger 128, 150
charts *see* maps
China 7, 12, 14, 18, 28, 52, 64, 136, 180–181
Christmas Island viii–xi, 2–3, 5, 8–9, 11–13, 47, 79–80, 85, 106–107, 111–112, 117–152, 153–154, 157, 159, 166, 179–180, 183–184, 187, 220n4
  crabs 136–137f, 146, 150
  early names 8, 13, 117–118, 125–126, 135, 159, 210n56

mapping 12–13, 25, 27, 29, 31, 59, 72, 117–118, 120, 125–126, 145f, 159, 182, 213n91
  phosphate x–xi, 128–129, 150–152, 184
  prior inhabitants 140, 147
  rats 136–137, 146, 150
  shipwrecks 4, 127–128, 138–149, 154–160, 163, 167–172f, 184–185
Clunies-Ross, Andrew 151
Clunies-Ross, George 128, 151–152f, 184
Clunies-Ross, John ix–xi, 48–51, 53, 82–83, 94, 106, 108, 110–116, 183, 205n17, 215n18
Clunies-Ross, Robert 113
Coco Islands (Bay of Bengal) x, 71f, 78, 83, 96, 100–102, 129, 131, 133, 153, 183, 213n89
Cocos Buff-banded Rail 11–12, 39, 56, 182
Cocos (Keeling) Islands viii–x, 2, 5, 9, 11, 44–64, 67–80, 81–91, 93–116, 125, 131, 133, 135, 154, 166, 171, 213n92
  Darwin's visit 48–51, 75–78, 102, 109, 164, 206n24, 206n25, 207n26, 208n41
  early names 8, 13, 34–35, 46, 54–60, 62, 64, 68, 69–70, 74–76, 78, 93, 100, 103, 133, 135, 182–183, 210n56, 212n80, 217n29
  geology 48–52, 76–78
  mapping 12–15, 25, 29–31, 34, 37, 39, 44, 54–60, 68–73, 81–83, 91, 96–99, 103–105, 113f, 118, 125, 182
  North Keeling Island x, 2, 34, 39, 48–52, 56–57, 62–64, 67, 70,

74–77f, 83, 93, 95, 105, 109, 154, 181, 183, 215n19
shipwrecks 4, 52, 81–83, 89–90, 93, 106–107–109, 114, 154–159, 162–164, 168, 170, 173–176
snakes 109–110
South Keeling Islands 34, 48, 49–50, 53, 57, 59, 67, 95, 110, 168, 170, 173–174, 185
  Direction Island 82, 154
  Home Island 2, 53, 59, 62, 76, 113, 165f, 166
  Horsburgh Island 48, 50–51, 109, 154, 184
  South Island 59
  West Island 2, 47, 59, 82, 114, 154, 163, 173–174f, 184
  see also greenstone
coconuts 11, 13, 44–47, 60, 66–67, 79–80, 82, 92, 95–96, 106, 113, 129–131, 133, 134f, 154, 164, 180, 183, 220n4
Coghlan, Megan 162, 165f, 173, 176, 187
Comberford, Nicholas 117–118, 126
Convention on the Protection of the Underwater Cultural Heritage viii, 231–232
Cortesão, Jaime 17–21, 201n18
Covington, Syms 39
cowrie shell 18–19f, 92, 182
Creemers, Thomas 170, 187
Curtin University 162, 165f
cyclones 46–47, 156, 159, 163–164
Cygnet 129, 133

d'Apres de Mannevillette, Jean-Baptiste 159
da Nova, Joao 15
da Pisa, Rustichello 13

Dalrymple, Alexander x, 35, 57, 67–68, 83, 95–98, 103–104, 183
Dampier, William x, 25, 64, 68, 88–90, 118, 127, 129–133, 137, 180, 183, 213n92, 220n4
Dana, James 46
Darwin, Charles 39, 44–53, 74–78, 102–103, 109, 164, 181, 206n24–25, 207n26, 208n41, 221n19
de Bry, Johann Theodor 26, 34, 57
de Gama, Vasco 8, 12, 14–15, 20
de Hoop, Robert William viii, 166, 233
de Jode, Gerard 8, 27–28f, 55, 70, 126, 208n43
De Lis 153, 221n1
de Marre, Jan 95
de Vlamingh, Willem 127, 135, 157–158, 183–184
Defoe, Daniel 88
Dekker, Ed 163–164, 166, 173–174, 184, 187
Desceliers, Pierre 21, 34, 54–55f, 80, 208n46
Desire 26
Detmold, Charles Maurice 38f
Dias, Bartolomeu 15
Diego Garcia 8, 19–22, 37, 54–55f, 56, 62, 73, 108–109, 182, 224n1
Diephout, Jan 159
Dieppe School 54, 80, 91, 208n43
Dixon, Susan 166
Doctrine of Discovery 110
dodo 26f, 41–42f, 62, 63f
  see also birds, giant
Dorr, Henry 136
Dragon 65, 66f
Drake, Francis 26
Drie Heuvelen 94
Driscoll, William 106–107, 109, 173–174, 184

Dudley, Robert x, 20, 34, 57, 68–78, 83–84, 91, 102–103, 105, 183, 212n80, 212n82, 212n84, 213n89, 213n92, 217n33
Duyfken 8, 56, 66, 118–119f, 121
Dunn, Samuel 35, 57, 67, 82, 96, 98–99, 216n22
Dutch cartographers 70, 78, 103, 213n93
  see also Goos, Pieter; Gerritsz, Hessel; Silo, Godlob; van Keulen, Johannes
Dutch East India Company *see* Verenigde Oostindische Compagnie (VOC)
Dutch East Indiamen 1, 85, 90, 109, 154, 159, 171, 173
  see also Aagtekerke; *De Lis*; *Fortuyn*; *'s-Graveland*; *Ridderschap van Holland*; *Rooswijk*
Dutch East Indies government 116, 122–123f
Dutch seafarers x, 18, 31, 41, 57, 59–60, 72–73, 88–89, 93, 103, 105, 175, 182

Earl of Liverpool 52–53, 83, 108–109, 154, 181
earthquakes 48, 50, 75, 206n25, 213n89
East India Company (EIC) 65–66, 98–100, 122, 124, 126, 183, 216n22
Easter Island 11, 52
Eckeberg, Charles G. 82, 95, 103–104f, 215n19
Eendracht 122
Eendrachtsland 155
Egeria 128, 151
Elcano, Juan Sebastian 8, 22–25, 37, 39
elephants 174–175

elephant tusk 161–166, 173–177, 184–185
Elizabeth 162
Emden ix
Enggano Island 27, 30, 59, 70, 120–121, 213n92
England 20, 34, 59, 72–73, 82, 88, 103, 182
  see also British Government

Fauvel, A. A. 20
Fitzherbert, Humfrey 125
Fitzroy, Robert 83, 99, 103, 181, 215n18
Flying Fish 128, 150
Fortuyn ix, 4, 81, 89, 93, 153, 155–160, 162, 166–168, 171–173, 184–185
France 18, 20, 54, 72, 80, 88, 93, 108, 151, 159, 175–176, 224n1
  see also Mauritius
Fremantle, Stephen x, 83, 100–103, 116, 183, 216n29

Gates of Hell 85
García de Toreno, Nuño 8, 25, 33, 37–39, 40f, 56, 62, 182
Geelvinck 135, 157
Gelderland 41
Germanus, Nicolaus 7, 14
Gerritsz, Hessel x, 34, 46, 56–62, 67, 70, 72–74, 80, 93, 105, 117, 125, 182, 209n53, 210n56, 212n81, 212n84
Gezo of Dahomey, King 18
Ghiberti, Lorenzo 84
Gibson-Hill, Carl Alexander 106–107
Glazier, Maurie 161
Golden Hind 26
Goos, Pieter 118
Gotha Lion 95

's-*Graveland* 81, 93, 158–159
greenstone 47–53, 181, 206n25, 207n26
Grenfell, Sidney 149
guano 25, 46, 57, 62, 64, 92, 218n49
Gulliver, Lemuel 88
gunpowder 57, 64, 92
Guppy, Henry 46, 50–51, 83, 102–105

Halls, Chris 158
Hamanaka, Hama 171–172f, 188
Hare, Alexander 82–83, 94, 108, 112, 115–116, 128, 176, 215n18
Harleian map 80, 91
Hartog, Dirk 3–4, 25, 59–60, 155
Hector 65, 67
Heesburg 95
Helen 53
Henderson, Graeme vii–viii, 162, 166, 207n26, 231
Hercole, Duke 17
Hippomenes 82, 113
Hoboken family 148–149
Hollandia 118–119f, 122
Holle, Lienhart 14
Holman, James 47, 109–111f, 114, 175–176, 180, 216n29
Hondius, Jodocus 34, 56, 58–59, 80, 182
Hooker, Joseph, 44
Horsburgh, James 82, 99, 107
Houtman Abrolhos 151, 156–158, 161–163, 173, 184–185, 214n5
Houtman, Cornelis de x, 8, 27, 37, 56–57, 68, 118–121, 125, 180, 183
Houtman, Frederik de 118

Imperieuse 128, 151
India 4, 7–9, 12, 14, 20, 27–28, 37, 79, 133

Indian Ocean Territories
  Australian 1–2, 155
  British 11, 116, 128, 151, 183
  see also Christmas Island; Cocos (Keeling) Islands; Diego Garcia
Indigenous Australians 9
Indonesia x, 9, 11, 15, 18, 20–21, 29, 79–80, 92, 139, 166, 181, 203n36
  see also Bali; Ceram; Enggano Island; Java; Spice Islands; Sumatra; Sunda Strait
Iran 180
International Union for Conservation of Nature 39
Italy 10, 13, 15, 17–18, 21, 57, 62, 64, 69, 84–85
  see also Cantino, Alberto; Pigafetta, Antonio; Polo, Marco

James Matthews viii
Jansz, Willem 66, 73
Java 5, 7–9, 13, 15, 17–18, 20–23, 25–29, 34, 47, 51–54, 112, 120, 124, 182
  Bantam 66–68, 102–103, 121–122, 124, 136
  Batavia 81, 90, 93–95, 112, 115–116, 122, 147, 150, 153–161, 174
Juno 116

Keating, Arthur 47, 106–108, 216n29
Keeling, William x, 34, 60, 83, 98–99, 183
  myth of first sighting of Cocos Islands 64–80, 83–84, 98–105, 115
Kerr, Robert 65

Lancaster, James 122–123
Langhenez, Bernardt 118, 120–121
Le Courier 108
Le Gour, Louis 106–109, 112
Liesk, William 48, 51, 53, 206n24, 207n26, 208n41
Lilliput 91
Linschoten, Jan Huygen van 9, 26, 34, 56, 60, 120
lizards 25, 27–28, 39
Lonach 106–107, 154
Lopes, Thome 8
Lucini, Antonio 69
Lyell, Charles 48–49, 51, 74

Maclear, John 128, 150
Madagascar 11, 13, 15, 20, 22, 29–30, 33–34, 36–37, 42, 48, 52, 79–80, 94, 108, 118, 156–157, 176
Magellan, Ferdinand 8, 22–26, 180
Malacca 26, 28, 120
Malay
    language 11
    peninsula 7–8, 14–15, 22, 28, 33
    people 62, 151, 215n18
    seafarers 23, 28–29, 53
    see also Malacca
Maldive-Chagos archipelago 8, 10–11, 13, 15, 18, 20–21, 37, 54, 56, 58–59, 66, 79–80, 108, 182
    Gan 20–21
Manguin, Pierre Yves 10
maps ix, 2, 12–31, 33–39, 46, 53–62, 64, 67–80, 81–84, 90–99, 103–105, 113f, 117–118, 122f, 125–126, 132f, 151, 181–182, 201n18, 209n47, 209n53, 210n56
Maritime Archaeology Association of Victoria 166

Mascarene Islands 20, 37, 78
    see also Mauritius
Mascarenhas, Pedro 21
Mauritius 20, 26f, 37, 41–42f, 53, 108, 156, 175
Mauritius 73, 82, 106–109, 112, 118–119f, 121, 154, 173, 216n29
Mauro, Fra 13–14, 33, 36
May, William 151
Mediterranean 14–15, 18, 222n20
Mentawai Islands 27, 30, 59, 70, 133
Mercator, Gerardus 8, 27–28, 34–35, 56–57
Middle East *see* Arab seafarers
Milton, John 84–87, 180
Milward, John x, 72, 117, 122, 124–125, 183
Moll, Herman 90–91
Mortier, Pierre 64
Moss, Alex 166, 167f, 188
Mota, Avelino Teixeria da 17–21, 201n18
Muirfield 159
Murray, John xi, 128, 150, 152, 221n19
Murray, Thomas 130f
Mynors, William 117, 126

navigational knowledge 12, 14–15
Nek Laisa 166
New Zealand 52, 181
Netherlands *see entries starting 'Dutch'*; RCE
Nijptangh 157

Olsen, Kenneth 44
Ortelius, Abraham 8, 24f, 56, 208n43
Otis, James 101

INDEX

Parkinson, James 166, 167f, 188
Pelsaert, Francisco 161
Philippines 22, 122
Phillip, William 120–121
Pigafetta, Antonio x, 23, 33, 37, 92, 179–180, 213n92
Plancius, Petrus 34, 56, 208n43, 212n81
planisphere *see* Cantino, Alberto
Poe, Edgar Allan 89–90, 180
Polo, Marco x, 7, 13, 15, 18, 22, 27–31, 34–37, 62, 66, 129, 179, 213n92
Portugal 4, 10, 15, 17–19, 23, 25, 27–28, 37, 39, 53–54, 64, 73, 96, 118–120, 182, 202n21
   see also de Gama, Vasco
Ptolemy 14, 22, 120–121
Purchas, Samuel 65, 67–68, 102
Putin, Vladimir 180

Queensland Museum 164

RCE (Cultural Heritage Agency of the Netherlands) viii, 4, 233
Rapid viii, 127, 136
Red Dragon see Dragon
refugees 47f, 167
   see also SIEV 221
Ridderschap van Holland 135, 153, 155, 157
roaring forties ix, 2, 122, 183
Rooswijk viii, 233
Rowe, Richard 124
Royal Exchange 125
Royal Mary 117, 126

Saint Paul Island 94, 111, 155, 157, 163
Saris, John 66–67, 105, 124
Scholes, Mieko 149, 188
scurvy 131

Semarang 147
Seychelles 8, 11, 20, 73, 108
shipwrecks 155–156, 161–162, 165f, 166, 172, 177, 184
   see also entries under Christmas Island; Cocos (Keeling) Islands
SIEV 221, 167–168, 171
Silo, Godlob 81, 93–95, 106, 112
Singapore 52–53, 106
Sir Francis Nicholas Burton 82, 108, 114–115, 154, 162, 173, 175–177
slave trade viii, 18, 37, 53, 82–83, 94, 108–109, 112–113, 115, 154, 175–177, 183, 185, 201n17, 215n18
Slocum, Joshua 112
South America 11, 37, 40f, 217n29
Spain 4, 8, 19, 22–25, 64, 122
Spice Islands 2, 4–5, 18–19, 22–23, 37, 56, 68, 182
spice trade x, 9, 27, 118, 155
Sri Lanka *see* Ceylon
Sumatra 5, 9, 13–14, 25, 27–30, 47, 59, 66, 91, 108, 111–112, 120–121, 124–125
Sunda Strait x, 10–11, 25, 27, 29–31, 34, 52, 57, 59, 66–67, 72, 79–80, 118, 120, 122, 124, 155
Swan, Charles 129
Swart, Fred 131
Swift, Jonathan x, 82, 88–92, 180
Sydney ix

Taprobana *see* Sumatra
Tent, Jan 27, 125, 188
Thomas 124
Thornton, John 84
Thornton, Samuel 118, 126
Timor 23, 25, 151
Treaty of London 111

INDEX

Treaty of Tordesillas 4, 19, 25, 39
Treaty of Zaragoza 4
Trial 73–74f, 82
turtles 46–47

Underwater Cultural Heritage Act, 2018 viii, 231–232
UNESCO viii, 231–232

van Braam, J. 81, 210n56
van der Aa, Pieter 29, 68
van der Aa, Robide 149–150
van der Jagt, H. 114, 116
van Keulen, Johannes 71f, 95–96f, 98, 133, 212n80, 216n21
Verenigde Oostindische Compagnie (VOC) 56, 93–95, 118, 122, 135, 153, 155, 157–158, 160–161, 163, 168, 171, 173, 183–184, 216n21, 216n21
Vergulde Draeck viii, 135, 155, 157, 161, 231
Vice Admiraal Rijk x, 128, 137–150, 154, 160, 170–172, 184
Victoria 22–23, 24f, 26, 39
Viduka, Andy viii, 166, 167f, 169f, 232
Vietnam 29, 31, 64
volcanoes 2, 50–51, 160, 168, 181

Waldseemuller, Martin 22, 25, 201n18
Wells, H. G. 43–44, 180, 205n15
Weseltje 157
Western Australia 4, 25, 42, 47, 59–60, 73, 129, 131, 136, 151, 155–159, 161–162, 168, 172, 185, 205n15, 207n26
  see also Houtman Abrolhos
Western Australian Museum viii, 158, 161–162, 164, 188, 231
Westrik, Pieter 157
whalers 108, 151
Whippey, James 151
Whitecar, William 151
Windhond 81, 93, 184
Witboom, Jan 160
Wood, Rachel 173, 177, 188–189
Wood-Jones, Frederic 103, 213n89
Wreck Check 3–4, 46–47, 149, 154–155, 162, 164–168, 171–173, 184, 188, 231–232

Yule, Henry 31f, 35–37, 36f

Zeewijk 155, 157, 160–163, 173
Zheng, Admiral 52, 180–181, 207n36
Zuytdorp 155, 161, 168

www.ingramcontent.com/pod-product-compliance
Lightning Source LLC
Chambersburg PA
CBHW041313240426
43669CB00024B/2975